# Farm Boy

# City Girl

# Farm Boy

## *City Girl*

### From **Gene** to *Miss Gina*

A Memoir
John "Gene" E. Dawson

Editor: Tamara Dawson Bonnicksen
Cover Design, Layout, Photo Editing, and Ebook: Connie Brooks, www.lindstromdesign.net
Typists: Judy Harris Hilleman, Twila Gerard, and Shelly Gerard
Photo Scanning: Geneva Dawson
Contributed Photography: Geoff Story, geoffstory.com, gayhomemovie.com
Photo Adjusting: Jane Swanson

Most of the photos in this book are from the author's personal collection.


ISBN: 978-1-7346260-0-1
Library of Congress Control Number: 2020902816


Published in the United States of America.

Order this book online at www.amazon.com.

For more information about the author, visit facebook.com/farmboycitygirlbook.

# Dedication

I dedicate this book to my family members—those who came before me and those who are younger. I'm very proud of all my relatives and the strides my parents made in this great country and land of opportunity where anything is possible if you put your mind and heart into it and employ some elbow grease.

My grandparents and great-grandparents, natives of Ireland and England, were all successful—especially Grandpa Edward Agnew, my maternal grandfather, and the Dawson family. Mother Nature did Grandpa Agnew in after hail wiped him out—there was no hail or crop insurance at the time. That left his children with nothing when they began their adult lives, but due to great faith and perseverance, they prevailed. Their mother/my grandmother would have lost everything during the Depression, including the homestead, if her priest hadn't intervened.

The calamitous hail that hit the Agnew farm missed my Grandpa Dawson's, but he still lost everything in the Great Depression. The Greenes, my paternal grandmother's family, also were reduced to poverty by the economics of the 1930s.

Many early families earned their livings through agriculture and farming—always a gamble but a most noble and satisfying occupation. Although I haven't lived on a farm for many, many years, I love to read, hear about, and observe farm life. I consider myself a farmer at heart.

So I'm really proud as I look around at my brothers and their families, my single brother Bernie, as well as my cousins and their families, and observe how each generation since has climbed the ladder of success. Of course, my most missed and beloved brother, Paul "Lee" Leroy, who died in 2000, was an inspiration to all of us with his examples of hard work, sound investment, and great kindness.

Even if they were still among the living, it would be impossible to repay my Mother and Dad for all the sacrifices they performed for me. They went without so much so I could have everything that I actually needed. They would go year after year wearing the same suits, dresses, shoes, etc. Mother didn't get new furniture, saying she would wait until the boys "grew up." But I knew she longed for new matching chairs or dishes. Most of our dishes, pots, pans, and furniture came from some unfortunate family's or individual's closing-out sale.

I thank God for my wonderful, loving, stern-but-fair, God-fearing parents. And for my younger brothers—since I am the oldest, I have been privileged to enjoy every minute of their lives, and I love them dearly. My brother Kenny passed away while this book was being finished, and I miss him. I am especially thankful for Paul Leroy, who I miss every day of my life.

I thank God for my grandparents and their values. I thank God for my sisters-in-law, my terrific nieces and nephews, and great-nieces and great-nephews. I thank God for my loving aunts and uncles and all my cousins and their families.

I thank God for creating me, my Catholic faith, and every minute of my life.

# Memories

*Memories will linger long*
*Of the things that have fled by,*
*Perhaps the title of a song*
*Or a starting, piercing cry.*

*Memories will reawaken*
*The times of yesteryear,*
*Tasks that were undertaken*
*Or given up in fear.*

*Quickly the days go by*
*While memories are stored away,*
*The months and years seem to fly*
*But memories will always stay.*

Gene Dawson, North English (Iowa) High School
*Songs of Youth, Young America Sings* Anthology, 1949

It is when I contemplate the evolution of everything that I realize that time marches on, doesn't stop and take breaks, and before I hardly realized it, I became old in years but definitely not in outlook or spirit. It is inevitable that birth ends in death, not only for mankind but also for all of God's creatures.

# Contents

# Foreword

In 1971, I finally got to know the family of my father Ken Dawson, brother of author Gene Dawson, a little better. Although my siblings and I grew up just a mile as the crow flies from my dad and Gene's father, my Grandpa John Dawson, I'm not sure I had even been in his house.

Gene and niece Tammy in 2000.

Of course, I knew my Grandma Mary Agnew Dawson died after a fire in that house in 1955, but I didn't know a lot more. Grandpa and his three youngest sons sometimes attended family events, and I knew that my older uncles, Gene and Leroy, were in far-away St. Louis, but I saw them very little.

When I did, I thought there was something different about Uncle Gene compared with the people I knew in Parnell, Iowa. No man in the Parnell area had flaming red hair combed from the back to the front! I didn't know—or even consciously think about—what the difference might be other than hair. But whatever it was, I thought Uncle Gene was great fun and loved his attention.

So in 1971, it happened that my dad was in the hospital 30 miles from home for a three-week period. Since my mom was at the hospital most days, arrangements were made for Grandpa and Gene, who was visiting from St. Louis, to take care of my siblings and me after school one day. I looked forward to this—partly because I would see Grandpa and get to spend time in the mysterious house but mostly to spend time with Uncle Gene.

"Welcome, welcome!" Uncle Gene said as we tromped in the door. He announced that we would be making sugar cookies. My mom mostly kept us away from cooking and baking, so we kids were delighted. There was no way to forget the day, but if I had, I have a written memory. Uncle Gene wrote, "Tammy, you're as sweet as sugar cookies!" in my autograph book, one of my favorite possessions at the time.

I don't think I saw much of the house that day, but not long after that, I was honored to be the only Dawson sibling to have time alone with Uncle Gene. He and I cleaned the house, which he somehow made a good time. I had never before thought that cleaning was fun!

Later he opened his suitcase and pulled out fishnet underwear—I certainly never had seen anything like that! Besides his red hair, I also noticed that he shaved his underarms (he wore shirts with the sleeves cut off) and that he had beautiful, long fingernails—not like the short, sometimes dirty fingernails of the local men and boys.

Yes, I knew there was something different about Uncle Gene.

In the 1980s, Uncle Gene and I grew closer, and I spent time with him during his visits to Iowa when Grandpa Dawson was suffering from cancer. By this time, it was obvious to me what was "different" about Uncle Gene. Gene is gay and transgender—he always felt that he should have been a girl/woman. Knowledge of his lifestyle didn't change my opinion of him.

I visited Gene and Uncle Leroy several times in the 1990s at their shared home in St.

Louis. In 2004, my family moved to St. Louis, and we were able to spend a lot of time with Uncle Gene. My husband and son also became fans of Uncle Gene/Aunt Gina—or, as I call him, "Your Highness" (since he is a queen!).

I also call Uncle Gene the family matriarch since he is the oldest of his first cousins on both sides of the family and the best at keeping in touch and sharing stories about his childhood and relatives who have passed away. Several family members (and I) encouraged him to write those memories. Finally, he **handwrote** the first part of his memoir in 2003–2004 and the rest 10 years later. When I first read his story, I was amazed at his writing flare as I could visualize every scene he describes.

After Gene wrote the second part of this memoir, it still was five more years before he decided he wanted to publish the book. He feels that now is the right time. Sadly, my dad, Ken, will not see the final book—he passed away just as it was being finished.

Gene's memoir really is two stories with a transition between. His growing-up years in rural Iowa were very, very different than his adult life in Cedar Rapids and St. Louis. It seemed as if he went from a somewhat sheltered childhood to living on the edge as an adult. He certainly doesn't portray himself as "Ms. Perfect"—some stories don't put him in the best light. But he wanted to tell all.

In Part One, the "Farm Boy" from Iowa County, Iowa, recounts his years growing up in the Great Depression and moving with his family from rental farm to rental farm until his parents could finally buy their own farmstead. Although he enjoyed the farm lifestyle, it was a great amount of work, including for the children. And when they "acted up," the old-fashioned paternal discipline could be harsh (before reading Gene's book, I had no idea this had happened, and it was hard for me to read).

In Part Two, after Gene left the farm and was transitioning to becoming a "City Girl," the tragic death of his mother/my grandmother sent him back to the farm for four years as he selflessly helped raise his three youngest brothers. He does not sugarcoat the devastating story of his mother's agonizing death and how Grandpa blamed him for it even though Gene was far away at the time of my Grandma's accident. But time eventually healed the wounds in Gene and Grandpa's relationship.

Finally, in Part Three, Gene could begin his uninterrupted journey as a "City Girl." Gene/Miss Gina lived in Cedar Rapids, Iowa, before moving to St. Louis to be with his brother Leroy, who also was gay. In the city, they both could be themselves, which really wasn't possible in rural Iowa in those days. Gene's life as Miss Gina in St. Louis sometimes led him to situations where he almost ended up dead—these stories also were hard for me to read. But he kept getting out there. The pioneers in the LGBTQ world had to be brave.

Uncle Gene's stories are interspersed with photos of his life on the farm and in the cities. The book is a labor of love. It is a gift to Uncle Gene's family, a gift to Iowa history lovers, and a gift to LGBTQ men and women.

*Tamara Dawson Bonnicksen*
*March 2020*

# PART ONE:

## Farm Boy

1931–1949

Four generations: My Great-Grandma Minnie Healy, Grandma Minnie Agnew, and Mother Mary Dawson, who is holding me (plus a photobombing chicken).

Mother and me in 1931.

Dad and me.

Aunt Ann Dawson Conroy is holding me with Mother behind. I am the oldest nephew (or niece) on both Mother's and Dad's sides of the family.

# Chapter 1

## 1931–1934

My life began in Iowa in 1931 during the Great Depression. But I never knew until much later that I actually grew up with very little. Everyone I knew lived the same way—hand to mouth. I was happy and felt loved in my extended Irish Catholic family. They had worked hard tending the land to get where they were by the time I was born.

My great-grandparents who immigrated from Ireland and England were hardy, wise, thrifty, and very intelligent. They passed these traits on to my grandparents.

My dad, John Paul Dawson, son of Thomas and Mary Greene Dawson, was born May 13, 1907, the sixth of 11 children. My mother, Mary Helen Agnew Dawson, was born on October 4, 1907, the second oldest of 14 children. Her parents were John Edward and Mary "Minnie" Healy Agnew.

Dad and Mother met while they were both working for his Uncle Jack Dawson. It was love at first sight, Mother told me and Dad later verified. I'm most certainly glad they met and fell deeply in love, as I was born February 18, 1931, just three months after they were married on November 19, 1930.

I was born that February day at 11:40 p.m. at the Agnew farmhouse on the homestead in Dayton Township, Iowa County, Iowa, in the Armah community. Dr. Harlan of Keswick delivered me with Great-Aunt Susie Healy O'Brien in attendance. At that time, most children were born in the home. A few days later, Father P.J. Ryan of the Armah, North English, and Millersburg Catholic parishes baptized me, and Aunt Anna Agnew and Uncle Tommy Dawson were my godparents.

Dad worked with his dad and brothers to try to coax a living from farming. The Great Depression was under way and, to compound matters, heat and drought covered the Midwest and the Dust Bowl resulted in the sky appearing cloudy even on sunny days. The southwest wind filled the air with topsoil, and dust settled on everything—even the windowsills, as dust has a way of getting in the smallest crack or opening. Gardens and pastures dried up, as did ponds, creeks, and many wells.

Prices were so low that it didn't pay to try to raise pigs, etc. How people survived, I don't really know. Being a child, I didn't realize we were living in poverty as my parents deprived themselves so I would have milk and other necessities.

Dad was a very good farmer. He always had crops that produced bountiful harvests and was patient to never work the soil while it was wet or to harvest crops before they were fully ripe. He had only a fifth-grade education but could read, write, and spell as well as I. I'm sure he was better than I am in arithmetic (hooray for calculators!).

We lived at my Grandpa and Grandma Agnew's house until June 1, 1931, when we moved to the "Berry Place" southwest of Millersburg and stayed there until November. Then we went to the "House on the Hill," which was midway between Keswick and Armah.

On March 1, 1932, we settled on a farmstead southeast of Keswick that was owned by Grandpa Tom Dawson. The first of March every year was the traditional moving day for farm renters as one family would move in to replace another who replaced another family that had rented a larger or better landed place. It almost seemed like musical chairs.

We lived on the Dawson farm for two years, and my childhood memories begin here. "Al," our big German shepherd, and I chased chickens until he nipped me for some indiscretion, causing a deep black-and-blue bruise on my arm. Later, Al "disappeared" after threatening to attack Dad instead of my Uncle Jim Dawson (Dad's brother) who had been stealing our chickens. Uncle Jim had won Al's loyalty by bringing him food while he did his nighttime thievery. (During the Great Depression, many neighbors raised chickens—they could be sold quite easily for there was not much else to eat.)

On December 23, 1932, I was presented a new baby brother, Kenneth Edward. I was not quite two, but I remember Aunt Ann Dawson (later Mrs. Harold Conroy) shaking a red hot-water bottle that made a gurgling sound and shook like Jell-O. Aunt Ann, a registered nurse, was there to care for Mother and the new baby. I was very frightened of the "hot bottle" and can still see her big, smiling, white teeth as she thoroughly enjoyed my fright. (Later in life, I really enjoyed my visits to the Aunt Ann Dawson Conroy place where she and her family raised white pigeons. I was so thrilled the first time I saw those pigeons, and since that time I've loved pigeons and raised them when I had the opportunity.)

I remember seeing Grandpa Agnew in the casket after he died (October 1933, so I was two years old) and Mother crying. As they held me to view him, I couldn't understand why he was asleep and dressed in his Sunday clothes. They said he was going to heaven, but I kept waiting for him to come back.

When we had visited Grandpa and Grandma Agnew on their farm on Sundays after Mass, he was always the first to come to the car—almost before we came to a halt—and then he would carry me into the house. One time, Dad drove Grandpa and Grandma to North English to shop, and Grandpa and I stayed in the car. I had just learned to talk, and as I watched everyone pass in front of us, I asked, "Who that?" His very courteous and polite answer was never a "man" or "woman," but always "That's a lady," or "That's a gentleman." He was a true gentleman himself.

Soon after Grandpa Agnew died in 1933, his poor widow, who had eight children still at home, nearly lost the farm. Grandpa had borrowed some money from two well-off farmer neighbors after hail and drought ruined his crops. Not long after his death, the neighbors demanded that the money be repaid or else they would take over ownership of the homestead and possibly evict the family. However, Father Ryan of Armah intervened, and I don't know what the conditions were, but Grandma's farmstead was saved.

My Aunt Theresa Agnew O'Rourke later told me that Grandma Agnew and her son/ my Uncle Emmett went to the White State Bank in nearby South English and received a loan—enough to pay back what was borrowed. The bank is still in business and has been patronized by the Agnew family and many of their descendants through the years.

Grandma Agnew's homestead was the one stable gathering place that the John and Mary Dawson family had because we moved so much through the years.

Grandma was a hard worker—she could milk a cow as quickly and as well as anyone. On muddy days, she would go barefoot while she pulled weeds in the garden or went about her poultry chores.

When I was little, Grandma Agnew let me accompany her to feed the chickens, geese, and ducks, and to gather their eggs. I liked to go with Grandma to gather eggs. She had big yellow chickens called Buff Orpingtons, which laid brown eggs. Grandma Agnew's house did not have a screen door with the back kitchen door, and an old yellow Orpington hen would slip in most every day and deposit an egg in a wood box that held wood chunks for the cooking stove. When the hen finished, she would jump out of the box, cackle loudly and proudly, and then rejoin her hen friends outside. (This was only a warm-weather event as she was confined to the henhouse during the colder months.)

In Grandma's "little house," a small building used for storage, there was often a fire going under the stove. On top of the stove was a huge kettle that contained a mix of ground corn, oats, and milk. Grandma let the mixture cook until it got rather crusty and then fed it to the poultry. I always ate some, too, although Grandma advised me that I really shouldn't. I loved its aroma, crustiness, and flavor after it simmered all day. The flies seemed to like it, too! I thought it was delicious—of course, I used to eat the burned parts of wooden matchsticks after they had been used to light a lamp or stove. Nice charcoal flavor! I never got sick from any of these delicacies.

A wooden-framed windmill with its wooden air wheel was the means of nature pumping water from a deep well into a cistern. Then it could be drawn out with a hand pump with a long handle. On warm days, a large bucket was used to lower butter, milk, and cream so they would not spoil. At noon, one of my uncles would pull the bucket up so we could eat. The deep well usually had heavy planks over the top, but one day, I was with Uncle Emmett or Uncle Harry when a young duck fell into the well while it was uncovered. It took quite some effort to dip the duck out.

It always was a treat to spend a few days every few weeks at Grandma Agnew's. Grandma would cut the crusts off her delicious homemade bread for me. When the Agnew kids and Grandma would gather around the kerosene-lit table to eat, they would exclaim, "Mom, what's the matter with the bread, where are the crusts?" Then several pairs of eyes would peer at me implying that I was guilty. Now I understand how distasteful the bread must have appeared ... I amend!

Grandma Agnew could make the best dressing from dried homemade bread chunks soaked in milk and fried in little balls with onion and sage. She then took the chunks like crumbled hamburger and stuffed a chicken. Turkeys were of the wild variety; the only person I knew at that time who raised turkeys was Manda Harris, and she had a big tom turkey that chased people. White big-breasted turkeys had not yet evolved—at least not in our neck of the woods.

Another specialty of Grandma Agnew's was hickory nut cake. Three or four hickory trees grew right next to the yard, and the Agnew kids picked the nuts in the fall. On winter days, Grandma and the girls would crack and pick out the pieces of hickory nutmeat for cake baking. I wish I had her recipe.

Occasionally, we would eat a meal of roast pigeon. I did not like the idea, but most everyone was glad to eat what was available. My uncles would catch the pigeons that lived among the rafters and in the cupolas of the two barns, and my aunts and Grandma would clean them. Then Grandma made her delicious dressing and each bird was stuffed. There were enough prepared so everyone could eat an entire pigeon, which mainly consisted of a very large, fine-tasting breast. I hate to admit that I actually ate a pigeon—I feel like a cannibal!

I have great memories of my aunts and uncles. On the Agnew side, my early memory of Aunt Anna Agnew (called Ann later) was how kind she was. She was the oldest of the siblings and my godmother. Aunt Anna remembered everyone's birthdays and always gave her godchildren $1 on that day. Birthdays actually were no big deal—I don't recall ever being the recipient of a cake or any special present except from Aunt Anna.

I remember Aunt Anna telling me about Great-Grandpa Healy, a convert to Catholicism, who said the rosary every day, even if no one joined him. Aunt Anna was impressed.

Aunt Anna always worked very hard. She worked for the Hurd family in the 1930s, and in the 1940s, she went to work for Mr. and Mrs. Dow Mason, who had the main grocery store in nearby North English. She had Sundays off but worked from 6 a.m. to 8 p.m. weekdays and 8 a.m. to 6 p.m. on Saturdays. She later moved with Grandma to North English and worked at Shorty's Café and Agnew's Tavern, which was owned by her brothers Emmett and Bernard after Bernard returned from World War II. Eventually, she found a job in the housekeeping department at the University of Iowa in Iowa City (about 35 miles from North English) and retired from there. She never married.

Mother was the second oldest of the 14 Agnew children. She had a case of diphtheria as a child and barely survived. She also nearly succumbed another time when she was attacked by an angry swarm of hornets while Grandpa Agnew was cutting weeds in a field. The hornets stung her repeatedly, and Grandpa fought them off with his large straw hat.

The summer after Mother completed 11th grade at St. John's boarding school in Victor, Iowa, a devastating hailstorm pounded through the Agnew homestead, breaking out windows, killing young chickens, and damaging roofs. The garden, corn, and other crops were pounded into the ground. The family was wiped out. When Mother's senior year rolled around in September, the family did not have enough money to pay her tuition, thus ending her formal education.

When Uncle Johnny and his wife Rose Furlong Agnew, who grew up in nearby Parnell, came to Grandma's on a Sunday, it was a rare and great occasion. Johnny lived in the next county east (Johnson), which was far away in the days of mud roads and unpaved highways. He was the first uncle who was not a laborer or farmer. Johnny had a "supper club" (tavern) in Tiffin, Iowa, called "Club 88" and drove a big sparkling car, and Aunt Rose had the most beautiful dresses and makeup.

Uncle Johnny had a very strong and pleasing personality—he was a natural-born leader. He was a success with every endeavor he undertook from bootlegging, to skirting the law, to operating his Tiffin nightclub and "The Flamingo" nightclub in Silvis, Illinois. Rose was equally dynamic, and they formed a successful team. One of Uncle Johnny's favorite sayings was "You can catch more flies with honey than you can with vinegar."

Mother revealed to me that it was no secret that Grandma Agnew favored her boys, especially Johnny, the oldest. She would give him money from selling a case of eggs to spend as his own. Grandpa favored the girls.

When they were little, Uncle Johnny and Mother were mischievous. They told how they were out walking one day and came across some horse manure (round little balls). Uncle Johnny had Mother carry them in her apron, and they proceeded to throw them on the neighbor's kitchen floor and then took off! Of course, they were reported and spanked. Older sister Aunt Anna was not as ornery, but one time, she, Mother, and Uncle Johnny locked themselves in the little house and had to break a window to get out. Mother and

Uncle Johnny got spanked, but Aunt Anna escaped punishment as she had cut her hand.

Aunt Marge, the fourth oldest of the Agnew siblings, was the first "liberated" woman I remember knowing—she was the first to drive a car, wear glasses, and smoke cigarettes! She had a very strong personality and left the farm in her early teens to live with her Aunt Nellie Healy Van Horn (Grandma Agnew's sister) in Millersburg. It was reported that she and my Uncle Johnny—two very independent people—did not get along.

Aunt Marge married Leo Costello, a handsome young man from Millersburg, whom she met while living with my Great-Aunt Nellie. He always referred to Aunt Marge as "Margaret." Evidently, he considered "Margaret" more respectful than the nickname that everyone else used.

Uncle Emmett Agnew was quiet, had very wavy-curly black hair, and was said to look like his Grandpa Healy. His voice was gruff and I thought a little intimidating, but he was very kind. He liked to go fishing, although you had to be very quiet if you went with him. Uncle Emmett later married Gloria Albert; he met her when she was working as a waitress in nearby Marengo, Iowa.

Uncle Emmett "took the rap" for Uncle Johnny and Dad after they were busted by the feds for bootlegging alcohol during Prohibition. Bootlegging kept bread on the table for many families during that era of Dillinger, Bonnie and Clyde, the Lindbergh kidnapping, and "poor little rich girl" Gloria Vanderbilt.

Uncle Emmett was sentenced to time at the state boys' reform school in Eldora, Iowa, and that is where Mother and Dad went on their honeymoon in November 1930. While in Eldora, Mother had to use the bathroom and there were no facilities, so Mother and Dad went into a hotel and Mother used the chamber pot in a room when its occupant was out! I remember them laughing about that incident later on and surmising what the occupants thought when they got back to their room.

Mother's sisters Ethel and Alice were glamour girls to me. Both were beautiful and had the glamorous fashions and styles of the 1930s. They always had their nails painted, but left the ends and the half-moons unpainted, which was the latest style at the time. When their beaus came to pick them up, the girls looked like movie stars. They were both very kind to me and would even paint my nails, too. Of course, Dad and my uncles called me a "sissy," but Mother and Grandma didn't seem to mind. Kenny had a nail job, too, so we both got some weird looks.

Mother and all of her sisters were very close, and Aunts Ethel and Alice stayed with us at various times. I remember Mother and her sisters' happy laughter while making "snow" ice cream—new fallen snow with sugar or powdered sugar and vanilla.

When I was four years old, I accompanied Aunt Ethel on an overnight visit to a friend who lived probably eight miles away. Uncle Emmett hitched the horse team to the buggy, and although the unpaved, ungraveled roads were very muddy, I very vividly remember a pleasant ride through the countryside. It took at least half a day.

Aunts Ethel and Alice both had cedar chests, which they called "hope" chests. When they received towels, sheets, or anything for setting up their own homes, those items went in the hope chests. Aunt Ethel apparently met her future husband, Richard Harris, when she assisted the Hurd family (Richard's grandparents) with their household chores. Aunt Alice met her eventual husband, Kermie Herr, while she worked at Uncle Johnny's first tavern, which was in nearby South English.

Shortly after Aunt Ethel and Richard Harris were married, I stayed with them on a farm one mile south of the Hurd family's general store. Richard was away all day working for the Hurds, while Aunt Ethel and I pumped many tanks of water for the Hurd cows as they came "mooing" to the tank. It was hot and dry, and there were no streams as they were all dried up because of drought, as well as dust storms. While I was staying there, Manda Harris, Richard's mother, stopped by one afternoon with a fresh peach upside-down cake—the first I ever tasted. It still makes my mouth water! Incidentally, Aunt Ethel could make terrific potato salad, and I recall that it had just the perfect amount of celery seed.

Uncles Harry and Bernard liked to hunt for squirrels and rabbits and were excellent marksmen. Uncle Harry used to suffer from very painful boils on the back of his neck. He offered my brother Leroy and me our first cigarette, which we gladly accepted while he enjoyed our effort to appear "cool" as we coughed and sputtered! We were approximately four and eight at the time.

When Uncle Bernard was born, Grandma was hospitalized for six weeks at the Amick hospital in Millersburg where Great-Aunt Nellie Van Horn worked as a nurse. Uncle Bernard was a "blue baby," as his blood was very "blue" and he had a bluish pallor. While Grandma recovered, Mother—then 12 years old—took care of baby Bernard while Aunt Anna was in charge of the housework.

Uncle Bernard was quiet and a very good worker who was employed by various farmers to help plant and harvest their crops. He was the first Agnew to enter the U.S. Army.

When the Agnews finally got a car, Uncle Bernard made the acquaintance of his future wife, Veronica Armstrong, at a Dayton (Township) Hall dance. Uncle Harry Agnew married Mary O'Rourke, whose sibling Leo O'Rourke married Aunt Theresa Agnew. (I actually am related to Mary and Leo O'Rourke, too, since their father, J.S., is Dad's first cousin.) Both the Agnews and O'Rourkes attended Immaculate Conception Catholic Church in Armah and their farm homes were less than two miles apart. At the time, most courtships started at school or at church, and often next-door neighbors' children would marry.

Aunt Theresa was 10 years older than I. She was a very good seamstress, and she and Aunt Helen made their own doll clothes. Sometimes I would play hide and seek with her, Aunt Helen, and Uncle Leo Agnew. I can recall usually finding Aunt Theresa because I could spot her black hair. After she was married, I would walk across the fields to visit her and her little son Jimmy, and she would always have delicious cinnamon rolls, which I thoroughly enjoyed.

Uncle Leo (Agnew—I also had Uncles Leo Costello and O'Rourke by marriage) was my favorite person—I was totally happy when I was with him. Whenever I could, I would go with him to hunt, check his traps, and catch and take care of his pigeons. He used to "fetch" the cows from the pasture, as Grandma would say, "It's time to go fetch the cows." On the way back, he would ride on the back of a very gentle and tame Polled Hereford bull named Old Wes.

Uncle Leo loved homemade ice cream, and in the winter, I would walk with him to a neighbor's house to borrow vanilla so we could make some. It seemed Grandma was always out of vanilla. Uncle Leo liked to turn the crank on the ice-cream freezer.

I served my first Catholic Mass as an altar boy with Uncle Leo, who was an altar server until he was taller than the priest. Uncle Leo loved dogs and his favorite was Mike, who was named after Mike Reilly from whom he was obtained. Mike could sit up, shake hands, play dead, sit down, and fetch. Uncle Leo even took Mike to the annual North English Creamery Picnic—the biggest area event of the summer—to perform his tricks.

Uncle Leo was the best climber I ever knew—he would climb in barns and up into the cupolas to catch pigeons. I was always happy when he got back down safely. He wasn't as lucky one time while he was sawing wood. He got his thumb nearly severed—it was hanging by the skin—but Doc Miller of North English stitched it back together.

Later on, Uncle Leo was rejected for the Army because of his thumb, but he insisted on joining. He was an expert marksman. He was a casualty of the World War II Italian campaign at Anzio after being shot through the heart by a German sniper on January 25, 1944.

Aunt Helen taught me how to make "mud cakes" and other playing-house "deli" courses. It seemed like I often was in a tug-of-war between Aunt Helen and Uncle Leo over who I would spend the day with! Aunt Helen's job at home was gathering clean dry corncobs (the hogs and chickens had eaten the corn off the cobs) to use to start the fire in the cookstove the following morning. I held the sack for her as she picked up the cobs.

Aunts Helen and Anna were the only Agnew siblings to graduate from high school. Aunt Helen met Lyle Hartzell at Keswick High, and they were going steady by the time they were both in 11th grade. Helen got straight As all through high school and was valedictorian of her Keswick school class. She taught rural school north of Millersburg and was employed in Cedar Rapids, Iowa, during World War II.

Before I even started school, another adventure I enjoyed with my Agnew aunts and uncles was mushroom hunting. With gunnysacks in hand, we would tramp through Grandma's pastures and Jim Cunningham's timber field (across the road from Grandma's homestead) and harvest lots and lots of the brown fungus delicacies. Grandma and the girls would soak them in salt water to wash them thoroughly and get the bugs out. Later we would enjoy mushrooms fried in butter—they were delicious.

I didn't meet the youngest two Agnew aunts, Charlotte and Bernadette. Aunt Charlotte died at the age of two in 1930, and Aunt Bernadette survived just a very short time in 1929.

My first memory of Grandpa Tom Dawson was when I was two years old. While Dad and I were visiting him, he gave me a piece of delicious-looking chocolate cake. I took one bite and refused to eat any more. They encouraged me to "eat your cake," but when they decided to have a piece, they knew whoever had baked the cake used salt instead of sugar! Yuck!

On the Dawson side of my family, my Dad's siblings were split apart by the Great Depression. Three farms, along with most everything else, were lost. Only a few of my aunts and uncles stayed in the area.

Dad was 13 years old when his brother, Uncle Willie, was killed in an automobile accident. For a long time afterwards, Dad said he would lay awake thinking about his oldest brother. Grandpa Dawson treated Uncle Willie as an equal—at the age of 12, he was allowed to go to sales and purchase stock. He also was designated to discipline his younger siblings. According to Dad, Uncle Willie was very mature both mentally and physically from a very young age.

Aunts Marie and Catherine "Katie" Dawson lived in far-away Minneapolis, and Aunt

Marie often sent us boxes of candies and fruitcakes at Christmastime. She would visit occasionally. I recall that Aunt Marie would go outside or upstairs to smoke—most women did not smoke in those days, and she didn't want to do it "in front of the kids." When she was in her early 40s, Aunt Marie wed Ray LaMere, a retired sailor.

After I graduated from high school, Aunt Katie moved to St. Louis. I found her to be very intellectual and very set in her ways. She never married and lived to be 91 years old.

Uncle Jim "Big Jim" Dawson and Dad did not get along very well. Uncle Jim's younger brothers and sisters considered him a bully, and I never did get to really know him although he and Dad reconciled in their later years. He never married.

As a very young child, I remember Uncle Joe "Joker" Dawson carrying me to the house when a pig was being butchered, as I was terrified due to the frantic squealing and blood. Joker died of the dreaded pneumonia when he was 28. I remember him only from that one day.

Aunt Ann Dawson Conroy was the nurse I described earlier who frightened me with the "hot bottle." Aunt Ann worked as a registered nurse at St. Joseph's Hospital in Ottumwa, Iowa. She met her future husband, Harold Conroy, while living in a room she rented at his grandmother's home.

Uncle Tommy Dawson, my godfather, had thick, black, wavy hair and was always jolly and smiling. He would play basketball with my brothers and me, and we had so much fun when he visited. He had a whirlwind courtship and marriage with Rose Reiland of Lone Tree, Iowa. They then left for California at the height of the Great Depression and came back a few years later in a beautiful car. Then with Uncle Johnny Agnew as a partner, Uncle Tommy operated a tavern in Lone Tree. He did very well until he began to enjoy too much of the merchandise and lost his tavern ownership.

Uncle Raymond Dawson attended Keswick High School and the University of Iowa. He babysat Kenny and Leroy when Mother accompanied me on my first day of school in September 1936. When we got home at noon, there was glass all over the kitchen floor. He had given them light bulbs to play with! In those days, they were very fragile and shattered in hundreds of pieces if dropped.

Uncle Raymond later moved to New Mexico, as he had sinus problems and asthma, and joined the Civilian Conservation Corps (CCC), a job program for the young unemployed that was part of President Franklin Roosevelt's New Deal. Uncle Raymond first laid eyes on the young Elisa Baldonado, his future wife, when he was stationed in New Mexico.

Aunt Elizabeth "Sis" Dawson was a frail child and suffered from epilepsy. She was very quiet, but when she wasn't in bed, she usually had a flyswatter. She declared a nonending war on all flies and insects. She also delighted in seeing Dad punish or "get after" us for some perceived wrong.

Aunt Winifred "Winnie" Dawson died of pneumonia at 17 just as she was going to graduate from Keswick High School in 1935. I remember Mother fixing her hair for her high-school graduation picture—she had beautiful wavy hair and always was smiling.

Dad and Grandma Dawson told me how Grandma was kept on edge by the high-spirited antics of her kids. Dad and Joker got into lots of mischief—one time they climbed to the top of a silo and walked around while a frantic Grandma pleaded for them to "come down right now." They didn't. Another time, they terrified little Aunt Elizabeth

"Sis" by placing her in a manure spreader and threatening to spread her on the acres! They talked their sister Aunt Ann into sticking her tongue on an iron pump handle when the temperature was zero.

At the age of nine, Dad started the family's Model T and took Joker and Aunt Ann on a joy ride with Aunt Catherine screaming in hot pursuit until she was left in a cloud of dust. Grandpa and Uncle Willie didn't punish Dad, and he even was allowed to drive into Keswick to pick up the mail. One neighbor farmer said Dad looked like a wise little rat sitting on the edge of the seat with both hands on the steering wheel, but barely able to see out the windshield.

Another Dawson story I heard occurred about 1857. Great-Grandma Catherine O'Meara Dawson was growing exasperated with Great-Grandpa William stopping at the "watering holes" of Columbus, Ohio, on his way home from his job as a tax collector. She went to the parish priest who advised her to buy a covered wagon and a good team of horses.

Before Great-Grandpa could object, Great-Grandma had the wagon loaded and, along with their kids Maggie, Catherine, and Mary, they were on their way west. The family ended up near Sigourney, Iowa, where they became homesteaders. Great-Grandpa William stopped drinking, and the family became very prosperous. How Great-Grandma Catherine tricked William into moving west was a favorite story of hers, according to Dad's first cousin Nelle Dawson Kelly, who also was her grandchild.

On Grandma Dawson's side, at one time, her father/my Great-Grandpa James "Neddie" Greene owned about 20 properties around Keswick. After Great-Grandma Ellen Boland Greene died in 1929, Great-Grandpa "auditioned" many women to be his housekeeper. He had lived next to the Keswick Catholic church where my Grandma lived, but then moved to another house in Keswick before his death in 1932. The Depression got him, too, and he was left only with the house where Grandma Dawson lived, which went to her sister Maggie.

Dad told how he would drive Great-Grandpa Greene to pick up potential female laborers from the surrounding area. He always admonished Dad, "Don't drive on Main Street in Keswick." Dad would, of course, "gun" the car down Main Street and get everyone's attention while Great-Grandpa slumped in the back seat, muttered curses and threats under his breath, and hoped no one detected the new "applicant."

During this time period, Dad would carry me in with him when he visited a Keswick saloon owned by Bessie Bender, a jovial lady who always gave me a stick of gum. One fall day in 1933, Mother put my all-red outside outfit on me so I could go outside. I immediately started walking to town to see Bessie. Aunt Ethel Agnew happened to see me start on the road and raced to retrieve me—much to my consternation!

When I was about three, I remember saying my prayers at Mother's knee one night. Out on the darkened back porch, a boisterous party was in progress—Dad had made a huge batch of home brew and was entertaining his clients and selling some bootleg whiskey, too.

Mother had a very pained expression on her face and said, "Pray that your Dad won't have to continue doing this."

"Why don't you divorce him?" I asked. I had learned about "divorce" by overhearing adults talk about the Vanderbilt custody battle that was headlining most newspapers.

Mother was startled and said, "He's your dad," and I was told never to suggest such a thing again.

In his later life, Dad told me about a time he was hauling a carload of bootleg alcohol near Millersburg when federal revenue agents suddenly were in pursuit. As they chased him down a narrow country road, he came over a hill head-to-head with an old farmer who had a load of wood chunks gathered from the timber. Dad could not stop and veered to the right where he plowed out a strip of fence and chugged through the pasture until he had to drive through another fence to get back on the road.

As he veered around the old farmer, the farmer let go a chunk of wood that crashed through the windshield and narrowly missed Dad's head. That was just one of Dad's hair-raising episodes with the feds.

Mother and Dad with me.

I sit outside at my Agnew grandparents' home next to a chicken (I think it's a chicken).

Brother Kenny and me (Kenny is on the tricycle).

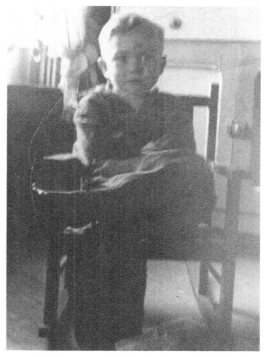

It looks like I'm thinking hard while I sit on my little rocking chair.

Kenny (right) and me at the Bair Place, 1935.

My family in 1935. Dad is holding my brother Leroy, and Mother is just behind Kenny. I am leaning next to Dad with what some might say is a typical look of mine.

Grandma Agnew is pictured with her four oldest grandchildren: Kenny, Leroy, Eddie Harris (in her lap), and me, 1938.

I received my First Communion at Our Lady of Lourdes in Keswick in the spring of 1938. This picture was taken later in the day at Grandma Agnew's homestead.

# Chapter 2

## 1935–1939

We had moved to the "Bair Place" on the west end of Keswick across the street from Mert Bair's dairy farm on March 1, 1934. While we lived here, I welcomed another new brother, Paul Leroy, born January 4, 1935. Kenny slapped Leroy the first time he saw him! In Kenny's defense, he had just turned two years old and had been told he was no longer the baby.

Dr. Harlan delivered Leroy at home. Mother was bedfast for a week, and a friend took care of her and Leroy during that time. Leroy had an outbreak of boils soon after he was born, and Dr. Doyle of Sigourney found a formula that returned him to health.

We had two or three pigs to eat table scraps and drink the slop composed of dishwater, grease, and assorted scraps. The slop was carried to them (carry-outs!) in five-gallon buckets. If you covered some corn or oats in a trough with the slop and a little skimmed or sour milk, the hogs gathered around as if they were enjoying a banquet. Chickens also would sneak in to get a few bites. Cows, horses, and sheep found it unappetizing.

My brothers and I played "pig" with chairs turned down to make pens and little bowls of cereal set out to "eat" while we crawled around and "oink-oinked." Mother, however, frowned when we got up on one another's rear quarters like we had seen the pigs "playing." We were discouraged from playing pig and "playing that way."

Back in these years, one of my first little friends was Richard Rickman, whose family lived in the next house to the east. Later their house caught fire, and Aunt Ethel Agnew, who was visiting for a few days, Mother, Kenny, and I stood on the Bair Place porch and watched the flames lick up the side of the house to the roof. The water-bucket brigade finally got the fire extinguished. I had bad dreams about that for some time and have been terrified of fires ever since.

When the Depression was at its peak of discouragement and hardship, young men left the farms, cities, and small towns in droves to seek employment elsewhere and eke out an existence. Many became hobos and rode the rails, which was very dangerous. A hobo was not a "tramp" or a "bum"—a hobo had skills for which there was no demand, just like many homeless today. Of course in the 1930s, there were no homeless shelters and very few soup lines where watery soup was available. A tramp only worked when forced, and a bum didn't work at all. Hobos, bums, and tramps all rode the rails, hopped freights, and stowed away in empty boxcars or even rode on top of the cars. The tramps and bums preyed on the innocent hobos.

It was the down-on-their-luck hobos who occasionally approached our back door while we lived at the Bair Place, which was near the railroad tracks. Sometimes when people saw them coming, doors were slammed in their faces as they were told to move on and get off the property.

Mother always treated the hobos with kindness and courtesy. She would bring a basin of warm water, soap, a washcloth, and a towel to the back porch, while Kenny and I hovered nearby very curious and rather frightened. Mother would fix a sandwich or a plate of whatever we were going to have for every hobo. They were very appreciative and not one ever failed to thank her profusely.

Thank God that President Franklin Roosevelt was elected in 1932 and began instituting programs like the Works Progress Administration (WPA) and CCC that put the unemployed to work building highways, developing national parks, organizing conservation programs, and constructing government buildings. This gave the population hope and a few dollars in their pockets. The morale of the country improved, hope was again alive, and a sense of pride returned. I could sense this even as a young child.

I didn't like being quiet and the "don't turn around" part of going to Mass at Our Lady of Lourdes in Keswick. However, the choir with Manda Harris in charge and the soloist were fascinating, and I liked seeing Grandma Dawson and Aunt Elizabeth "Sis" Dawson always smiling when I could sneak a look back. They sat in the last pew nearest the exit door. I wondered why Grandma Dawson could smile and look happy while my parents and all the other kids' parents looked so stern. I was uncomfortable around priests and terrified of the hooded nuns with their huge rosaries clanking. I was only three to four years old.

Kenny and I played "Mass" when we lived in west Keswick. We put two kitchen chairs side by side and Kenny—as the priest—used a Sears catalog for the prayer book and a glass of water was the wine. Pieces of soda crackers were communion. He mumbled in "Latin" and "said" Mass. I was the choir and sang out "O lawsy, O lawsy," which I thought was what Manda Harris was singing during Mass. She was probably singing, "O Lord, we love Thee." Mother looked on happily with a little smile on her face—her two little angels playing Mass—surely at least one would be a priest!

Grandma Dawson and Aunt Sis lived next to the Keswick church, and we always visited with them and many Greene and a few Dawson relatives after Sunday Mass. (Grandpa Dawson and my Uncle Jim Dawson were then living in south Keswick.) After visiting Grandma and Sis, we got in the truck Dad used for hauling livestock, coal, and rock and rode seven miles over dirt—which was sometimes very muddy and slippery—to Grandma Agnew's farm home.

At Grandma Agnew's, the aunts would fix a big dinner while the uncles would play cards or horseshoes, go hunting, or just sit outside in the shade or by the big coal-heating stove in the living room. Since I am not much younger than Aunt Helen and Uncle Leo, they were my main playmates, along with my brothers. Uncle Leo had pet pigeons, and I loved them.

Grandma Dawson was a storyteller. She told of the times when roving bands of gypsies raided area farmsteads. These were lightning-fast raids—the daylight robbery could be finished in 10 minutes, and the gypsies would be on their way to the next unsuspecting victim. Dad recalled one such raid that happened when he was very small. I enjoyed hearing Grandma's tales of their cunning and boldness.

Grandma Dawson was a schoolteacher before her marriage and well educated for the time. When we would stay with her when Mother and Dad were at some function, she would have Kenny, Leroy, and me at full attention as she told the most hair-raising Irish ghost stories—always portrayed in a local setting with local names. She would have us too scared to move and when she would throw up her arms and exclaim, "The burning bush was really the devil" and holy water had miraculously extinguished the evil one, we were happy he had been repelled!

One of my memories of Grandma Dawson is that her house always smelled good—there were six to eight varieties of pine trees surrounding it, and she grew many perennial flowers. Whenever flowers were blooming, she would cut and take armloads of blooms to the church and decorate the main and side altars for Sunday Mass. I would accompany her, and she would let me go into the choir loft and "play" the organ. Of course, I had no organ training, but she always acted as if my singing and "playing" were heavenly.

In the summers when Father Quinlan was working in the Keswick church, Grandma and I would catch the best-looking, healthiest chicken, tie its legs, and put it in a gunnysack. We would sneak around the outside of the church—peeking around so Father wouldn't see us—and hastily run to his car and put the chicken, along with a bag of fresh vegetables, on the floor of his back seat. She didn't want any praise or thanks, but I'm sure he knew they were gifts from Grandma, who was so poor herself that she couldn't even afford a three-cent stamp (the cost of mailing a letter in the 1930s). She steamed stamps off letters she received and then reused them.

At Grandma Dawson's, we could do just about anything we wished. She had two pianos that we enjoyed "playing," and she let us make and drink tea, which wasn't allowed at home. I liked to put her false teeth in my mouth—they were always in a cup of water by her bed as she only wore them when she attended Mass or went uptown.

Grandmas Dawson and Agnew, along with Mother, had varicose veins that used to fascinate me, as well as worry me.

Grandpa Dawson passed away in 1936. He had Parkinson's disease, had lost his first wife and child in childbirth, lost two sons in their 20s and a daughter at 17, and lost all three of his farms and $7,000—a lot of money at that time. He lent money to neighbors and friends with a handshake and, of course, was never repaid because everyone was broke except for the big land banks that took over many, many farms.

Anyhow, Grandpa Dawson died a sick and defeated man. His parents, immigrants from Ireland, had been very successful and prosperous and had left or given each of their surviving children approximately 160 acres of good land.

We went to Grandpa Dawson's wake at Grandma's house in Keswick next to the church. Mother had Kenny and I dressed in starched white shirts, ties, and little corduroy trousers. I hated the stiff white shirt and felt the tie was choking me. J.S. O'Rourke, Dad's first cousin, told Kenny and me he would "cut off our ears" if we weren't good boys. When he reached in his pocket to show us a pocketknife, we raced to the nearest bedroom and dived under the bed. Evidently, it had not been dusted under there for quite some time because when Dad finally pulled us out, we were covered with dust bunnies, our hair was all messed, and Mother was "fit to be tied" after all her efforts to make us look presentable.

This is the first I remember of Aunt Katie and of disagreements among siblings. When Grandpa's first wife, Winnie Stanton Dawson, died at age 21, on her deathbed she asked him to be buried next to her. But many of his children wanted him to be buried next to their mother/my Grandma. Aunt Katie said he should honor his first wife's wishes, and she prevailed. He was laid to rest next to Winnie, and Grandma's plot is surrounded by some of her unmarried children in another section of Pleasant Grove Cemetery in Sigourney.

There was nothing left for Grandpa's children to inherit except a few undeveloped acres that Uncle Jim took. Grandma remained in the small house by the church, which actually was owned by her sister Maggie Greene, who operated a boarding house in far-away Cedar Rapids.

We moved to the "Big House" just south of Main Street in Keswick soon after Grandpa Dawson died there (March 20, 1936). It was a huge house with three floors and a watch-tower, but it was no longer the grand place that it had been when a doctor had it built many years earlier. It was so cold upstairs that Mother and Dad would wrap heated bricks and irons to put into the beds. Kenny and I huddled up, cozy under tons of covers.

We had a chicken house and barn, so we got our first cow, Floozie, whose ears and tail had been frozen off as a calf. She was probably the ugliest cow ever, but she had a new calf every year and furnished us with milk and cream. Mother then churned our own butter. Floozie did not like children and would "bunt" us if we approached her head.

We also had chickens for eggs and food, and Mother had a large productive garden. She baked bread, made cottage cheese, and made our shirts, pajamas, and underwear from printed feed sacks. She made our sheets and pillowcases from bleached flour sacks.

I was thrilled that pigeons lived in the barn, and I spent many hours thinking how I could catch them. I never could!

We got our first dog since Al; Mother named him Ginger because of his coloring. He was very protective of Kenny, Leroy, and me, and proceeded to bite the paperboy and a door-to-door salesman from Oskaloosa. Dad had to buy the man a new pair of pants and warned him to never come to Keswick again.

Ginger chased cars and was struck one day. He was in very bad physical shape and lay out in a clump of weeds. Mother took him scraps and water. After two and a half weeks, he hobbled to the back porch. The elderly neighbor exclaimed, "He'll never chase cars again." However, Ginger was soon back at it, urged on by me! Before long, he mysteriously was gone and never seen again.

In 1936, I first heard a strange, unnerving sound. I even considered that it might be a ringing-buzzing in my head that only I heard. But it was the emergence of the 17 Year Locusts. In the subsequent years of 1953, 1970, 1987, and again in 2004, as I was penning this, it was a depressing sound that I equated with sad stories of events I heard about at that time. Adding to the dust storms, drought, soup lines, and extreme heat were an invasion of grasshoppers that devoured every green leaf in their paths, and chinch bugs that invaded fields of oats. Those are remembrances of the "Trying Thirties."

In the 1930s, sometimes the heat was so intense that people would sleep outside on their lawns or on their shaded porches where the sun had not hit during the day. There were no air conditioners and few fans since no rural homes and few towns had been wired for electricity.

In 1936, the summer heat was like a furnace. For a few hot summer days, Kenny and I stayed with Aunt Marge and Uncle Leo Costello in their tiny rented frame house in Mill-ersburg. I accompanied Aunt Marge as she drove her car, and we visited her friends and got groceries and the mail. Leo had a Chevrolet car dealership, and Kenny went with him to the garage and brought back several car sales books. We enjoyed cutting out the cars and "driving" them around the floor while crawling on our hands and knees. At night, we slept on the dining-room linoleum floor, and a noisy fan—the first one I had seen—at least stirred the hot air around us.

When everyone was so poor during the Depression years, the adults in the Agnew family drew names one Christmas. Kenny, Leroy, and I had each received a fountain pen from Santa Claus, but no toys. But Grandma Agnew remembered us. As the adults opened their presents, she gave each of us a pocket comb with a clip that could be attached to our overall-bibs. I was thrilled to no end! I was not expecting anything, and that little brown comb was one of my favorite gifts ever.

At Christmas, there always were lots of peanuts in the shell and other Christmas nuts to crack. We kids used to make a big mess behind the stove with our peanut hulls and nutshells. One of the aunts periodically arrived with a broom and dustpan to sweep up the mess.

I was four years old when I told Mother that a little girl who lived nearby had "wet" for me and Richard, and—to my amazement—hers had been cut off as it came out of a hole! Much to my surprise, Mother immediately told me I no longer could play with them. It was my first lesson about not telling my parents everything that was questionable.

Later, when I was six or seven, I told Mother, "I'm going to marry Albert [my best friend at the time] when I get big." (I never would say "grow up," it was always "get big.") Much to my consternation, Mother said that I couldn't because "boys don't marry other boys."

I was dumbfounded thinking Albert and I wouldn't be able to play with our toys and be together all day. Mother and I never discussed it again, and I'm sure Albert's mother felt relieved when we agreed that we were both supposed to marry girls, not each other.

I did like doing what were considered more "womanly" things. Whenever Mother would bake a cake, I stood on a chair next to her wanting to stir, beat the egg whites, or do anything to help. The best part was licking the bowl after she poured the batter in the baking pan. I would have been satisfied to just eat the batter. However, I was warned that if I persisted, I would "get worms." Back then, kids were "wormed" periodically.

Drinking a teaspoon of cod liver oil every day was said to prevent illness. Laxatives consisted of Ex-Lax, Syrup Pepsin, Sal Hepatica (awful), and the gagging, horrible castor oil. If an adult really wanted to get "cleaned out," he/she took a dose of Epsom salts. Mother drank mineral oil each morning and ate 100-percent all-bran.

In the 1930s, it seemed we had all the childhood diseases. I hardly remember having the mumps, but they weren't as bad for children as for adults.

When I was six and living in the Big House, scarlet fever swept through the area, hitting and missing various families. Of course, we were victims. We were quarantined for three weeks with a sign on the door: "QUARANTINED—CONTAGIOUS." Other than Dr. Doyle, Dad was the only one who could enter.

I was in bed with a "sheet tent" over the top to keep in the moisture and whatever it was the Doc had prepared. I pretended to be in a tepee—one of my daydreams at that time was to live as an Indian (Native American).

I recovered first, and Mother was soon in the "tent," as were Kenny and Leroy. Dad cooked lots of eggs and fresh fried potatoes; he was a very good cook although his gravy was almost as thick as fresh concrete!

My job was to answer the phone, and I had to climb up on a chair to get to the mouthpiece. It was a party line, and I had to crank for one long ring to get "central." The operator would say, "Keswick," I would name the person I was calling in Keswick, and the operator would put the call through. I did not enjoy the phone job, especially calling Elick's grocery to tell Dad to bring bread or whatever home.

When I was seven or eight, I was chosen to "lead the horse" at Grandma Agnew's farm to pull the forks of hay from a hayrack (it was all loose hay) up into the haymow. I had to lead it though a patch of smartweeds. If you touched those weeds and then touched your face or eyes, they made an itchy, smart feeling. The feeling only worsened each time you touched your mouth or rubbed your eyes.

I also had pneumonia, and it was feared that the Dawsons had weak lungs as Aunt Winnie and Uncle Joker had both perished from the dreaded malady. Kenny was susceptible to nosebleeds; Leroy had boils, as did I.

It seemed there always was someone ailing. Perhaps it's that way in most families with small kids.

In 1936, Uncle Emmett Agnew dated Catherine Gregan, Dad's cousin. On a very warm August evening, Dad and Uncle Emmett hovered close to the radio as Catherine, a schoolteacher, tried to teach Kenny to print his name. Dad and Uncle Emmett were listening as Joe Louis, a black man, had just knocked out Jack Sharkey, a white man, in three rounds of boxing. It was the first time I even knew that there were black human beings.

Of course, today my original Irish Caucasian family now includes members with African-American, Hispanic, and Native American blood. My friends and loved ones are from all races, cultures, and sexual orientations—being color-blind is a virtue in this regard!

But as a youngster growing up in rural Iowa in the 1930s, it would be many years before I laid eyes on a black individual, although Dad was a little more worldly since he had been to Chicago. (As an aside, Dad had my eyes "bug out wide" as he tried to portray the area and hugeness of Chicago. He announced that it stretched as far as from Keswick to Cedar Rapids—which I thought was pronounced "See the Rabbits," and most certainly had a huge hare population. I just couldn't fathom such immensity, and it was frightening. I could have gotten lost in Sigourney with a population of just over 2,000!)

I started school in Keswick in 1936. We did not have primary or preschool but went directly to first grade. I was in a country school that had one teacher for all the grades (first through eighth). Miss Margery Weiss, my first- and second-grade teacher, was tall, blond, wore glasses, and looked mean.

There were five in my first-grade class, and three named "Gene" or "Jean" of which two were girls. I was very confused and wondered why I had a girl's name. I did not like school and seemed to be the dumbest student in class. But by second grade, I had caught up, surpassed the other four, found school rather fun, and Miss Weiss was OK.

At school, girls were considered to be good, obedient, and intelligent. Boys always were getting dirty and picking on the girls. They were less obedient and more ornery. They weren't as studious as the girls—they were just boys!

When I was in second grade, I got my first pair of clamp-on roller skates and immediately took them to school. As the kids gathered around at noon, I put them on and immediately rolled out of control in an embarrassing fall!

Gene Harris, who was in fifth or sixth grade, came to my aid, and I recall Gene O'Rourke (a cousin on the Dawson side) laughing hilariously. It took me many weeks to learn to skate. Kenny and I would each put on a skate and "one skate" up and down the sidewalk in front of our house.

At the time, Keswick had a great boys' basketball team, and most of the players made a fuss over me, especially Dean Hartzell, the older brother of Lyle Hartzell, who would become the husband of Aunt Helen Agnew. Dean ranked right up there with Uncle Leo Agnew as a super hero.

I dreamed of being a basketball player. I started staying after school to watch practice, but Mother put an end to that and demanded I return home as soon as school was out. I had a little brother (Kenny) in first grade to look out for.

On entering third grade, Miss Velma McClung was my teacher, and she looked mean all the time. By this age, I had become a "dreamer" and couldn't concentrate on the "three Rs" (reading, 'riting and 'rithmetic). I felt so dumb and always looked forward to recess.

One nice fall day, Kenny and I returned from school to find that Mother, Dad, and Leroy were away. We decided to make some mud cakes, and why not use some real ingredients? We went to the chicken house and found about 10 to 12 eggs—we left two or three so there wouldn't be questions about the hens' lack of production—and proceeded to mix the eggs and fine dirt to make a wonderful, sticky batter.

We were just ready to put it in the pans (jar lids) when Mother, Dad, and Leroy returned home. We waved and smiled, but they were not smiling and Leroy was pointing. It was only then that I noticed the pile of eggshells that we failed to dispose. Needless to say, we got a good scolding and spanking. Now I realize how our survival partly depended on those eggs.

Our parents meted out various types of punishment, usually in accordance with the severity of the offense. When I was in grade school, if a student got a spanking or any kind of punishment, the offender could count on receiving a whipping when his/her parents found out—and they always did. Folks did not challenge a teacher's authority—she was in charge until we got home from school. None of us Dawsons were ever on the end of any physical punishment in the classroom, but it seems to me that verbal assaults sometimes are just as devastating, have an equal or better "hurting" range, and are remembered as well as the corporal variety.

Dad's main method of administering "justice" was via his foot. When he kicked my rear end, his kick often lifted me off the ground. I swear he could have set distance records for field goals as an NFL kicker. Although he was a terrific and successful farmer, I'm afraid he missed his calling to immortality.

Another of his weapons—and, to me, they were weapons—was his belt. I was always glad when he wore overalls or coveralls since they didn't require one. When I saw him unbuckle his belt, my butt cheeks quivered in anticipation. Even worse than belts were razor straps that were used to sharpen straight razors, which were in vogue in the 1930s. But they only were accessible if the perpetrator was cornered in the kitchen or wherever Dad was shaving.

Occasionally, we were "invited" (told) to select our own switch from a branch of a tree. I would try to delay the inevitable, and Dad would exhort me to "Hurry up, let's get this over with. Don't take all day 'cause you won't like the one I select."

Now I'm glad that he was a firm disciplinarian and wish today's parents were in his mold.

We were told—and it was enforced—that we were to be seen and not heard, and if we had company, we were to be seldom seen and never heard! If I broke that rule, one devastating look from either parent or whoever was in charge was enough to send me scurrying away like a rabbit. I knew that the person delivering the withering look also was making a mental follow-up ... and wouldn't forget.

Mother's arsenal included a hairbrush with a long, flat, porcelain handle. She wielded it occasionally when we were small, especially when it got to the point that her hand spankings would make Kenny and me laugh. Later on, she brought sober looks to our faces when she would announce that she would tell Dad about our behavior as soon as he returned. With those words, I became very meek, humble, and contrite, hoping she wouldn't tell him. Often that was effective.

After two years (March 1, 1938), we moved from the Big House to the "Sauter Place" in east Keswick. By now, we had lived in west, south, and east Keswick.

The Sauter Place included a barn, garage, chicken house, and two to three acres, so Floozie, the chickens, and the pigs had plenty of room. Here I had pigeons—wild ones I had caught at the town elevator with the aid of my friend Georgie Van Fleet. I clipped the pigeons' wings, and they lived in a small space under the garage and only came out when I wasn't around—no fun!

Our neighbors here were Nora (Hubbell) Morgan and her children: Mary Jean; my classmate Bobby; and Betty, Leroy's age. Several Keswick residents were of interest to me by now. One was Mr. Lawrence "Buck" Bender, who was the husband of Bessie, the owner of Bessie's Tavern. He would walk by our house with a bucket of fresh milk from a cow he owned; Bessie used the fresh milk and cream at the tavern. Buck was a very friendly gentleman, and on many pleasant mornings, three-year-old Leroy tried to "sell" Floozie to him! Even at the age of three, Leroy was trying to make some money. Buck got a big kick out of it and related the incidents to Dad.

The elderly Mrs. Cameron lived directly across the street in a large two-story house. Each summer, Mrs. Cameron's unmarried daughter, along with a partner, who also was a schoolteacher, arrived from Chicago. Mr. Sherman Wilhite used his car as their "taxi" and took them to various social events. The women returned to the big city in the late summer.

Mrs. Cameron's son also had "escaped" Keswick and moved to California. He would visit for a week or two in the summer, bringing along his son and a male friend. I was a year or two younger than the son, and even though he and his friend played catch with a football in our "Floozie" pasture, they ignored me completely. It was the first time I had ever seen a ball that wasn't round—Keswick did not have a football team—and I longed to join them, but I was too shy.

Also living nearby was a family that included a teenage son who was very attractive and effeminate—his mannerisms made me wonder if he were really a boy or a girl. I spent much time observing him and was very fascinated. He always was with teen girls, who seemed very fond of him, but I noticed he never played games with or had close male friends. When Aunt Helen started Keswick High School, I heard her telling my other aunts about him and how his male peers teased him, called him a "sissy," and had him miserable and in tears. Shortly after that, the family moved to a distant town.

I felt a certain kinship with him and felt sorry for him. I have often wondered what happened to the "beautiful" son.

Dad was a full-time truck driver with his own truck. Dad hauled livestock for area farmers, coal from the mines for fuel and warmth, and gravel from the pits for roads. He supplemented our family income during the Depression, Dust Bowl, and Prohibition by making "home brew" and providing it to thirsty consumers (bootlegging). But the bootleg business "dried up" when Prohibition came to an end and taverns sold alcoholic beverages.

Of course, there was little crime in rural Iowa, although when I was quite small, I do recall hearing about a bank robbery in Keswick. It wasn't Bonnie and Clyde, Dillinger, Pretty Boy Floyd, or the Ma Barker gang, but two locals who made many blunders and soon were caught. I remember another crime that happened around 1935. In the very hot Depression days of summer, a man who lived on an area farm went berserk and shot his wife and stepdaughter to death. Neighbors heard their cows bawling and pleading for water and went to investigate. They saw the swollen bodies through a window. The man was soon apprehended and didn't spend very long in prison. I had accompanied Dad when he hauled livestock for him, and I had seen the victims when they were alive.

During the late 1930s, there were some deaths from heat stroke, and many animals and poultry were victims. One thing that haunts me to this day occurred at the Sauter Place. We had quite a few chickens, Floozie, a yearling calf, and a pig or two to drink the slop and supplement the family income when they were sold.

On a very hot summer day, I went to the barn and observed many chickens and a 175-pound pig inside (Floozie and the calf were in the shade of a tree). I shut the door and proceeded to chase the chickens and pig from stall to stall, back and forth. Finally, they got so hot and tired that they wouldn't even run anymore. The pig was panting and I, too, was exhausted. I opened the door, released the suffering victims, and then went to the house to lie down on the cool, linoleum-covered dining-room floor.

When I went outside early that evening, I was surprised to see Dad and his friend Arnie Wagner, both sweat-covered, digging a hole under Floozie's shade tree. Lying next to the excavation was the pig—now dead.

I was shocked and very ashamed as I slunk away knowing that I had caused its death and was depriving our poverty-stricken family. Dad never questioned me about this since many animals were dying at the time. I just hope God has forgiven me.

We raised lots of young chickens. We bought "settings" (15 eggs) from Manda Harris so we could raise big White Rock chickens like she had, and 15 more from Kate Noonan who had many beautiful chickens. The eggs were put under "setting" hens; they hatched and mothered the chicks until they got feathers.

Grandma Dawson also had her chickens, along with a cow and a pig where she and Aunt Sis lived. Everyone had big gardens and fruit trees. I recall Vera McBride, a neighbor from down the street, telling me she would give me a dime to catch a big white chicken—ours—that had strolled into her yard. I declined and hurried home wishing our chickens would stay at home.

In the 1930s, an outbreak of hog cholera broke out—what else could happen in the Trying Thirties? There was the Depression, drought, dust storms, and now for the farmers, highly contagious and deadly hog cholera. In my opinion, other than the swine deaths, the worst thing about the hog cholera was that the farm pigeon was singled out as the carrier from farm to farm. An edict was announced that I had to get rid of my pet pigeons.

I took them to Grandma Agnew's and gave them to Uncle Leo. The Agnew family was more realistic about the situation—they understood that birds, rabbits, pheasants, squirrels, rats, or any varmints could be the carriers. Actually, it was caused by unsanitary conditions and, if not carried airborne, it probably was on the shoes and boots of farmers themselves. It was a damned shame to put the blame on pigeons and try to eradicate them from the farms. Everyone started vaccinating very young pigs to prevent the disease, and the situation was brought under control.

During those Keswick years, young men would torment L.D. Toothman, the local druggist, on Halloween. He would sit in his store all night with the lights on. Even then, they would divert his attention long enough to get a farmer's wagon ("borrowed" from an unsuspecting victim) or a young calf up on the flat roof of the building. Of course, they were enjoying a few "beverages" while this was taking place.

The Toothmans also owned a hardware store, and Mrs. L.D. (Selva) Toothman opened a beauty salon in the back of the building. During this time period, Mother made an appointment to get a permanent wave, even though she had naturally wavy hair. Kenny and I accompanied her. I recall her very pained expression as she had her hair rolled in metal-type rollers and large clamps for forming waves. Each roller was hooked to an electrical cord—something like Christmas tree lights. Then a huge lid was lowered over her head, and we waited for what seemed like hours as I yawned and stretched. After a long time, she was disconnected and a mass of curls was the result.

When the local women got together, they would discuss who got "burned" the worst and if Mrs. Toothman had administered any salve to relieve the pain. Sometimes those hot electrical coils would burn the scalp, as well as curl the hair. I really thought Mother's hair looked frizzy and unattractive for about the first six weeks until it relaxed somewhat. Of course, I didn't tell her though.

Sometimes Mrs. Toothman cut Kenny's and my hair while Mother "cooked." She charged only a dime for our cuts. Uncle Tommy Dawson heard Mother talk about our 10-cent haircuts, and he soon strolled into Mrs. Toothman's shop asking for the same deal. Of course, she was surprised and directed him up the street to the town barbers, Mr. Bill Rickman and his sons, Walter and Hubert.

A few years later, Dad took me to the Rickman shop and told them to "Cut it damn short. I know he'll [me] tell you not to make it too short, but I don't want to have to pay for this again for two to three months." Much to my dismay, the barber cut it even shorter than Dad suggested. I felt like a plucked chicken, and my immense "calf-sized ears" were even more visible. (Don't believe that "all-the-better-to-hear-you" crap. I believe a wolf said that to Little Red Riding Hood!)

When I got older, one of my barbers was "Dubbin" Mason, who once nipped one of my ears. No wonder—it was so big! He quickly doused it with alcohol while acting as if nothing had happened. After he finished cutting my hair, he put so much scented oil on it that the oil ran down the back of my neck. At that time, everyone used oil for shine and to lubricate dry hair.

After the nipping, I switched to his fellow barber, Mr. R.G. Litzenberg, who used only scissors—no clippers—and took forever to cut my hair while he spoke softly right next to my ear about threshing crews' hardships and bygone days. He was very old.

After that, I began to cut my own hair and have ever since. Leroy tried Mr. Ernie Claypool, a barber who worked down the street and found him to be even slower than Mr. Litzenberg. Seems every barber I visited was either bald or nearly hairless. Wonder why. Hmm ...

When I stayed overnight at Grandma Agnew's in the 1930s and 1940s, I could see large searchlights tower about and above the countryside. Two searchlights were located a few miles from the Agnew farm—one was to the west and the other was north. They turned in 360-degree circles to illuminate the night sky and serve as beacons for mail planes.

I would lie awake at night next to my sleeping uncles and listen to their peaceful breathing and the drone of a mail plane as it passed in the blackness of the night. At the same time, I would watch the large arc of light as it completed a cycle across the south wall of the bedroom. These were peaceful and mystical moments of tranquility and nice memories.

The "big" summer events also provided great memories. The Creamery Picnic in North English and the Keokuk County Fair in What Cheer were big social events and anticipated for months. There were Ferris wheels, parades, midways, lots of food booths, and local talent contests, which sometimes included tricks performed by Uncle Leo Agnew's dog, Mike. For us kids, most of the time was spent mingling with lots of youngsters from miles around while the oldsters enjoyed the camaraderie.

At What Cheer, the organizers also judged livestock, and there was a booth where you could get a photo taken for 25 cents. We bought lots of pictures and exchanged them with friends. Everyone had a grand time. Those carnivals were the highlights of a summer.

Entertainment in the 1930s also included traveling tent vaudeville shows that occasionally stopped in small towns. Everyone enjoyed these live productions, and it seemed the entire town and surrounding area turned out. I remember one that featured a man with his mule that did tricks. What I actually recall were their names: "Si Sizzle Sickle and his mule Tommy Tucker." For some reason, I enjoyed saying that over and over again.

Each year, we looked forward to the arrival of Christmas catalogs. They became well-worn as we thumbed through them and dreamed of the things we wished Santa Claus would bring. Leroy and I would get under the covers with a flashlight and delight in all our fantasies as we pored over the pages of wonderful portrayals. Finally, Dad would hear us chattering and shout, "Get to sleep! Don't make me come in there!"

However, when I was seven, Christmas became not nearly as much fun after Georgie Van Fleet told me the most devastating and god-awful lie. He said there was no Santa and our parents had been tricking us all this time. I didn't want to believe him but then happened across a pencil box hidden on top of the cupboard that Santa supposedly brought to me later.

When I was in the age range of five to eight, the culmination of the annual vacation Catechism classes at our Keswick church was the "Queen of May" festival, which featured the crowning of the Blessed Virgin (the statue of the Holy Mother) with a garland of flowers. Keswick, What Cheer, and Webster kids went to vacation Catechism together.

While the priest and nuns were dining at a parishioner's home during the noon hour on these class days, there would be wars of words with much shouting, insults, and threats between the What Cheer and the Keswick-Webster kids. This often pitted cousins against cousins who were members of the different parishes. Kids can say very insensitive things, and one year, an obese girl from an orphanage was "auditioning" to be adopted by a neighbor. This girl was originally from Tennessee, and we kids pestered her constantly and called her "two-ton Tessie from Tennessee." Now I'm sorry for what we put her through.

I remember the Catholic Church's rule of the time that every female had to have her head covered inside the church. In my mind, I still can picture the ladies' big floppy hats that also served as sun umbrellas. In the summer, the church windows were open and hand fans advertising the local funeral home were in the seats. Some women carried their own fold-up, Japanese-type fans in their purses. Usually an older child (me) would fan a baby in attendance. Men didn't fan as vigorously—if at all—as women; they considered fanning to be feminine behavior.

I would go with Mother to pick out her Easter bonnet. She would try on dozens at Graham's in Sigourney before eventually buying the one I had selected for her. When she would get complimented on it, she would proclaim, "Gene picked it out," and I would beam proudly. The person who bestowed the compliment would look puzzled—wondering why a little boy would pick out his mother's hat.

I received my First Holy Communion in the spring of 1938. Shortly after that, I ate a peanut after 12 midnight one Sunday morning and received the Holy Eucharist at Sunday morning's Mass (Catholic rules then forbade receiving communion at morning Mass if you ate or drank after midnight earlier that day).

We had stopped at Grandma Dawson's before Mass and a piece of peanut brittle was on the table. One little peanut had escaped from that hardened mass of brown sweetness! I ate it and didn't think about it until communion time. I was afraid to not get up—I knew Dad would yank me out of the pew. I was scared to say I'd broken my fast, so I sighed and quickly decided to avoid the danger at hand and worry about hell later.

It seemed a dark cloud enveloped me, and I was afraid to confess in the confessional that I had done the unthinkable and received communion with a peanut in my belly.

Another first in my Catholic life was attending a funeral. I was about seven years old when it was decided I was old enough to attend. The deceased was a very aged and frail gentleman. I thought about the funeral for days after seeing his lifeless body in the casket and then dirt covering the casket later. I can still visualize those scenes today.

When I was seven and Kenny was five, we had our tonsils and adenoids removed at Dr. Doyle's office in Sigourney. We were "knocked out" with ether and had very sore throats for a few days. Later on, Leroy was subjected to the same. At that time, when kids reached the ages of five to seven, most everyone went through it. The only pleasant part was that we had lots of ice cream because it was the only thing easy to swallow.

Wisdom teeth, teeth "pulling," and huge "foot-long" needles were subjects I had heard adults discuss—they would frown and look like they were in pain as they talked about the torture. Kenny and I had our first dental appointments on a Saturday with Dr. Boland (a distant cousin) in Sigourney. The ride to Sigourney over dirt roads in our 1932 Chevy was a dreadful trip of fear.

We arrived at the reception room shaking in our boots and had just settled down when Dr. Boland emerged in his white coat. I broke like a frightened fawn and dove for cover behind the furniture. That set Kenny off, and we began crying and screaming. Doc Boland stood in the doorway making grabs at us as we scurried by with Dad in hot pursuit.

When you think you are going to be tortured, you become very elusive.

Finally, Doc Boland threw up his hands and said to come another day. Death and torture were avoided at the moment, but I knew dreadful punishment awaited me, especially since I was the oldest and supposed to set a good example. During the height of the chase, Miss Weiss, my first- and second-grade teacher, walked in for an appointment. Miss Weiss had never seen that side of me, so I knew there would be added consequences for disobeying Dad in front of her.

Mother was quite disappointed in the dentist-office episode and cast sad looks in my direction, probably thinking that all her preaching and instruction had been in vain. Mother, I amend and am sorry I ever disappointed you.

I avoided dentists until after I graduated from high school and reluctantly went on my own to have my teeth cleaned. Now I rather enjoy a dental visit and nearly fall asleep in the chair. Maybe I don't have as much sensitivity to pain at this advanced age—one advantage of growing old.

I never dreaded the visits to Dr. Harlan in Keswick, but after the tonsillectomy, I was very leery of doctors. So my fear list now consisted of "God will get you, he sees you being bad," priests, stern-looking nuns with chain-looking rosary beads, dentists, doctors, most teachers, J.S. O'Rourke and other middle-aged men who might "cut off your ears," old ladies (not relatives) dressed in black with no teeth, lightning, thunder, fires, the end of the world, slippery and muddy roads, and that Mother, Dad, Kenny, or Leroy would die.

I would silently pray to be the first of our family to die—even though I knew I was doomed to hell's fire for eating that peanut and then going to communion.

On March 1, 1939, we were on the move again to the 80-acre "Lucas Place," a few miles north of Keswick. Dad still had the truck and also had some crops. We got more cows to go with Floozie and a few more pigs and chickens.

We didn't have electricity here—the rural electric association was not yet in place (we had electricity at our Keswick homes). We carried kerosene lanterns to do winter chores and had kerosene lamps in the house. We had no basement; a man-made cave in the yard was used for storage, and we had our cream separator down there. It was never too hot or too cold in the cave and was a haven when storms came roaring out of the northwest—it seemed the black clouds and jagged, cracking lightning always came from the northwest.

Most of our relatives moved a lot of times, but it seemed like none of them moved as often as us. Uncle Johnny and Rose Agnew lived in Tiffin, and they also briefly rented a house in North English. Aunt Marge and Leo Costello moved within Millersburg to two different houses, and one was a historical brick that they purchased. Aunt Ethel and Richard Harris started at the "Stewart Place" (where we later lived) one mile south of Hurd's country store. From there, they lived in three places near Keswick and another next to Dayton Hall. Then they moved to Vinton, Colo, and finally Haverhill, Iowa.

Aunt Alice and Kermie Herr resided with his mother in Harper, south of Parnell in a house that later became the Kenny Dawson compound, west of Keswick, both west and northeast of North English, and then in Delta, Iowa. Aunt Theresa and Leo O'Rourke lived both southeast and southwest of Millersburg, southeast of Armah, west of Parnell, and then the O'Rourke farm southwest of Armah. Uncle Bernard and Veronica Agnew lived in North English above their tavern and at the Agnew homestead near Armah.

Uncle Emmett and Gloria Agnew lived northeast of Armah and east of North English. After Uncle Emmett and Gloria divorced, he resided with Grandma in North English. Aunt Helen and Lyle Hartzell made their homes in Keswick; North English; Denver, Colorado; with Grandma in North English while Lyle attended railroad school; Madrid, Iowa; and then on to Shawnee Mission, Kansas. Uncle Harry and Mary Agnew started at the Agnew homestead, then purchased the Jim Cunningham farm, and retired to Lakeside Acres north of Millersburg.

Our John Dawson family was the only one of Dad's siblings' families that moved often. However, Aunt Catherine Dawson worked for the U.S. Government in Minneapolis, St. Louis, Chicago, and Indianapolis before retiring to Cedar Rapids, Iowa.

My brothers and I spent a lot of time with our aunts and uncles in the late 1930s/early 1940s. Aunt Theresa and Uncle Leo O'Rourke lived in a big, white house on a hill southeast of Millersburg after they married in 1939. Kenny and I stayed a few days with them. Aunt Theresa baked her own bread, and she made wonderful hamburger sandwiches with horseradish on them. I recall her watery eyes as she ground the horseradish that grew on the farm.

There were pigeons up in the rafters of their large hog house, and one night, Uncle Leo, Aunt Theresa, Kenny, and I went out to catch some for me to take home. We looked for them and were disappointed when Uncle Leo said there were none there. But Aunt Theresa cried, "Yes there is, one just shit and it's running down my nose!"

We all thought that was quite funny—except for Aunt Theresa, of course. I was secretly glad that it did because Uncle Leo O'Rourke then caught the pigeon and I got to take it home.

When I was eight or nine, Kenny, Leroy, and I visited Aunt Marge and Uncle Leo

Costello at the house they had purchased a block south of St. Bernard's Catholic Church in Millersburg. During our stay, Aunt Marge made her version of Maid-Rites, the first I ever had. She made them with crumbled hamburger and an egg or two mixed in. I have loved them ever since.

There was a barn on the place, and we climbed into the mow and discovered a case of beer hidden in the hay. We somehow got a bottle open, and I remember how it foamed—hot! We each had a sip and thought we had done something daring. It didn't taste good, and I never really liked the taste of beer. I just liked the result of feeling uninhibited—later in life of course.

About once a year, Aunt Marge cooked dinner for her Agnew siblings and their families at her place. The thing I remember most was the delicious strawberry Jell-O and whipped cream salad that she fixed—always a specialty of hers. Group photos also were taken at her place.

Aunt Marge and Uncle Leo mainly used their kitchen, dining room, and a downstairs bedroom. The front room and upstairs were strictly "off limits" to kids. An adult accompanied us to the upstairs bathroom, which had a real toilet and sink, so we wouldn't waste running water—a flush toilet seemed like Niagara Falls!

Uncle Emmett and Aunt Gloria Agnew lived two miles east across the fields from Grandma Agnew's place. They didn't have any children and liked to have kids around. Aunt Gloria had a special fondness for Leroy and vice versa.

Aunt Gloria always had lots of "store-bought" cookies on hand. We considered them great treats as we always had homemade cookies. Now it's just the other way around. The same thing can be said for bread. We kids used to wish we had some "boughten" bread.

The couple raised chickens, geese, pigs, cows, and the whole bit, like most farmers. One sunny morning, I looked out in their yard, and a large rat had grabbed a small chicken by the leg and was trying to drag it to the rat burrow. I called Aunt Gloria, who was washing clothes on a washboard, and she beckoned Uncle Emmett. The rat released the poor small chicken and scampered down the hole.

It was so dry that rats burrowed down into the ground right out in the open. It seems that when one misfortune occurs it is compounded by others, as the drought forced rats and mice from the fields closer to buildings and living quarters. We began pumping buckets of water, and Uncle Emmett put a stone over the second rat entrance (or back door) while their rat terrier waited in anticipation of a successful hunt. Uncle Emmett poured bucket after bucket of water down the rat hole. Finally, a very wet and soaked fat rat emerged, and the dog pounced on it. The ground was so dry that it took many gallons of water to drown out the rat.

When adults would ask what I wanted to be when I "got big" (grew up), I would say a schoolteacher. Even then, I wanted a desk job. When Kenny and Leroy were asked the same question, they would exclaim, "I want lots of money and be rich like Uncle Johnny Agnew!"

At the age of eight, I was allowed to stay with Uncle Johnny and Aunt Rose Agnew for a few days. They had their supper club, Club 88, in the tiny town of Tiffin. While visiting them, I made friends with the boy and girl who lived next door and were around my age. I also met a nine-year-old boy who did not have much supervision and rode around town on his bike. I was told by Aunt Rose not to become friends with this boy but to stick with the very proper neighbor kids—no fun! Of course, I found this boy to be very wise and interesting.

On the second day of my visit, Uncle Johnny, Aunt Rose, and I set off in their fancy car to go to an afternoon movie in Iowa City, about 10 miles away. I had never been to a "show" so was very excited and talked incessantly from the back seat. Before long, Aunt Rose asked me to be quiet as they were going to say their prayers. It was silent as we sped along. I really think they just wanted me to be quiet!

I was so overwhelmed and amazed by the huge screen and picture that I sat on the theater seat without turning it down. Uncle Johnny and Aunt Rose chuckled and finally got me settled. Oh me, oh my, what an afternoon. First movie, first movie cartoon, and first popcorn I ever had!

During this visit, I also ate French fries for the first time. Oh, the wonderful potato!

Uncle Johnny had slot machines in his club—although they were illegal in most of Iowa. Johnson County was what was called "wide open" with slot machines allowed and mixed drinks served in establishments. Beer was the only alcoholic beverage that was served to customers in most of Iowa at that time.

Uncle Johnny and Aunt Rose lived in a large room in the rear of the club, so I could hear the music and laughter from the dance floor when I went to bed. During my visit, I asked Uncle Johnny for a dime to play the slots; the club had 5-, 10-, 25-, and 50-cent machines. To my delight, after putting the dime in, immediately out popped three dimes!

I reached for the dimes elatedly and was ready to put in another when Uncle Johnny said, "Wait, now give me back my dime." I was shocked, but I gave it to him and promptly lost the other two to the machine. He taught me that when you borrow something, give it back as soon as possible and don't just expect someone to give you something when you ask—earn it.

While I was in Tiffin, I caught the most beautiful red and white pigeon I had seen up to that time. Aunt Rose got an old beer case and fashioned a cage for it. We gave it water and pieces of bread and kept it in the beer-storage room.

One afternoon, unbeknownst to Aunt Rose, the nine-year-old boy and I were playing in an old barn when he told me that doctors did not bring babies. He proceeded to lie on his stomach on my back (we were fully clothed) and told me that was what my Dad did to my Mother to make babies. I thought it seemed very mean of Dad to be on Mother's back, as it felt uncomfortable to me.

I thought this couldn't be true—no wonder Aunt Rose said to avoid this boy. Of course, I couldn't check with her because I wasn't supposed to see him anyhow. What a quandary.

When I got home, I watched Mother and Dad with a jaundiced eye. A couple of years later, Jimmy, Dean, and Joe Bender, who were all near my age, convinced me that what the neighbor said was right all along.

The day after the disclosure, Aunt Rose and I visited a friend of hers who worked as the housekeeper for Father Ryan, the former Armah priest. Father Ryan now was stationed in nearby Oxford, Iowa. Here I was, bewildered by these sexual revelations and sitting in the house of a priest who could drop-kick you into hell!

Dad came through Oxford that day hauling something in the truck, and I was glad to see that Kenny also had come to spend the night with Uncle Johnny and Aunt Rose. The five of us had supper together. The next day, Uncle Johnny and Aunt Rose returned us to our parents along with my beautiful new pigeon—which Dad did not appreciate.

The birds and the bees always was a taboo subject. We were forbidden from observing the mating of cattle and hogs. I wondered why a group of men could watch and we couldn't. It only made me more determined to sneak around and peek or find a good viewing point from a window in the house or a crack in a barn wall.

We also heard "Don't look at anyone else's private parts," and "Don't touch yourself." I wondered just how I was supposed to pee! My young uncles and aunts occasionally gave me hints about various things, but I think they just wanted to know how much I actually knew.

The first I ever heard of or enjoyed potato chips was in 1938 or 1939 when Uncle Raymond Dawson came from New Mexico for a visit. He and Dad came out of Bessie's Tavern, and he tossed a bag of open chips into the back seat. They spilled over the seat and the floor of the 1932 Chevy while Kenny, Leroy, and I dived after them like chickens do for grains of corn.

I was amazed that a potato could taste that good and, at that moment, it was the most delightful taste that my taste buds had ever encountered!

It was still the era of the Depression, Dust Bowl, and drought—the "Trying Thirties." Mother and I would sit under the walnut tree trying to catch a breeze while we would shell peas or do other tasks. The heat blistered down, and it was difficult to sleep at night.

On top of all of that, the newscasts from Des Moines-based WHO (we had acquired a chest-type radio) told of a terrible war in far-away England and Germany and that the Japanese had been slaughtering Chinese people.

I recall visiting Uncle Emmett and Aunt Gloria's place and watching the adults hover around the radio as a terrible frightening person named Hitler addressed the world through an interpreter. Everyone was very quiet and looked worried—and children pick up on those vibes. I was afraid Dad would have to fight Hitler and be killed. Or he would have to kill Hitler and the Japanese. Dads were considered very brave and indestructible, even if very stern.

In addition to school, lightning, fires, and punishments, now there was a war to worry about!

When we moved to the Lucas Place, I was close to finishing third grade and Kenny was in first. Miss Lois Moore was our teacher at Aurora, the Adams Township Country School, which was located just across the road from our home. Kenny and I were attending school with our three cousins, Kathleen, Roy, and Richard Greene, along with Kenny McKinney, Charles and Rex Shafranek, and eighth grader Phyllis Smith.

Miss Moore would read a chapter from a good book after school started at 9 a.m. On one particular morning, I felt gas pressure as we had beans for supper the night before. At the very moment when everyone could have heard a pin drop, I lifted slightly to let a little "quiet" gas escape. Much to my embarrassment and alarm, a long noise came rushing out, which seemed to go on for five minutes. I couldn't stop it. It took a couple of days to get over the shame of that audio blunder.

Rural schools had to have at least eight children enrolled, equivalent to one for each grade, to stay open. That September, our school had only seven students, so Leroy was permitted to enroll at the age of four years and eight months to keep the school open. The new teacher, Miss Margaret Smith, spoiled him, and he could do no wrong.

On a fall Saturday in 1939, nine-year-old Kathleen and eight-year-old Richard Greene came to visit and play with us kids. For some reason, we ended up across the road at the schoolhouse. The inner door of the schoolhouse was locked, but the entryway, where we left our overshoes and boots, was not. In the coalhouse, a separate building, there was a small hatchet and an old broom that Miss Smith used to sweep up cobs to carry to the big stove inside.

Kathleen decided that we should take a peek at the grade book. Before long, she somehow got the doorknob off the inside door. I was outside with Richard, who proceeded to chop the broomstick with the small hatchet into about six-inch pieces. By this time, I had begun to enjoy myself as I hadn't done any damage yet and could see no trouble brewing involving me. I joyously started to toss pieces of the mutilated broomstick in the air.

Well, when you throw those things up, they don't come straight down ...

I heard the sound of glass breaking as I watched one of the broomstick pieces cut right through one of the north schoolhouse windows. It was like slow motion and time was coming to a stop. Kenny stood in amazement, Kathleen whooped "oh boy," Richard fell to the ground in convulsions of laughter, and my life flashed before my eyes.

The Greenes suddenly decided to go home, and I began about 36 hours of agony. We went to Grandma Agnew's after Mass the next day, and I didn't enjoy it one bit. By bedtime, I knew the time was short and I hardly slept.

About 8:30 a.m. on Monday, Miss Smith came frantically to our door to say that someone had broken into the school—the knob was off the door. Dad hurriedly accompanied her across the road. I heard her say that there was probably a bum or some dangerous lunatic inside. Dad got the knob back on, and they were surprised to see shattered glass over a portion of the floor and the broken window.

Dad returned home a few minutes later. "It looked like kid's work to me," he said as he cast an accusing glance my way.

We hurried across the road to school, and at morning recess time, Miss Smith "invited" Kathleen, Richard, Kenny, and me to stay in our seats. Kathleen testified that it had all been my idea and that I wanted to see the grade book! Richard chimed in to agree with Kathleen, and Kenny was excused because he was the youngest and not mischievous.

Miss Smith shocked us by saying we could see the grade book anytime if we just asked. Then she asked me, "Did you break the window?" I said I did—what else could I say? Miss Smith said she was disappointed in us, but since I didn't tell a lie, there would be no punishment. By that time, a member of the school board was putting cardboard over the window to keep the draft out as the first late fall storm was roaring in from the northwest.

I can still see that piece of broomstick going through the window! I learned there is no use of worrying if you tell the truth because the consequences are never as bad as you think they will be after hours of stress. Plus, no one else will remember it 10 years later. But I'll sure never forget.

As for me, it seemed like I always got myself in trouble when I threw objects up in the air. The first time was when I broke the schoolhouse window. One time at the Lucas Place, when our road was newly covered with nice white chunks of gravel that were fun to throw or made good ammunition, I picked up a fairly good-sized piece and threw it straight up in the air. It seemed to get off target, however, and came down on the windshield of Dad's truck, our only transportation.

The windshield was shatterproof, thank goodness, but the gravel nearly made a hole on the passenger's side. There also were many spider-web-like cracks spreading out from the damaged spot. Every time Dad hauled something, he was asked, "Johnny, did a piece of loose rock fly up and hit your windshield?" Of course, he told the true story, so I was glad when he got a different truck.

When I was eight, I picked up a nice-size piece of gravel off the street in front of Grandma Dawson's house. I threw it up as hard as I could and, unfortunately, it came down and struck Richard Greene's head. He dropped and wailed like a banshee. I thought his older siblings—Frank, Roy, and Kathleen—were going to jump on me. But their dad, Jim Greene (Grandma's brother/my Dad's uncle), heard the noise and came out and saved me. I apologized profusely, and after the "knot" on Richard's head went away, all was well again.

I finally gave up throwing objects. I seemed to lack any control as to where they would land!

Grandma Agnew and her children in late 1939. Front row: Helen Hartzell, Anna Agnew, Grandma Minnie Agnew, and my Mother Mary Dawson. Middle row: Theresa O'Rourke, Marge Costello, Ethel Harris, and Alice Herr. Back row: Johnny Agnew, Leo Agnew, Harry Agnew, Bernard Agnew, and Emmett Agnew.

Dawson and Harris cousins in Aunt Ethel and Uncle Richard Harris's yard in 1942. Leroy is in the back with his hands on his hips, and I am sitting just below him. Kenny is standing by the pump. Sitting in front are brother Bernie, Eddie Harris, and MaryAnn Harris (later Petermeier). Dayton Hall is in the background.

Leroy, 1940.

At the Wagner Place. I am in the middle with cousin Eddie Harris and brother Leroy.

Mother and her boys in 1940. She is holding Bernie while Kenny is on the left, Leroy is in front, and I am on the right.

# Chapter 3

## 1940–1944

By this time, Aunt Ann Dawson and Aunts Marge, Ethel, Alice, and Theresa Agnew had married. The Dawson run of having the only grandchildren on either side of the family was over with the births of our oldest first cousins, Joe Conroy (Ann's son) and Eddie Harris (Ethel's son).

I was Eddie Harris's "babysitter" when he could sit up and was just beginning to crawl. When I was at the Harris house, most days we had eggs and potatoes for dinner, and I can still hear Aunt Ethel say, "There goes the sandwich," as I made an egg sandwich at each meal. (I have always loved sandwiches—I'll make them out of gravy, mashed potatoes, tomatoes, cheese, and anything that will stay between two slices of bread.)

Since these five aunts were married, when I said my prayers at Mother's knees each night, I would ask God to tell the doctor to deliver to them. I also would ask God to have the doctor bring me a baby sister.

Lo and behold, I was astonished when Donnie Herr (Alice's son) and MaryAnn Harris appeared, and our Dawson family welcomed Bernard Joseph on April 23, 1940. He was named after Uncles Bernard Agnew and Joe Dawson. Although I didn't get a sister, Bernie was a good addition to a basketball team. Now there were four brothers—just one to go for the team!

Dr. Doyle delivered Bernie in his black bag—I had been told that doctors brought babies to people they thought deserved them. And would you believe that God told the doctor to bring Jimmy to Aunt Theresa in 1941?

Wow, by the power of prayer and the benevolent doctors!

Now wasn't I really dumb? My Agnew uncles had told me I was delivered by an "old crow" that deposited me on a fence post, and Aunt Theresa once had me in tears saying that I was adopted. Aunt Helen agreed wholeheartedly!

Kenny, Leroy, and I each weighed about 7½ pounds when we were born, but Bernie weighed 9 pounds. I remember the day he was born as being dreary and rainy. Dad came over to our school that morning and conferred with Miss Smith, our Aurora teacher.

Kenny, Leroy, and I always went home for lunch at noon since we lived right across the road. But on this day, Dad brought scrambled egg sandwiches to us. We were much surprised! And when he again conferred with Miss Smith at about 1 p.m., the Greene kids started to whisper, "Your Dad is courting the teacher."

I had never heard the word "courting," and it conjured up thoughts that I didn't dare entertain. Dad and Miss Smith chatted again around 3 p.m., and an hour later, she told us we would be going home with her after school. She lived with her parents just over a mile away.

We were delighted—this meant no chores! (At the farm, Kenny's and my duties included helping milk cows, feed calves, and slop hogs.) Canned strawberries were the highlight of our supper at Miss Smith's, and Leroy loved strawberries.

After dark, Dad came for us and told us we had a new brother. When we went into the bedroom at home, Mother had tears on her cheeks and a healthy baby beside her. Later I understood what all the commotion was about. "We almost lost your Mother," Dad told us.

It was not unheard of for a woman to die while giving birth—this was before Caesarean operations, and children were born at home. Learning about Mother's difficulties during Bernie's birth broke the spell of babies arriving in a doctor's bag.

For the first two to three weeks after Bernie was born, Doris Rank arrived to do the housework and care for Mother. Doris had tissues in her room and a box of cherry chocolates—neither of which I had ever seen before. Needless to say, I sneaked in and used some tissues. I even remember the smell.

I also indulged in stealing a superbly delicious piece of candy—the best I ever had! I knew it was a sin, but I already knew I was going to hell since I had yet to confess that I broke my fast before communion more than two years earlier.

When Bernie was a few months old, he got rheumatic fever, and I was taken out of school to hold and rock him so Mother could get the housework done. I was disappointed to return to school—I preferred babysitting over arithmetic!

Bernie was on formula (bottle-fed) as Mother had "milk fever" and couldn't nurse. I remember her pained expression and cries when she used a breast pump. The other aunts were breastfeeding during this time, so I was banished from Grandma Agnew's kitchen during nursing time on Sunday visits. Of course, I peeked around to see whatever I could.

We always had a sandpile on the farm. Dad bought sand at the lumberyard and dumped it under the shade of a large tree in the backyard. The sand under the top layer usually was damp, which was nice and cool on bare feet. The sandpile spread out a ways, as it was usually the amount of sand held in an almost-full bed of a pickup truck.

Kenny, Leroy, and I played in the sandpile often where we would create our own little "farms." When we would dig in the sand, we often uncovered hidden "treasures" in the form of dried cat turds. Our outside barn cats found the sandpile to be the equivalent of today's toilets. We would toss the turd away without giving it much thought. It was not a nice experience to uncover fresher deposits.

We went barefoot and basically played in the dirt all day when weather permitted. Then we went to bed without washing our feet whenever we could get by with it. Since Mother was often busy preparing a younger brother for bed, when she would ask if we had cleaned our feet, sometimes we outright lied and assured her that we had done so.

Pepper was our family card game. Spades or Hearts occasionally were dealt, as was 500. Mother enjoyed a game of Checkers and, in the 1940s, a game played on a board with marbles—Chinese checkers—was popular. And who can forget the Old Maid card game? We played by the light of flickering kerosene lamps.

We were encouraged to read books, and I would get lost in time as I read accounts of Indian wars and the Natives' great chiefs. I would wish I were an Indian, carefree with no chores or school or church (I did not like to attend Mass, Catechism, or other church activities geared toward children).

In my romanticized Indian daydreams, I didn't think about frigid winters and the nomadic life to follow game, the main source of food. Or that there would be no potato chips, ice cream, dressing, gravy—or pure cold water. And wouldn't I miss the outhouses and thunder mugs?

It is best when daydreaming to not go too deep or the daydream could become a "day-mare."

On Sundays at Grandma Agnew's, we had a noon meal and then the men went outside to play horseshoes and talk. After the dishes were washed and dried (and when my aunts weren't nursing), I would hide behind the kitchen cookstove. I listened as Grandma and her daughters sat around the big table and discussed the most "taboo" things including who was dating whom and who was going to have a baby. They also talked about who had a new hat—we would see some fantastic and outlandish creations at Mass since women had to cover their heads inside the Catholic Church.

Also at Grandma Agnew's (and our homes as well) were "privies," "backhouses," and "outhouses"—the outside convenience shacks. Most outhouses had three holes of varying sizes, with one even small enough for a child. It seemed that two of the Agnew women or girls always went together, especially if they had something secretive to divulge. As a little kid, I was permitted to accompany them and sit on the tiny hole while looking disinterested and hearing all the most interesting and mysterious things they said. But by the age of 5½ or 6, I was deemed too old to go with the ladies for these "retreats."

On the farm, men hardly ever used the outhouse, and the Agnew men never did. If you saw a man or boy selecting a clean, soft-appearing corncob—if one could ever be— you knew he was preparing to go behind a tree or building to find a clump of weeds to "do his duty."

Inside at night, we used "slop jars," "chamber pots," or "thunder mugs." Then each day it was someone's job to see that they were emptied, rinsed, and turned upside down in a place out of view of passersby. Then they would be dry and fresh for the next night. At the Dawson house, poor Leroy usually was chosen to do that job, and Aunt Anna Agnew dubbed him "the pot rusher." Our family did not have indoor facilities until we moved and bought our house southeast of Parnell in 1949, when I was 18 years old.

At Grandma Agnew's on these Sunday afternoons, most of the conversations seemed to focus on current gossip. Grandma, Mother, and Aunt Ethel mostly just listened, and Aunt Anna gave accounts of her work. Aunt Marge was very vocal in her dislike of those who she thought were trying to "run" the local Catholic parishes. Aunts Theresa and Marge talked the most. Aunt Alice would make some amusing comments and how they would laugh!

Eventually, someone would get up to get a drink of water and since the bucket containing the common drinking dipper was near the stove, I would be flushed out with questions: "How long have you been back there?" They would then demand I go out and play with the other kids.

After our road had just been graveled, cars would whiz by churning up huge clouds of white dust. One neighbor drove about the fastest in his big car. After one of our guineas was run over, a family discussion concluded that he probably had caused the bird's death.

A few days later, this neighbor stopped by to ask Dad to haul some livestock. Leroy came running out of the house and hollered accusingly, "You did run over our guinea!" (Even as a child, Leroy was the most outspoken Dawson brother.) The neighbor looked startled and Dad tried to hush Leroy up, but Leroy just repeated his accusation. Dad did get the job, but we were admonished not to repeat what we heard in family discussions.

Leroy also was a comedian and should have been on stage. He always was the center of attention. Although when he was at work later in life, he was all business—and extremely successful.

When Leroy was little, he called anyone (me) who displeased him a "stink-pot dumb-bell." Mother tried to get him to stop; she was afraid that he would call kids at school by the uncomplimentary moniker and perhaps even address the teacher as such! I don't recall that he did use it at school.

Leroy was very thoughtful of Mother and all of us. When Mother was extremely tired and taking a rest, he would go out to the well, pump a very cold drink of water, and bring the water to a very surprised and grateful Mother.

One Sunday morning, we awoke to find that Dad was not home. Mother put on a brave front, and she, Kenny, and I decided we'd better milk the cows. When Floozie kicked at Mother, we abandoned that chore and went to slop the pigs. Mother was carrying a large bucket of slop when she tripped on a piece of old wire fence and fell with slop flying all over her. She was so exasperated that she just cried—and so did we kids. It is so hard to see your Mother cry.

At Ed Fry's tavern the night before, Dad had tipped a few drinks and had a few harsh words with a local resident. I don't know who started it, but the man decked Dad and Dad rose up like Samson and got the guy's head under his arm and proceeded to pound away. The man begged for mercy and finally broke free with Dad in hot pursuit. They headed north and then east on the street where the man lived. As Dad gained on him, the man dashed right through a neighbor's front screen door calling out, "Save me, save me, Johnny Dawson is going to kill me." The man hid in a bedroom before crawling out a window and heading home. He then called the sheriff.

So on that Sunday morning, Dad was in the Keokuk County Jail in Sigourney! We found out after Mass. Our cousins Tommy and Raymond Gregan came to do the chores. Uncle Johnny Agnew hastily was called via long distance to help bail Dad out.

Dad arrived home grinning and looking sheepish, as Mother, Kenny, Leroy, and I greeted him on the front porch. I talked first, asking, "What did you have for dinner?"

That broke the ice and everybody laughed. We were so happy to have him home. It made a good story to rehash and for teasing Dad.

Oh, and Dad said he had bologna sandwiches as his jailhouse dinner.

When Kenny didn't like something I did and deemed that a threat was necessary, he very seriously would announce, "I'm going to put you in jail!" We thought that being locked in jail was the same as being gone for good—until Dad's episode landed him in the hoosegow only overnight. Then we understood that sometimes you could get out soon if someone like Uncle Johnny Agnew would "bail" you out.

A very old man and his two sons lived just north of us. Their old, gray house was surrounded by many large trees and dilapidated farm buildings. We were warned to never go near that place. However, Dad rented a plot near their barn, and I got to go with him to plant potatoes.

While Dad was talking to his cousin James Hannon, who also was helping, I slipped away and approached this mysterious house and folks. The house didn't seem clean, and the furniture was in disrepair. I was delighted to find that they had a tame pigeon that roosted on the wall telephone, which no longer was operational. They called the pigeon "Pouter," and all I thought was that it was a terrific deal to have a tame pigeon in the house!

One summer, the elder man's grandchild came to stay at the house. The grandson was my age, but I was told to avoid him as his manners were not top-drawer and no one made him wash himself. Naturally, I slipped away and made his acquaintance. I thought he was real "cool" with nobody telling him "don't do this, don't do that." I even got upstairs at the house and saw closets full of furs and fine women's clothes; the family had been wealthy many years earlier. The grandson gave me a near-white pigeon he had wounded with a BB gun, and I took it home and nursed it back to health. I'm glad I met this boy.

When large farm animals died from disease, lightning, foundering (overeating for cattle), giving birth, or however, Henry Simmons was called to come quickly before they started to smell. He had a large truck with a box rack and hoist he used to load the swollen carcasses. Everyone called him "The Dead Man."

He trucked the dead animals to a rendering plant in Montezuma, Iowa, about 25 miles to the west, where they were cooked so the meat and bones could be ground into powder. This was sold as "tankage," and farmers occasionally fed it to their livestock as protein. It was said that the Simmons family had the healthiest chickens that laid the most eggs from eating a diet consisting of only tankage. Mr. Simmons actually performed a much-needed service to all who needed his assistance.

A neighbor was convicted of stealing chickens—including many of ours—when some he had stolen returned to their regular roost after the sheriff released them. I had noticed chicken crates and feathers in the open trunk of the neighbor's car when I was on a pigeon-catching expedition to his farm (he was in the field). I put two and two together after he was caught.

Nobody locked doors at that time. In fact, we didn't even have keys to our doors, and a master key that could be purchased at any dime store would work on most any door. Most folks left their doors and windows open anyway in the hope of getting a refreshing breeze through the house. To combat the flies that would come in a house, several rolls of fly stickers would hang from the ceilings. They were coated with a sticky sweet substance.

One neighbor family had a screened-in porch that wrapped around two sides of their large house. I caught a pigeon one day at that farm and went to the house to show it to the mother. When no one answered my knock, I entered and released the pigeon. Of course, it started to fly around. I didn't get frantic until I saw the pigeon walking over two pies that had been set out on the porch to cool.

I had just captured the bird and was walking out the door when the family members arrived home. My sweat-covered self showed them my bird, and they were concerned that I might get a heat stroke from chasing and catching pigeons.

I carried my pigeon home, and I'm sure they enjoyed pie for their supper!

On another afternoon, I briefly watched a local couple do some "couple things" under a leafy canopy in the timber. Leroy refused to have any part of watching it and held it over my head for many years. Whenever I miffed him, he threatened, "I'll tell about the timber deal!" I was young and merely satisfying human curiosity. There were no sins committed!

I learned another lesson of titillating sexual nature when reading the writings on toilet walls. The first time I ever saw these "writings" was when I was about nine and in the outside privy at Strohman Implement in Keswick. After settling on the uncomfortable hole, I read the most unimaginable suggestions, proclamations, and outright invitations, accompanied by crude drawings. I knew better than to ask any adult for explanations and decided to wait until I encountered the Bender boys or Georgie Van Fleet, who was very knowledgeable on many subjects about which most kids barely whispered.

I spent a lengthy amount of time in the privy until Dad broke the spell and inquired, "Did you fall in? I'll have to get a team of horses to pull you out."

At home, Mother could bake the best homemade breads, rolls, pies, and cakes. Anything she cooked was delicious. She made homemade noodles, cottage cheese, and soaps with lye—you name it and she could make it.

But of all her creations, the best were her icebox cake and made-from-scratch angel food cake. She was known in the Keswick Ladies Circle, a monthly church group, for her angel food cake. Each cake took about a dozen egg whites, and I often helped her separate the yolks from the whites. Thank goodness we raised our own chickens! The yolks were used to make scrambled eggs or noodles.

On one particular occasion, two angel food cakes that Mother made "fell" slightly and were not to her liking or standards. It pleased me—we had two cakes for home and lots of scrambled eggs. After we spent all day baking, a third cake came out perfect.

After school the next day, I walked to the Strohman home where the meeting was taking place. Mary Agnes Strohman told me what a beautiful and delicious angel food cake that Mother brought to the meeting. I never could keep my mouth shut at the proper time, and I exclaimed that the "other two" were just about as nice. She said, "You mean she baked three?" I said yes as she wanted a perfect one.

And then I looked at Mother and she just laughed, but I still wish I hadn't said it. Do other people say things without thinking or am I the only one?

It seemed all the local women were very good cooks. There were no ready mixes or fast food. If you ate out, it was at a local diner, tavern, or beer joint. Ice cream was dipped by hand and put in a cone or dish. Soda came in basic orange, strawberry, cream, and root-beer flavors, and kids weren't to have Cokes. Cokes were for the men to mix with their whiskey.

There were no large grocery stores but only mom-and-pop operations where everyone knew everyone else or rural stores, such as Hurd's in Dayton Township, where even farm implements and machinery could be ordered by catalog. Lots of people ran a "tab" and paid when they sold their hogs. At these rural stores, peanut butter was dipped from huge barrels and put in jars. And it was good. People bought 50-pound sacks of flour and sugar. Flour sacks were used for many things including dishtowels, garments, and sheets.

Ice cream socials and church picnics were happy events for all the kids. We would run and play happily and get sweaty and hot. Everyone was in a good mood, and there was much laughter and the most delicious pies and cakes. (I always have preferred pie, especially lemon and coconut cream, to cake.)

At the ice cream socials, people brought freezers of homemade ice cream packed in ice, salt, and water. What a wonderful ending to a hot summer night. Around 10 p.m., the dads would start rounding up us kids and tell us to calm down and quit acting like we had never been to town before or had just "come in out of the sticks."

In the early 1940s, I again stayed with Aunt Ethel and Uncle Richard Harris; they had moved to a farm east of Al Bender's home. Richard worked for the Hurds and the Benders, but he had some crops, and the family raised lots of guineas and white chickens. I remember chicken hawks circling to try to get the chickens and Uncle Richard shooting them—or at least at them as they were quite elusive.

It seemed like there was a terrific electrical thunderstorm every time I stayed with the Harris family. I was terrified and thought we would be struck and the house would burn. During one storm, I cowered under the covers, head and all, and counted 31 "crash bangs" (as I called them)—awfully loud and crackling thunderclaps that seemed to be right outside the window. I thought the Harrises were living in the center of a "lightning belt" and didn't stay with them at that location anymore.

When our family would look for a place to move, I would check to see if the house and the buildings had lightning rods. If they didn't, I tried to discourage Dad from renting the place. If we did end up in a place with no protection, Uncle Tommy Dawson was summoned since he had a lightning rod-installing business.

Lightning struck many barns and trees and started fires. Cattle often were victims of lightning and would be found dead after a storm. To this day, I run for cover to the basement or the center of the house when I'm fearful that lightning is about to flash.

Summer storms often caused small ditches and creeks that didn't even have names to become rushing rivers that overflowed their banks onto pastures and cropland. They washed out fences in the ditch area between the farms, and it was a dangerous and dreaded job to separate two families' cowherds and repair the fence. It especially was bad if bulls got together and began fighting. The herds could get completely alarmed.

In the 1940s, rushing water resulted in a tragedy near North English. A young man, Franklin Brower, was swept with his horse into a swollen creek. The horse came home that night, but Franklin's body was found a few weeks later among some logs several miles downstream. It seems like only yesterday that everywhere we went, or if anyone stopped by, the first thing that was asked or talked about was, "Have they found Franklin Brower?"

When I saw large banks of clouds in the west and northwest and flashes of sheet lightning as the sun set, I tried to gear my mind to prepare for dangerous thunderstorms. I would start praying that all our family, friends, and dwellings would be spared. Sure enough, just as sleep would come over me, "CRASH, BANG"! I worried about the world coming to an end and cowered under the covers during those nighttime thunderstorms. Then the next morning, the air would smell so good, the birds would be singing, and there had been no lightning strikes, so we survived another storm.

Never did I stay with Aunt Alice and Uncle Kermie Herr—they lived in far-away Harper, and Kermie's mother made her home with them. What I do recall from Sunday visits there was that Kermie had the meanest, crossest Hampshire sows that would "take a kid" even if they didn't have small pigs at their sides. I also remember that Aunt Alice made the most delicious lemon pies. And I remember that their son Donnie, when he learned to speak, addressed his parents as "Alice" and "Kermie," not "Mother" and "Dad," which was what we Dawsons and our cousins called our respective parents.

In 1940, we got electricity after a new well was dug, which had an electric engine to pump it. Our road also was graveled all the way to Keswick and to the Iowa County line near Armah; our house was in Adams Township of Keokuk County.

On the magic day of March 1, 1941, we again loaded moving trucks and wagons and went a few miles northwest to the Stewart Place, which was south of the Hurd farm and store in Iowa County's Dayton Township and the Sherman rural school. This was the same place I stayed while Aunt Ethel and Uncle Richard Harris lived there; they were now residing in Vinton, Iowa. By this time, we also had sheep and geese, as well as the other livestock. Floozie was getting old, and I sadly knew she would be sold soon.

We were two miles from school, and the hilly roads were all dirt and tree-lined with brush. Gritter Creek flowed in the hollow between the Hurd farm and our place.

Miss Doris Shaull was our new teacher, and there were many more kids at Sherman. Plus, there was a merry-go-round on the school playground! At recess on the first day of school, we new kids took turns riding the merry-go-round as if we were spinning the *Wheel of Fortune* on TV. By the time recess was over, the three new Dawsons were all dizzy.

I was now 10, Kenny was 8, and Leroy was 6, and our best friends were Jimmy, Dean, and Joe, sons of Albert and Gertie Bender. They liked to ride horses, go "swimming" in little streams that were knee-deep at the deepest, and catch pigeons. Mildred, Ambrose, and George Van Dee Jr. also were classmates at Sherman, and we felt sorry that their mother had been killed in an auto accident. Their grandma Emma Van Dee and their dad were their caregivers.

At recess, DareBase was a favorite game. We also raced and played hide-and-seek, Andy over, softball, and if we were really lucky, basketball with a net-less hoop on a—usually—wobbly pole. There were teeter-totters on the grounds. Winter and snow brought the fox and geese game, snowball fights, and making snow angels and snowmen. We got plenty of fresh air and exercise. The teachers usually played the games with us, were mediators of arguments, and served as comfort-givers if someone fell or was hit in the face with a snowball.

Before getting ready for school each morning, we had chores to do: milking cows, separating cream from the milk, and feeding calves. Mother fixed our lunches that we carried in "dinner buckets," which usually were cans with handles that once contained Karo syrup. By the time we ate breakfast and walked two miles to school, we often were late for the 9 a.m. bell.

One spring day, there was so much mud that our overshoes sunk so deep in its thickness that it was exhausting just to put one foot in front of the other. Poor little Leroy got stuck and cried, and Kenny and I tried to assist him.

After what seemed like hours, we finally arrived in front of the Hurd store with yet another mile to go. It actually was about 10:45 a.m. Lambert Hurd came out chuckling and inquired if we were going to "night school." We decided it must be 4 p.m. and time for school to let out. So we turned around to return home.

On the way back, we discovered some anthills by the side of the road. We disturbed their muddy mounds and were having fun watching the ants scramble when we heard this tremendous shout, "Get your asses home!" When he let it roar, Dad had a voice that could be heard for three miles if the wind was in the right direction. On a still day, it reverberated in a circumference of two miles.

We finally staggered to the house about 45 minutes later in time for the noon meal. Dad said that we were going outside to fix fence—a hated job—that afternoon, and "I'll make you wish you had gone to school." And he did. I don't think he realized how the mud had tired us—he thought we were just trying to play hooky from school.

One day at Hurd's store, Joan Harris, who was in my grade at Sherman, announced that Dean Bender wasn't her boyfriend anymore—it was now Gene Dawson. Aunt Anna Agnew delivered that news at the dinner table one Sunday at Grandma's, and the adults all started teasing me. Naturally, my face turned crimson, and I wanted to crawl under the table and hide. Besides, it was news to me that I was her guy and probably to Dean that he ever had been!

Boys at that age rarely were interested in girls as real girlfriends. But I do recall that I called older girls, like sixth to eighth graders who were real nice to me, including Margie Bender, Phyllis Smith, and Colleen Butler, my "girlfriends."

"Get on your knees," Dad would order at night, as Mother fingered her rosary beads. So we would kneel, and then Mother led the rosary and overnight prayers just before bedtime. Bernie, who was going on two, would cut up and keep us entertained as he had just learned to walk.

It seemed that we kids oftentimes lost interest and acted up. This would result in a quick swat from Dad—evidently he was very athletic and agile for it seemed he would get our attention from a distance away. Mother showed her disapproval with facial expressions.

In the mornings after breakfast, we did morning prayers and always ended with the *Morning Offering*.

During the school year, the Bender boys and we three Dawsons occasionally stayed overnight at each other's homes. On one particular night, Joe Bender was my guest for an overnight visit, and as we were kneeling in prayer, Bernie picked up a good-sized lightweight pan with a handle on it. I watched as he approached Joe from behind and proceeded to conk the unsuspecting boy on the head. Joe let out a tremendous yell, and I was so mad at Bernie's antics. Poor Joe wanted to be taken home immediately, and the prayer service came to an end. Finally, the poor child was soothed, and I kept a wary eye on the cavorting toddler.

The Bender boys' parents were one of the few couples in the area who owned their own farm. We considered them well off as they got new shoes and overalls more often than we did. They always had oyster soup (oysters were very expensive) on Friday nights; Catholics could not eat meat on Fridays at that time. (We had learned that Catholics who did eat meat were at risk of losing their immortal souls to the eternal brimstone fires of hell, which was presided over by Satan and his petrifying-appearing pitchfork.)

Of course, I repeat, I knew at this point that I was doomed for eating the peanut before communion and not confessing it.

One dark night, our family visited the Bender family. What sticks out in my mind is racing in pitch darkness while being pursued by one of the Bender boys. I ran full speed into a clothesline—a strand of wire strung tightly between two poles embedded in concrete in the ground. The wires were so taut that if pulled, they sprung back and made a sound similar to that of a musical instrument. I hit one at neck level and found myself flat on my back thinking that I might be dead or at least approaching that state.

It was one of the strangest feelings I ever experienced and not at all pleasant. My neck and Adam's apple were sore for days, and Dad said I was lucky I didn't break my neck. I can relate when I watch a football game and see the defensive back "clothesline" a receiver—he lifts the receiver right off the ground and hurls him back flat on the surface.

On Saturday nights in town when the Bender boys bought something and got change, they would take the pennies and throw them on the sidewalk. I showed no hesitation as I dived and scrambled for the coins. Ironically, though, not long after, the Bender home caught fire while they were away, and the house and contents were a total loss.

Soon the poor Bender boys were in our boat and wearing patched overalls, darned socks, and hand-me-down shoes. When I would see them, I would think of the old saying, "A penny saved is a penny earned," and resolved always to value all my pennies. The Benders soon sold their land and moved away, and I never saw them again.

On the last night that I spent with the Bender boys shortly before the devastating fire, upon arising the next morning, they started having pillow fights. For some reason, there was a pause, and I can still "see" each of them eyeballing me. I dived on the bed, as a barrage of pillows descended on me from all sides. I covered my head and wondered if the onslaught would ever end. Finally worn out, they stopped and I cautiously raised my head. All was well again, thank goodness.

Before the Bender boys left the area, they introduced me to the "F" word. It was the first time I had ever heard it uttered—let alone described in eye-popping detail! Of course, I relayed this new revelation to Kenny and Leroy (I thought I told Leroy anyway) but not to cousin Eddie Harris or anyone else.

So I was a stunned witness at Grandma Agnew's not long after that when, as Art Linkletter would say, "Kids say the darndest things." I was sitting under the shady and cool canopy of leaves adorning a large oak tree with Kenny, Leroy, Eddie and MaryAnn Harris, and Donnie Herr. It was after a Sunday dinner, and Grandma and her daughters were in the house chatting, washing dishes, and watching the youngest cousins, Jimmy Lee O'Rourke and my brother Bernie.

As we were relaxing, Leroy asked a question out of the blue that sent a shock wave of panic through me and Eddie shrieking into the house. MaryAnn sat in uncomprehending bewilderment. Not really knowing what he was requesting, Leroy had asked, "MaryAnn, could I f--- you?"

Eddie shrieked, "Leroy's going to f--- sister." I couldn't stop him—let alone corral him before he burst into the house. The Agnew women immediately descended from the back, front, and side doors. We all sat quietly as they surrounded us and peered with questioning eyes at Leroy, the main culprit. MaryAnn smiled, unaware of the tempest.

Leroy sat calmly, but I thought my heart was going to leap right out of my chest. Since I was the oldest, I became the object of intense scrutiny. After seeing that nothing seemed to be amiss, one after the other admonished us, "Now you kids play nice." For the rest of the afternoon and the following Sundays, rest assured at least one of the Agnew women kept us under surveillance.

I remonstrated Leroy and asked him why he would say such a thing, and I told him I would never tell him anything again. He replied, "You didn't tell me anyhow. I heard you tell Kenny." Another crisis had been averted, and I was not questioned as to how I had heard of such a terrible, terrible word.

At vacation Catechism week in Millersburg in the summer, Father Vincent Walsh said he wanted to train some new altar boys (girls were not allowed to serve Mass in the 1940s) and said, "Where's that Dawson boy?"

I was hoping he meant Kenny, as I was very, very shy and bashful as a child. When I was embarrassed, my face would get hot with a burning feeling. My face and ears would become as red as a beet and noticeably warmer. They would get worse when people would notice and say, "Oh, his face is so red." It was a horrible feeling.

This happened when I was teased or attention was focused on me. My aunts and uncles were great teasers, and so was Dad, but they didn't do it maliciously. It would be hard for anyone who had not been a bashful and insecure child to know how miserable it feels.

Anyhow, back to vacation Catechism. Father Walsh was asking about me, so I began to learn the Latin responses to the Mass dialogue. I soon made my "debut" with my wonderful Uncle Leo Agnew as my mentor and fellow Mass server at Armah, our home parish.

After every Mass, Grandma Agnew and my other relatives visited the graves of our deceased loved ones. They were very reverent, spoke softly, and admonished me not to step on the graves. We prayed at Grandpa Agnew's, Great-Grandpa Healy's, and Great-Grandma Agnew Towler's tombstones in the cemetery on the church grounds.

Our Sunday visits after Mass with Grandma Dawson were over, as we were out of the Keswick parish. We would visit her sometimes during the week; on Sundays we still went to the Agnew homestead.

Mother came down with the flu that summer, and Grandma Dawson and Aunt Sis came to stay for a few days to care for Mother, cook, wash clothes, and do the other housework. I was amazed at the energy and strength Grandma Dawson exhibited as she drug mattresses and rugs outside and proceeded to beat the dust out of them by turning them over and over and pounding them with a metal rug beater. How the dust flew!

Mr. Davidson from Keswick came to the Stewart Place to wire the house for electricity. He had wired the Lucas Place during the time we lived there. These were disruptive times as holes had to be made in the walls and ceilings to pass the wires and install outlets and fixtures—a big mess for overworked Mother to clean up. It usually took two weeks to complete, and Mr. Davidson had dinner with us when he was on the job. Around this same time, Grandma Agnew also got electricity and then a small refrigerator.

Some home remedies that were used when I was small probably would be beneficial today. If one of us was thought to have a chest cold and in danger of pneumonia, Mother created a "mustard plaster," a dishtowel spread with a liberal amount of mustard and then wrapped around the back and chest. It burned intensely for 10 to 15 minutes before it was removed. The skin would be bright rosy red, and it seemed that it was easier to breathe once again.

Vicks VapoRub was said to prevent and cure head colds. When we were sick in the wintertime, Vicks VapoRub was applied liberally to our chest and around the neck. Then a rag was folded and safely pinned around the neck so the body warmth would cause the fumes to rise and help with breathing. How I hated those Vicks rags! We even had to wear them to school and church. When a rag was finally removed, there was a great sense of relief and liberation. (I would think a dog must really dislike wearing a collar.)

Soap and sugar mixed together, or bread and milk, were used as a poultice to draw up a splinter deeply embedded in a finger or to break a boil and quell the intense pressure pain. These remedies worked.

Nearly every farm had a flock of geese, so when one was butchered, the fat (goose grease) was saved and used as a healing salve and lotion. The downy feathers from a goose's breast were used for stuffing pillows and comforters.

In the winter, we stayed warm by bundling up in long underwear, long-sleeved shirts and sweaters, two pairs of overalls, long wool socks (sometimes two pairs), high-top shoes, and overshoes. A neck scarf completed the outfit. We looked like Ralphie's little brother in the movie *A Christmas Story*, which takes place in the 1940s. (I watch it several times every holiday season and can relate to its contents.)

Potatoes and eggs were sometimes fried in butter for good flavor, but butter burned easily and had to be watched so it didn't get too hot. Lard was one of the mainstays of cooking during this time. It was used for frying, baking, and many, many more things. Cookies made with lard were delightful. Lard made flaky piecrusts and delicious sugar cookies and was wonderful for deep-frying fish.

Large chunks of fat and hairless hog skin were fried in huge skillets at high heat to "render" the lard. Then it was strained through cheesecloth and poured into containers—when it set, it was a beautiful white. "Cracklings," the fried skins and fat, became hard, tasty, crunchy treats after they dried—although we were discouraged from eating them. They were used in the soapmaking process and sometimes fed to the chickens or dog.

The latest convenience to appear in North English was a "locker." The owners would pick up your hog or steer, butcher it, cut it up, and wrap the meat in labeled freezer paper noting the date and cut. About once a week, families visited their individual storage lockers in an ice-cold room to take the meat they needed. Each locker had its own key.

Meat no longer had to be canned or cured with salt, so fresh meat was available throughout the entire year. This was before the advent of deep freezers for homes. I can recall Grandma saying, "We have to go to the locker today." By this time, the family had acquired a car, and Uncles Harry and Bernard were driving. They no longer had to walk to Armah or go in the horse and buggy or horse-drawn wagon.

Uncles Johnny and Harry Agnew enjoyed coon hunting, and Uncle Johnny kept his coonhounds with Uncle Harry's dogs at Grandma Agnew's farm. One day when I was about 10 and staying a few days at Grandma's, a hound named Old Blue, Leo's dog Mike, and I walked down the hill to the English River, which flowed about three-fourths of a mile away to the north. As we walked along the riverbank, Old Blue jumped in among some jammed logs and started baying. Soon a large muskrat jumped on his back and tried to put his head under water to drown him. I was excited and didn't know what to do.

The muskrat ripped at the dog's back with sharp teeth, but it was not heavy enough to pull off a drowning. The muskrat's razor-sharp weapons peeled back a large patch of skin from Old Blue's back, and he came howling out of the water. It seems that Old Blue had invaded the mother muskrat's nursery, and she was quick to defend it. Uncles Harry and Leo enjoyed hearing of our adventure and were a little skeptical about it at first, but the huge wound on Old Blue's back was the clincher. They felt sorry for him and vowed to trap Mrs. Muskrat when trapping season arrived.

Corn was handpicked and then the husks were taken off. Then farmers threw the husk-free ears of corn into a wagon pulled by a team of horses. When the wagon was full, its contents were scooped into a corncrib. (The only corn shellers available took just one ear at a time and were hand-cranked. The grains went into a bucket below, and the cobs came out the other end. It took a long time and many ears to get three to four gallons for the little calves and the chickens.)

Some young fellows got very adept at husking corn and, in the fall, you could hear "bong-bong" and "bong-bang" as the ears hit the sideboards and fell into the wagons. Uncles Bernard and Leo Agnew were experts and hired by many farmers to get their corn harvested. The uncles furnished the wagon, team of horses, scoop shovel, and gloves— many of which were worn out before leather gloves became a necessary accessory. The two uncles entered "husking bees" with competitors trying to harvest the fastest with the most husk-free ears of corn. One or the other often was the winner. Husking was a job I found tedious and tiring, and I often felt like my feet, ears, and hands were freezing.

A few farmers had purchased the amazing tractor that could do things that teams of horses could not. The tractors were started by hand-cranking, and their exhaust could be seen and smelled as it emitted from their hoods.

World War II was in progress as the Japanese had sneak-attacked Pearl Harbor in the early dawn hours of Sunday, December 7, 1941. The next day was a Catholic holy day, the Feast of the Immaculate Conception, and we attended Mass at Millersburg on this bitterly cold day. Everyone bundled up in sheepskin coats, scarves, and gloves and listened as Father Walsh gave a very serious and scary sermon on the evils of war.

Everyone was worried about who would have to go to the army. Later that day, we gathered around the radio to hear the wonderful President Roosevelt ask Congress to declare war on Japan. Roosevelt gave a heartfelt and stirring speech that ended with "We will gain the inevitable triumph. So help us God." A great surge of patriotism surged through me, and I wanted to do whatever I could to protect our country.

Soon butter, sugar, lard, gasoline, some meat, and other things were rationed. Every family had books of ration cards and stamps. Farmers were fortunate because they could raise their own meat, eggs, butter, and other items. Sugar, which was used for canning, cakes, pies, and many other things, and gasoline were the main hardships. A new spread— margarine—was developed, and Crisco replaced lard. Karo syrup was used in place of sugar. A black market developed, and farmers would exchange meat and eggs for sugar with town folks.

Farmers got extra rations of gas for their tractors as "victory gardens" sprung up on vacant lots and yards, as we had to supply food for our soldiers. Silk supplies from Japan were nonexistent. Folks waited to purchase a new car with their names on a list up to two to three years.

Women left the farms in droves to work in war plants, and married women were now allowed to teach country school—rural schoolteachers previously had to be single. Except for superintendents, very few men were teachers, and they could be married.

Kids were given defense stamp books for the war effort; stamps were sold for 10 cents each at the post office. People bought war bonds for $18.75 each, and they were worth $25 when they matured.

At school, we played war games by building snow forts and using nice pieces of wood as "guns." Toys were in short supply during the Depression and war.

When we played "farm" at home, corncobs were horses—if a rare white cob was found, it was a precious white horse. A small cheese box would be a wagon drawn by the cob horses. Cardboard boxes became barns with windows cut out on the sides. Small pieces of wood were cattle of varying hues, and pine cones were hogs—we had a variety of hogs because Grandma Dawson had several varieties of pine trees in her yard and each had a differently shaped cone. Marble-sized rocks were chickens, and the smaller pretty rocks were pigeons. I always had pigeons in the barn on my farm.

We protected our "toys" just like kids do nowadays and squabbled over who saw a particular cob or rock first to claim it as their own. We had lots of fun, and the "toys" seemed real to me.

We pushed around the lawn mower or a small red wagon with one wheel off for a "car." Wheelbarrows were pretend trucks, rubber bands were wristwatches, and cigar rings were rings—although naturally we didn't dare get them wet.

We built ovens out of bricks to bake mud cakes, but we were more interested in building the fire inside using wadded-up newspapers and then watching smoke roll out. We had to keep the ovens out of view since we were forbidden to play with matches.

One fine day, we constructed a wonderful brick stove behind the chicken house and had a nice smoky "bakery" going with a pan of cake. Then we heard Mother shrieking and frightened—she had seen plumes of smoke billowing over the top of the chicken house and thought it was on fire. She said she wouldn't tell Dad if we promised to stop building stoves and lighting fires. So that ended our bakery business.

Many rural kids of that era went barefoot for most of summer vacation and even to country school on warm fall days. We were supposed to wash our feet every night, but sometimes we would sneak into bed with them unwashed if they didn't look too dirty or Mother hadn't checked. It was hard to cram our feet into shoes on Sundays as they had spread out and become toughened from walking in mud and over rocks and "cow puddles."

However, the worst thing about going barefoot was stepping on sharp objects. I recall stepping on broken jars and getting severe cuts, and I also once stepped on a broken glass medicine dropper and embedded it in my foot.

There were pieces of broken glass and dishes in most yards as many who lived at the homesteads in prior years used the backyards as dumping grounds. They also emptied ashes from the coal/wood-burning stoves in the backyards (ashes had to be emptied daily or they overflowed the ash pans, which caused a big mess and impeded a stove's heating ability).

One time, I ran into a pitchfork tine and came yelling into the house dragging the pitchfork and trailing blood. It seemed it hurt more when it came out than when it went in. Mother got pans of cold water, and soon the pan was crimson. It looked like I had lost a gallon of blood. I was sure I was going to bleed to death and silently prayed that God would stop the bleeding. Mother's gentle way and soothing words worked wonders, and soon the bleeding stopped. The foot was swollen and very tender for a few days as I hobbled about shoeless—I definitely couldn't get that swollen foot into a shoe.

Mother made soap out of old lard and grease mixed with lye and 20 Mule Team Borax powder. After the mix had set, she cut it into bars to use to get out mud, manure, and other dirt that was on our work clothes—mostly overalls and coveralls. Washing took an entire day, and the first step was carrying water into the house and heating it in a huge boiler. Then the water was carried to the wash machine that was powered by a kerosene engine and sounded like a John Deere tractor—"pop-Pop-pop-Pop"—as blue fumes belched out the flexible-metal exhaust hose that hung out the window. This infuriated the dog, which barked incessantly and tried to attack the hose. I always knew who was washing in the surrounding area when I heard the "pop-Pop" and a barking dog.

Really, really dirty clothes and delicate pieces were handwashed and scrubbed on a washboard—a backbreaking job. Every backyard had rows of clotheslines so clothes could be hung out to dry. In the coldest weather, clothes would "freeze dry."

Every male wore white shirts, which had to be starched and ironed, to Sunday Mass. This was before "wash and wear" clothing, so Mother ironed clothes until 2 or 3 a.m. many nights. Before we had steam electrical irons, irons were heated on top of kitchen cookstoves until they were almost red hot. Clothes that had been sprinkled with water and rolled individually to set for a few hours were then placed on the ironing board. It seemed the folding ironing board was "up" and in use almost half the time.

Saturday night was bath night. A round tub was placed near the stove, usually in back so there was a little privacy. Kenny, Leroy, and I all fit in the tub at once. Soft water that had collected in a barrel via a rainspout from the roof of the house was used to wash our hair. "Hard" well water didn't remove soap and left our hair gummy. If we did have to use well water, we rinsed our hair with vinegar and water. The rinse left our hair soft and soap-free, but we smelled of vinegar for some time.

Usually the bath ended with Dad dumping a large container of very cold water over our heads after warning us to "shut your eyes tight." I would shiver in anticipation of the cascade of ice water—not knowing for sure when exactly it was coming. When it did, I thought for sure I was drowning. The cold-water rinse was not done cruelly—it is an old-home remedy for closing pores and preventing head colds. To this day, I still rinse with cold water when I shampoo, and I can't recall having a head cold.

We boys had only one pair of shoes each, and on Saturday nights, they had to be cleaned and polished for Sunday Mass. We had two sets of striped overalls and two shirts for Mass. Blue was the "work" overall color. School clothes had to be changed immediately after school for they had to last from Monday to Friday.

We also were supposed to change our school clothes quickly so we could get outside to do chores. I was a daydreaming, lazy child, and it seemed such an effort to change clothes—it could take me an hour. Dad and Mother constantly were telling me to hurry up. One such day, Kenny and I were upstairs changing and decided it really would be daring to stick our naked rear ends out the window.

The very first mooning?

After we finished our audacious act, we turned back to see what farm animal had been mystified by our display—only to see Leroy clutching Dad's hand with his other hand pointing at us. We were lectured sternly on the terrible sin of immodesty, and dire consequences were suggested if we ever even thought of doing such a thing again.

Mother liked the Stewart Place for its big, cozy henhouse that housed her chickens. She sold the eggs, and the egg check was hers to spend as she wanted. But 99 percent of it, it seemed, always went for "the boys," as she would say.

During the year we resided at the Stewart Place, many young chickens drowned when they were unable to get to the shelter of the brooder house due to sudden intense storms with lots of wind.

We had bought some bantam chickens, and these multicolored and beautiful birds crossed with our chickens. We soon had several midsized chickens that laid midsized eggs, which we kept. People didn't want to pay for smaller eggs and, for certain, produce companies did not pay top price for them.

Our "egg man," Homer Means, picked up our eggs weekly and culled the hens periodically and bought the non-producers. In the fall, he arrived with his trucks and crates, weighed the chickens, and issued a check. Mr. Means also bought geese, ducks, turkeys, and guineas, and each of those commodity checks was eagerly awaited, as was the "wool" check.

We had started to raise sheep at the Stewart Place. They were not then—or since—one of my favorite farm animals. I much preferred the swine, cattle, and poultry. The buck sheep were mean to kids, as were ganders (geese) and sometimes a belligerent rooster.

Each spring, Mr. Evan "Pussy" (as in "pus") Drum arrived to shear the sheep of their winter wool. Each adult sheep had its wool removed and tied into a square. It was stored until it was sold to the "wool man," who traveled the back roads. Sheep that didn't produce heavy wool, had twin lambs, or got old, were sold.

Arnold "Cub" Bair was our "cream man." He arrived weekly to pick up our cream and leave cheese and butter if we wanted.

Other income periodically came from the sale of hogs or steers to the stockyards. These are some of the ways that we paid for clothes, groceries, and other necessities during the 1930s and early 1940s. It was a hand-to-mouth existence most of the time.

Right after World War II started, there was a huge shortage of meat. Dad would go to the local sale barn and buy huge boars at very cheap prices. Usually the boars were lean, muscular, mean, and had long tusks. People did not want to eat meat from these boars because it was tough and had a boar flavor—ugh! But once a boar was castrated and his tusks cut off, he would heal in about a month and become very docile. The boars then were more interested in eating than pursuing sows, and they would pack on the pounds and take on the appearance of a very large and fat "butcher hog." Then the meat would be tender and lose its boar-smelling flavor.

We put off castrating young boars until they weighed more than 100 pounds, which made the task of catching and holding them very difficult. Some groups, such as the Knights of Columbus, had us save the testicles. Then they sponsored get-togethers that featured "Mountain Oysters" as the main entree, served with copious amounts of beer. I was never invited and wouldn't have gone anyway since the very thought of eating them was a turnoff.

When a castration was finished, it usually took about a week for the ex-boar to heal and begin his regimen, which was to eat all the corn and ground oats he could gorge into his tummy and then wash them down with tasty buttermilk slop. Sounds like a great hog's life? At the packing plant, they brought top dollar, and Dad always made money from them. I was glad that tremendously fat hogs were no longer wanted after the war since lard was no longer needed.

Another swine activity was to gather all the hogs into a very tightly enclosed area for "cleaning." We used a mixture of wash water that Mother had saved after washing clothes and a very strong and unpleasant-smelling insecticide and germ killer called "dip." We would spray the pigs until their skin was completely clean of all dirt, scurf, and lice. They always were healthier afterwards and gained weight quickly so they were soon ready for market.

After observing what the awful-smelling dip had done for the hogs, I decided that since I had dandruff, a shampoo with a little dip might be a cure. Please don't try it! The concoction made my head feel like a blowtorch was being held to it, so I had to make a nude dash to plunge my head into a bucket of cold water. Eventually, that put out the "fire" feeling, but my head was very tender for a while when I combed my hair. I don't remember if the dip cured dandruff—maybe it did because I don't have it anymore!

The Stewart Place's big red barn was home to several pairs of pigeons. While living at the Stewart Place, I went on pigeon-hunting expeditions to the Hurd, Fisher, Drum, and George's neighboring farms. The Georges had a son, Leonard, who was married to Aunt Theresa Agnew O'Rourke's best friend, Orpha Ladely.

The Georges all resided in the same house, and I thought Orpha was very beautiful. She would even come out and try to help me catch beautiful cream-colored pigeons (the first I had seen of that coloration). I knew there would be a fresh hatching every six weeks, so I started going to the Georges' house on that cycle.

About the third time, I walked over in the afternoon and knocked at the door. Leonard answered and said, "So you're the one who has been coming over here to visit my wife!" (I was 10 to 11 years old, and he was in his mid-20s.) Of course, he was teasing, but that never entered my mind. So he helped me catch some pigeons. Later when I would see him at Mass or about, he would "warn" me with a smile to "stay away from my wife."

March 1, 1942, arrived and, with it, another moving day. The Stewart Place had been sold. The U.S. had entered World War II three months earlier. I was 11 years and a few days old.

On the night of February 28, 22-month-old Bernie and I were taken to Grandma Agnew's so I could take care of him. Outside it was very cold and windy with lots of snow. I was happy to be in the warm house, and Bernie was no problem. Uncle Leo was recuperating from his thumb nearly being severed in a chain-saw mishap, Aunt Helen was in school (Keswick High), Uncle Harry was being his charming self, and Grandma and Aunt Anna were washing clothes.

Grandma announced that "We are having canned peaches for dinner," to which Bernie repeated "canned peters." Uncles Harry and Leo immediately picked up on that and kept asking, "Bernie, what are we having for dinner?"

Of course, he always loudly announced "peters." I was getting a silent charge out of the proceedings, but finally Bernie became aware that he was being made sport of and started crying loudly.

Grandma Agnew ordered all to be quiet, and Aunt Anna chimed in about those sitting around and being ornery. Uncle Harry had been teasing her all morning about the most un-couth and despicable bachelors in the area. He had turned to me and said, "Ann is as tough as a boiled owl!" I had never heard anyone say that before and thought it was hilarious.

Our new home, the "Wagner Place," was the homestead of the Theodore Wagner family and their children who included daughter Charlotte, the late wife of J.S. O'Rourke, Dad's first cousin. The Wagner Place was devoid of electricity so was a rung below the Stewart Place, but we had to be happy with what we had and could afford. On our first night there, a big rat emerged from a hole in the floor and was found drowned in the slop bucket the next morning.

We now attended the Hawkeye Dayton School about two miles east of the Armah church. I was in sixth, Kenny was in fourth, and Leroy was in second grade. Miss Mary G. O'Rourke, who lived about three miles away with her dad, J.S. O'Rourke, and stepmoth-er, Grace, was our teacher. So our new teacher also was a Dawson second cousin. Miss O'Rourke also was familiar to me from my time at school in Keswick—the glamorous high-school girls Mary O'Rourke and Margaret Smith walked me nearly home to the Big House for lunch as there were no school lunches at that time. Margaret also had been my teacher when I went to the Aurora school.

Also attending Hawkeye Dayton were Billy, Catherine Ann, and Monica Bender, first cousins of Jimmy, Dean, and Joe Bender, who attended the school we had just left. Our new classmates' mother, Mary Greene Bender, is Dad's first cousin, so we had lots of relatives in this school.

Eighth-grader Herman Redwine was the first country-school kid who could beat me in a race. He was two years older than I and much taller. I was disappointed as I'd overheard the Bender boys' dad say that I could run like a deer just like all the Agnew boys (my uncles), who were very speedy.

Our pasture was a mile away from the Wagner Place, so we had to drive the cows to pasture each morning and fetch them each evening. There were several large hills on the road to the pasture, and Gritter Creek flowed at its entrance. In normal weather, we could walk, wade, or jump across it easily. After extensive heavy rains though, it overflowed and sometimes threatened to wash the bridge away that spanned it. Not realizing the danger, Kenny and I would force the cows to swim to the other side, sometimes almost having to push them or twist their tails to make them jump in.

Our mongrel dog, Shep, helped us perform the dangerous deed. In some places, the water could be 12 to 15 feet deep, and the cows would jump in and rise to the top of the rapidly flowing water and eventually swim to the other side. We never considered that an aged cow or a calf might drown or that we might be dragged into the raging current. Mrs. Charles Wyant and son Herman would stand on their porch high on the hill overlooking the proceedings and admonish us to "stop that," "be careful," "watch out," and "I'm going to call your Mother," but we ignored them and continued defiantly. Eventually some-one did tell Dad, so our version of "Damp Rodeo" was discontinued.

One of my favorite places to play while living at the Wagner Place was under a bridge that spanned Gritter Creek. It was next to our cow pasture. After driving the cows to pasture, I would make my way under the steel structure that had floors of very heavy planks. I liked to hear the rumble of the planks as vehicles passed overhead, as I enjoyed the cool, shady playground underneath.

I spent dreamy, peaceful hours building dams and fashioning crude "ships" to float on my "lake." Sometimes I would find a pool with tadpoles and small frogs, and sometimes the cattle would join me to seek the same refreshing breeze and relief from the sun's hot rays. These were wonderful, carefree hours, and the memories seem even more enjoyable and precious as I grow older—and older—and older.

Dad had purchased our first tractor, a John Deere Model B with steel-lugged wheels in the back. It was a great help and replaced the horses that Dad had acquired at a farm sale four or five years earlier when we resided at the Lucas Place. The horses also served as "riding" horses when we rode four miles west to visit the Bender boys on Sunday afternoons.

Wonderful afternoons were spent visiting neighbors' barns and buildings, hunting pigeons, or going swimming in a small creek. On one such occasion, a cousin of the Benders was visiting. He was about a year older than the rest of us and looked more grown-up. He explained that boys "changed" when they reached a certain age, just like girls did when they first showed signs of breast development. That explained the phenomenon to me, as I found that observation to be mysterious before this "class" on sex education. Listening to "seminars" given by other kids was the only way we learned anything about "the birds and the bees"—sex questions were strictly taboo.

Tommy Joe, Uncle Tommy and Rose Dawson's oldest son, occasionally spent a few summer days with us. T.J. was seven years younger than me but very wise for his age. Uncle Tommy had a tavern in Lone Tree, Iowa, at that time. Tommy Joe told the most intriguing stories. Not long after, Uncle Tommy lost the tavern, Rose, and the family. He died in California in 1974.

Leroy and I got into several shenanigans together. At one point, we got tired of smoking corn silks and cornhusk cigarettes, and we decided to get the real deal to "puff" on. We started saving all the pennies we could find to reach the total of 20 cents that we needed to purchase a pack of Camel cigarettes.

Finally, we reached our goal, and on a Saturday night when Leroy was 7 and I was 11, we entered Mahannah's Café in North English and were greeted by Miss Susie Carter, the waitress. Leroy, who was not even as tall as the glass case that served as a counter, announced that he wanted a pack of Camels for his dad.

She went to get them, and we lined our 20 pennies on the case when, lo and behold, Dad came in the door. He asked, "What are you boys getting?"

"Nothing," we said, as we hightailed it out the door leaving Dad and our 20 cents.

"Whose little boys were they?" Susie asked when she came back. Dad said "mine," and she told him, "They just said you sent them in to get a pack of Camels for you, and there's the money. But where are they?"

Dad took them so, of course, he had the evidence. Needless to say, we avoided running into him until it was time to go home. I took the major assault on this one as I had "put Leroy up to it," Dad claimed.

But we had many good times with Dad, too. He took us hunting and showed us how to set traps so we could sell mink and muskrat pelts. He skinned and stretched the pelts for us, and we used them to pay for our first sled and our first very weak BB guns. (I don't believe we could have "put our eye out" as kids with BB guns and air rifles constantly were admonished.)

Dad got a horse and buggy for us. He told many amusing stories of his days as a child and growing up around Keswick.

I liked to carry the lantern when we made a final check late at night to see if the animals were resting comfortably and had plenty of hay, feed, and bedding. It would be very still and cold, and it looked like you could touch the stars. Across the fields, you could hear an occasional dog bark and see flickering kerosene lamps in the distant farmhouses. It seemed all was right in the world at least at that particular time and place, and I could truly feel safe, secure, happy, and tired.

But, sadly, a tragedy occurred with my pet pigeons when we were living at the Wagner Place. One night, a varmint entered and killed most of my pet pigeons that were housed in a small, dilapidated building. The survivors flew off and never came back because it had so terrified them.

While residing at the Wagner Place, Kenny and I were altar boys at a funeral. On Sundays that I had to serve Mass, I would have intense diarrhea before we left for church. I was extremely nervous and tense—afraid I would make a mistake on the altar. All Masses were prayed in Latin, and servers had to learn the Latin responses. I wasn't really sure what I was saying, but I learned them by heart and did not have to rely on altar cards as cues.

Our neighbors to the west across the field were the Berry brothers, Doc and Dean, and their aged mother, Nellie. We worked with them to make hay, thresh, and do other tasks.

One day we got up at 4 a.m. to get the chores done so we could make the journey to Parnell, about 15 miles away, where Dean Berry and Margaret Murphy (of Parnell) were being married. A few days after the wedding, it was custom to "chivaree" or "bell" newlyweds, and neighbors from miles around would gather at the newlyweds' home.

It almost was like a game as the bride and bridegroom would try to slip out and go to a movie or visit friends so they wouldn't be home. If they were home, a tremendous racket would ensue as folks pounded on pots and pans, rang cowbells, and made a deafening noise. If the newlyweds didn't appear within a reasonable time, someone would climb to the roof and cover the chimney to smoke them out.

Finally, a light would appear in a window, everyone would hoot, holler, and clap, and the newlyweds would emerge. Then the crowd would demand that the couple sponsor an oyster supper or a dance. Folks did not participate in "belling" their relatives; Dean and Margaret's chivaree was my one and only participation.

Dean and Margaret agreed to sponsor a dance on a Saturday night at Dayton Hall. Kenny, Leroy, and I, as well as the Bender boys, anxiously anticipated the event. I was delighted to see the nicely dressed men and gorgeous women twirling around the floor. The Parnell Irish were well represented and really could dance.

We Dawson and Bender boys scurried around to pick up half-burned cigarette butts to smoke. There was much drinking outside, and we sucked the last drop out of a whiskey bottle—knowing we really were being daring and living dangerously.

There was no electricity at Dayton Hall, and some folks brought their new state-of-the-art Aladdin kerosene burning lamps that threw off three to four times more light than the usual wick-burning lamps. The light was white and not the usual yellow. So that was my first dance at the age of 11.

Aunt Theresa and second cousin Leo O'Rourke (our teacher Mary O'Rourke's brother) sponsored an oyster supper at the J.S. O'Rourke residence after their "belling" in 1939. Soon belling passed into history as newlyweds started to sponsor some social gathering as part of their wedding festivities. Now nearly all weddings conclude with a dance or a dining reception.

On December 28, 1942, Uncle Harry Agnew and our schoolteacher/Dawson second cousin Mary O'Rourke were married at Armah. Billy Bender, Kenny, and I were altar boys on this very cold and snow-covered day. Afterwards, we attended a wedding dinner at the J.S. O'Rourke residence. That was the first time I ate dressing with raisins. We kids were all sick during the Christmas holiday vacation after the dinner—I blamed the raisin dressing. It is strange how I identified feeling terrible with those raisins; I haven't liked raisins since.

When school began again in January, the new Mrs. Mary O'Rourke Agnew told us not to call her Aunt Mary or Mrs. Agnew at school. She was to be addressed as Miss O'Rourke for the next few months until school was out. One day after we bundled up and got ready to walk home after school, Kenny got a safe distance head start and shouted back, "Good night Aunt Mary Agnew!"

I knew he had crossed the line, and she was ready the next morning. "Kenneth Dawson will not be joining us at recess for a few days," she announced.

As for me, Dad accused me of daydreaming, being "pigeon crazy," and standing around with my "finger in my ass" instead of concentrating on my schoolwork, taking care of my little brothers, helping him or Mother, or, in other words, being just plain good-for-nothing lazy.

However, I continued daydreaming and sometimes would have to stay in during recess because I couldn't concentrate on long division, which I absolutely hated. I liked history and geography—got straight As—as they were like reading good true stories. During my sixth and seventh grades, English became one of my favorite subjects because Aunt Mary

O'Rourke Agnew, the best teacher I ever had, pounded into my thick skull how to diagram sentences and the definitions of infinitives, conjunctions, participles, and gerunds. I always liked spelling, too.

At the end of each country-school year, the entire neighborhood attended a cooperative picnic on the school grounds. Each family brought their own plates, silverware, and napkins, and everyone brought food, which was placed buffet-style on a large table. But after gathering all the food together, strangely enough, it seemed the kids mostly ate only what their own mothers had prepared. We were very leery of the food brought by the other families—especially the Protestants! And our Protestant friends felt the same about the "Catholic" food.

I would eat what Mary Greene Bender or Aunt Mary O'Rourke Agnew brought since they were relatives. In fact, I had my first grilled cheese sandwich, prepared by Mrs. Bender, at the Hawkeye Dayton picnic. I nagged at Mother from then on to prepare grilled cheese, but during the war, cheese was a scarce and rationed item.

The war effort was in high gear. Prices were up as everything was scarce—even candy bars were in short supply as people wanted to send candy and cookies to their loved ones on the front lines in far-off lands.

Dad started raising 12 to 15 litters of pigs each spring and fall; three or four had been considered plenty to farrow in prior years. Dad would ask me to mark 20 of the best young gilts because he always proclaimed that I was good at picking out the best stock for our next group of mother hogs (sows). One time, however, a neighbor came by and offered a price Dad couldn't refuse, so our best group became that neighbor's breeding stock. We had to keep another group that wasn't quite as quality for our next brood sows.

Many young men were being drafted. Uncles Bernard Agnew and Jim and Raymond Dawson already were in the military, and Aunt Helen's fiancé, Lyle Hartzell, soon would join the Marine Corps. Uncle Leo Agnew could have been rejected by the draft board because of his thumb, but he would have none of that talk and insisted on joining his brother and friends in defending our country.

Early in 1943, I accompanied Aunt Mary O'Rourke Agnew to the Agnew homestead that she and Uncle Harry shared with Grandma, Uncle Leo, and Aunt Helen. Uncle Leo was leaving for basic training the next day, so I got to spend his last night at the Agnew home with him. Large families often had two and sometimes three of the same gender share a bed because of space. It always was a great honor to share a bed with an uncle, aunt, or Grandma; of course, when I got to be about 10, the sleep-ins with the females stopped.

As I left for school the next morning with teacher Aunt Mary, Uncle Leo leaned over the railing and said, "Come sleep with me again sometime."

I replied that I would—never dreaming that he had slept in that bed for the last time.

Later that day during afternoon recess, he drove his Model A by the school on his way to his induction. He waved, smiled, and honked the horn—"ooga, ooga."

That was the last time I saw my beloved Uncle Leo. He was 19 years old. In just about a year, he would lose his life fighting for freedom.

March 1, 1943, found us packed and ready to move again—this time to the "Swain Place," a 299-acre spread between North English and Millersburg. On moving day, Billy

Bender and Kenny were on horses and I was on foot to drive our cattle seven miles via winding country roads to their new quarters. It was mid-afternoon when we finally arrived, and I was totally exhausted.

After moving to the Swain Place, our new school was Hawkeye in English Township with Ruby Herdliska as the teacher. I had turned 12 just before moving day, and again I was the only student in my grade (seventh). Other than my brothers, I had no relatives at school, which was a first for me.

In May of that year, all seventh graders from rural schools had to go to a town school—I chose Millersburg—to take a geography test. Administrators were testing results of rural versus town students because it was rumored that kids got better educations in town schools.

I was pleased to receive a grade of 97 percent, the third highest in Iowa County; second cousin John Joseph Kelly of the neighboring Gehry School got the fifth highest with 96 percent. So we country kids did OK.

We didn't have a well at the Hawkeye school so at 10 a.m. every day, two students were appointed to walk a half mile to a neighboring farm to get a bucket of water and bring it back. It took two to carry the bucket, which was very large with a tight-fitting lid. Everyone used a common dipper to get a drink from the bucket. Water also was put in a basin so we could wash our hands after we used the outside toilets (there was one toilet for the girls and one for the boys).

Kids can be so unkind to each other. It usually is not planned, and I'm sorry to say I was guilty of such behavior on a few occasions. I can remember we three older Dawsons chasing a girl around the schoolhouse and then pulling up her dress to expose her "bloomers," as we called them. Eventually, either Miss Herdliska observed this from her window or someone told on us, so that "game" was ended.

We also were verbally unkind to others. On reflection, I understand how I hurt other kids' feelings. I never considered being in their shoes, and I now try to compensate for those early "injuries" by trying to be more considerate of others. I just hope the Lord has forgiven me.

It rained and rained and rained during our first spring at the Swain Place—so much that Dad could not even get 40 acres plowed to put in crops. So weeds covered the fields and grew as high as small trees. That fall, the field was plowed, and all the vegetation turned under made for great fertilizer. So the following year, we had a bumper crop of corn.

At the Swain Place, I nailed boxes to the rafters in the corncrib granary and soon had another flock of fairly tame pigeons. I became so adept at climbing among the rafters of the building that I could actually run and leap from sill to sill and keep my balance—almost like a monkey! Fortunately, I never made a miscalculation or would have fallen at least 20 feet.

I never was adept at handling machinery and driving tractors with attachments. While pulling a harrow at the Swain Place one day, I turned too short and it caught a big tractor tire and nearly came up over my head before I got stopped. Mr. Cram, a neighbor, viewed my predicament and came with wrenches to get the thing back together. I am forever thankful to him.

Another time, I turned too close to a fence and ripped out several feet of wire fencing. I couldn't cover that up and suffered the verbal consequences. Sometimes I would get on the wrong row when cultivating corn and look back to see the corn had been cut off on one row. I would quickly stop, run back, and stick the cornstalks back in the loose soil—not realizing that in a few minutes the sun would have them wilted and dead. There was no way to hide that error either.

I wasn't meant to be a farmer except to care for the stock who became my pets. I could pet a sow like a dog, and each had a name and responded just like a dog or cat. Hogs are very, very intelligent, as are most all animals and God's creatures.

At the Swain Place, Mother had a large black-and-white spotted gander (male goose) that followed her everywhere when she was outside. He waited patiently outside the back door for her appearance. He stood guard outside the chicken house, the outside outhouse, granary, or garden gate—wherever she went. He hissed and ruffled his feathers and sometimes attacked Dad, us kids, the dog, or anyone that he thought was too close to his beloved Mary. He did not stay with the other geese and looked upon them with disdain (I think!).

Mother raised large flocks of geese to augment her income—99 percent of which was spent on the rest of the family. However, her "Goosie" had no offspring, as he was completely devoted to the human object of his affection. Eventually, he was killed by a dog that got tired of being the victim of his attacks. This happened when there were no human witnesses to the murder—or was it self-defense?

Walter was a very talented young man with black wavy hair. Women of the Armah and Millersburg area employed Walter to wallpaper their rooms, paint, etc. He came to the Swain Place to wallpaper several rooms, and he always spent the nights so he could get an early start every day.

Mother enjoyed Walter very much, and they talked, laughed, and discussed cooking, sewing, and all sorts of gossipy things. I was quite fascinated and pondered why he never did any "man's" work—the women seemed so comfortable with him, but Dad didn't have too much to say.

While residing at the Swain Place, Dad rented some hayfields about a mile east along Iowa Highway 149. Brothers Pete and Albert West, who were older and never married, owned the fields. Pete took care of the house, garden, chickens, and had raised pigeons, so I just had to make his acquaintance. Albert cared for their Shorthorn cattle.

We spent several summer days baling hay and storing it in barns and stacks. I was impressed that the Wests' pastures always looked like golf courses. Pete and Albert each carried a very, very sharp pocketknife so when they spied a weed anywhere in a pasture, hayfield, or along a fencerow, that particular plant was dead. They would cut it off clear down below the soil line to make sure it didn't grow back. (I practiced that lesson the rest of my life and kept a sharp tool around to eradicate my weed population, making sure to cut below the growing level. But it was a never-ending battle as new weeds kept appearing.)

The Swain Place was our residence for six years, from 1943 to 1949, longer than we had ever lived in one place so far. While we lived there, two new families moved into the area.

The sons became very good summer buddies, and we had many enjoyable times playing basketball, swimming, catching pigeons, sneaking around to smoke ill-gotten cigarettes, etc.

A family with many boys lived nearby. When we drove by their house one time, I commented on the rust streaks running down the side of the house from some of the upstairs windows. Dad replied that evidently the boys must pee out those windows during the summer. I made a hasty mental note to refrain from doing the same.

A little neighbor girl about Leroy's age was game for any activities we would prescribe. One warm afternoon, Leroy and I convinced her that she should remove her clothes and get in a cool, muddy, hog-wallowing hole, which was in a small ditch along the road. We had said we would join her, but then reneged. The poor girl was covered with mud up to her chest; thank goodness no one drove by as there was no place to hide!

Suddenly it dawned on us that it was nearly time for her to go home. We had to sneak her up to the water-filled stock tank where the cows and horses drank. She got in and, with our help, got cleaned up. Fortunately, her clothes were not muddy. She dried herself with some old gunnysacks and made her way home.

Another narrow escape! Of course, I had known for five years that my destination was hell, but it was very beneficial to avoid the suffering that could be inflicted on this earth by irate parents or priests.

It wasn't until I reached the age of Confirmation that I mustered up enough courage to confess to my 1938 sin of eating a peanut before communion. I knew that if I received the sacrament of Confirmation in a state of mortal sin that an indelible mark would be put on my soul.

However, the priest did not seem to be alarmed, thunder didn't clap, and I received a regular penance! I was immensely relieved and almost disappointed that it had been so easy. I wondered if he actually heard me—maybe he was daydreaming. Well, that curtain was lifted, and I've tried to "tell all" and feel sincere sorrow ever since then.

Uncle Leo Agnew was killed at Monte Cassino, Italy, on January 25, 1944, a casualty of the Italian campaign at Anzio. I remember him telling me how old he would be in the year 2000 and often thought of that after we heard of his death.

In the spring of 1944, we returned from school to find that Dad had just returned home and Mother and Bernie were gone. Dad broke the heartbreaking news that Uncle Leo had been killed in January.

There had been much concern for weeks as no letters had been forthcoming. Every day, the Agnews had phoned one another asking, "Have you heard from Leo?"

Aunt Mary O'Rourke Agnew had heard from her brother Mike O'Rourke, stationed in Italy, that he knew something that the Agnews would not like to hear. During the war, military personnel censored letters to protect their positions.

After Dad gave us the news on that terrible day, we did hurried chores. I took a coal bucket to gather the eggs and was crying so hard that I missed a step on the outside porch and many of the about 60 eggs were broken. Dad did not even chew me out but said, "The hens will lay some more."

We arrived at Grandma Agnew's to find all the aunts, uncles, spouses, and our little cousins gathered. Everyone was red-eyed and teary.

The War Department first had alerted Uncle Emmett, and he summoned the Armah priest, Father Patrick Duggan (he had replaced Father Walsh, who had been drafted as a military chaplain). Father Duggan walked across the muddy field to tell Grandma. When he got there, Grandma Agnew came to the door and said, "I know why you're here."

He nodded, and her wail was unearthly.

When Grandma heard that Leo—her youngest son at age 20—had been killed, she got a headache that she had for the rest of her life. She practically lived on aspirin for years. Doc Miller of North English came out that day to give Grandma a shot for her nerves.

A memorial service was held shortly thereafter, but a funeral was not held until more than four years later when Uncle Leo's body was returned for burial.

In the fall of 1944, I began high school in North English (I wanted to go to Millersburg High School but North English was closer). Of the 107 students in North English High School, only five were Catholic, so we certainly were a minority. One of my fellow Catholics was 11th-grader Larry O'Brien, Great-Aunt Susie's youngest son and Mother's first cousin, so I knew at least one person.

In August, just before school started, I became very ill with fever, vomiting, nausea, and aches all over. I lay around upstairs most of the time except during milking time—I always managed to milk cows. We were milking 14 cows by hand each morning and evening, so all hands were needed.

In September, I had recovered sufficiently and could start high school. There were no school buses, so Dad bought a bay mare for me to ride the 4½ miles to North English. I was 13 years old, small for my age, and could not control the horse. She moseyed along eating grass from roadside ditches, and I often was very late—sometimes arriving at 10:30 or 11 a.m. I wore a brown, wool, over-the-head sweater and, thank goodness, the mare was the same color because by the time I arrived at school, I was practically covered with horsehair that clung to the wool like tiny magnets.

When I would get to North English, I would tie her in a stall Dad had rented and then walk on to school. But on several occasions, I just tied her up in the old barn and browsed through papers collected for the war effort that were sitting there. I probably learned more from devouring those old newspapers and magazines than I would have at school. We had not been able to afford to subscribe to a daily paper; all of our news was capsulated in radio newscasts.

When I would deem it was time for school to be out, I'd climb on Miss Horse for the trip back home. How I hated, hated riding that stubborn mare. I also was beginning to have trouble getting on her, as my left leg was weak and numb.

One afternoon, I asked Superintendent McCurdy if I could skip physical education class and told him about my leg. He sent me uptown to Dr. Miller. After an examination, he told a stunned me that I previously had polio! Dr. Miller surmised that I probably picked up the polio germ while cavorting in a creek in the dog days of that August.

I walked back to school in a daze and later rode the horse home. There was nobody there when I arrived, and I went into Mother and Bernie's room (one parent always slept with the youngest) and sat on the bed trying to figure out what I was going to tell Mother and Dad.

Soon they got home and came in looking very concerned and still surprised—they had just been to Doc Miller's for Mother's exam as she was six months pregnant with Patrick Leo. The doctor had informed them that I had been in earlier that afternoon and gave them the details.

I no longer had polio—or "infantile paralysis" as it was called then—but had a weak and numb leg and was unable to move my toes on my left foot as a result. About 10 years later, a vaccine was discovered that all but eliminated polio. I'm the last person from that area that I can recall to be afflicted.

In the 1930s and early 1940s, the dreaded malady left many young people unable to walk and some survived only by using an "Iron Lung," a huge device in which the patient was confined. I adapted but still have numbness, and my left leg is weaker than the right one. I believe it damaged only the nerves, and I'm very fortunate.

Uncle Harry and Aunt Mary O'Rourke Agnew had taken over operation of the Agnew homestead, so that same fall, Grandma Agnew moved to a two-story house west of North English's Main Street. After winter arrived and it had been revealed that I'd had polio, I was permitted to stay with Grandma Agnew during the week so I was close to school. The Agnew aunts and uncles, along with Mother and Dad, also did not want Grandma to be alone as she was in rather fragile condition health-wise after learning of Leo's heroic death.

Grandma Agnew was very religious and a devout Catholic. One of the reasons she later moved east of Main Street in North English was to be close to St. Joseph's Catholic Church. When I stayed with her, we attended morning Mass daily at the priest's house, where the buffet served as the altar. I served as the altar boy. Usually Grandma, her sister/ my Great-Aunt Susie O'Brien, and the priest's housekeeper were the only other attendees. What is rather amazing is the fact that Grandma and Great-Aunt Susie were teenagers when they converted to Catholicism after trying other churches. Their parents had been members of the Church of England before coming to the United States.

My jobs at Grandma's were emptying the ashes from the furnace and carrying the chamber pots to the outside privy for dumping. While I was performing these duties, I tried to avoid encountering the neighbors. Of course, I should have realized that they emptied their chamber pots, too, as indoor facilities had not arrived at this location.

While I was staying with Grandma, I discovered the local library and checked out many books. I missed school many days by telling Grandma that I didn't feel good. Then I would huddle under the covers and read interesting books about Indian tribes and Wild West adventures. I was still disappointed I had not been born a Native. I certainly would have been a great chief and driven the foreigners from our land!

Kenny, who was now in seventh grade at the rural school, and I were given permission to attend the first high-school basketball game of the season. We walked into the packed gymnasium, and I was amazed and shocked at the noise and colorful uniforms. I hadn't witnessed any basketball since a Keswick boys' high-school practice back in 1936 or 1937, and I didn't know the rules of the game at all. We arrived during warm-up for the first game, and each team was practicing free throws. I was still so dumb that I thought the team that made the most free throws won the game!

We found seats in the bleachers and—lo and behold—a striped-attired gentleman blew a shrill whistle and all kinds of commotion ensued. Then it dawned on me that "this" was the game! It was a girls' game and a heated rivalry between Millersburg and archrival North English. It ended in a tie, 22 all. You would have thought it was a war—the two towns' fans berated and threatened one another, and it was not all in jest.

From then on, I was crazy about basketball, so we nailed up rims taken off old barrels and had our own basketball "courts" in the haymow, tree, or wherever I could attach a hoop. We saved our pennies and soon purchased a real rim with a net and a game-type basketball. We nailed an old barn door to a tree in the front yard to use as our backboard.

Some of our friends began spending Sunday afternoons with us on our dusty basketball court. We would even shoot baskets after dark by the light of the moon or bundle up with coats, hats, and gloves when it was bitterly cold and windy.

Kenny eventually played for three years at North English and one at Parnell; Leroy played all four years at Parnell. I never played on a high-school team since polio had weakened my left leg and I had numbness of the foot.

However, I was a sports reporter for North English High School and phoned in scores and game statistics to *The Tait Cummins Show* at WMT in Cedar Rapids. I also wrote reports on our football teams, as well as the boys' and girls' basketball squads, which Tait would read over the air. A side benefit was that I got in free to all the games.

The fall and winter of 1944 were extremely cold with lots of snow. The mud roads had been used during the fall rainy season, so they had deep, irregular ruts and cracks. When the winter freeze set in, riding in a car over these roads felt like riding over a washboard. Passengers almost felt like they were on a trampoline!

On one early cloudy Saturday, December 16, I heard Dad bundle up Kenny, Leroy, and Bernie and leave. I wondered why he didn't get me up to chore, but I didn't mind and enjoyed the warm bed with flannel sheets piled high with blankets and comforters.

I was awakened from my slumber by the cry of a baby! By this time, I knew a doctor's "bag" containing babies was a myth. I came downstairs and saw a hungry baby in the baby carriage sucking his thumb.

Later I learned that after depositing Kenny, Leroy, and Bernie at Uncle Emmett and Aunt Gloria Agnew's house, Dad had arranged to pick up a local woman whose role in life, it seemed, was to be present when new babies arrived. Her skills at new mother and baby care, as well as household management, were valued highly. But "Mrs. B" had to be contacted and scheduled in plenty of time. Mrs. B soon had 8½-pound Patrick Leo and Mother doing well.

About two weeks later, Mother, Dad, and Patrick Leo set out for Patrick Leo's baptism over those washboard roads. I remember Mrs. B watching out the window saying, "Oh my God, I hope she carries him real tight."

Of course, mouthy-me later reported that to Mother. She did not appreciate the comment and said, "Does she think I'm dumb and never held a baby before?"

Mrs. B was very bossy and badgered us kids to do this and do that. Leroy always was very feisty and would defy her, saying "you're not my boss," and continued doing whatever he had been. She was always threatening to tell Dad on us. I would butter her up by telling her she made the most delicious baked goods and, sure enough, soon we would have pies and cinnamon rolls. Kenny seemed to escape her wrath and Bernie was too young, but she and poor Leroy were in constant clashes. He wouldn't tell her anything she did was good and always informed her that Mother did everything so much better.

When Bernie would fall or get hurt, he would cry loudly with tears streaming down his face and scare all of us, including Mother, Dad, and whoever else was around, by holding his breath. His face would turn very red and then blue while Dad and Mother tried to get him to take a breath. I would pray that he wouldn't die. Eventually, he would go limp, get very pale, and begin to breathe. All of us would breathe a sigh of relief, and he was worn out afterwards. Mrs. B was there during one such episode. She said to take him outside and pump cold water over his face. That snapped him back to life, and he never again scared us with a "holding breath" episode.

Bernie was a very handsome little child and could ask many questions. When Bernie was small, he dreamed of having a pony farm, raising mushrooms in the basement, or owning a worm farm for fishermen. One time, I took him with me to get some English assignments for the weekend. My teacher said he was the best-looking child she had ever seen, gave him candy, and made a big fuss.

Not long after Patrick Leo's birth, I got a first—I had my "hind-end" kicked all the way up the stairs from the basement on through the kitchen and dining room and finally up the stairs to my second-floor bedroom.

It started when Dad heard Kenny, Leroy, and me enter the basement from the outside steps. He decided to hide in the coal room and surprise us while we were taking off our boots and winter chore clothes. Dad remained quiet while listening to us surmise about various sexual topics and parts of the anatomy—until I made a reference to his penis as being "so damn little."

I barely had it out of my mouth before a shocking bear-sounding voice roared, "I've heard enough!" He proceeded to twirl a shocked me around while kicking my butt all the way up and through the downstairs and then on up the stairs where he knocked or threw me across the room to the bed. He announced that I would have no supper and he was going to reveal the words of the terrible conversation "to your Mother!"

All of this happened in a matter of seconds, and as I gathered my thoughts and tried to remember what all had been said and what the horrible consequences could possibly be, I wondered how I could ever face Dad again or look him in the eye. I dreaded thinking of the blow that hearing such filthy talk would be to Mother.

To top it off, since Patrick Leo was only a few weeks old, Mrs. B was there. I got the usual sad looks from Mother and mean ones from Dad. My rear was sore for a few days. Mrs. B gave me questioning looks wondering what I could have done to bring that exhibition of kicking through the house.

Many, many years later in the 1980s, I was taking a bath while visiting Dad. Also visiting at the time were some of my nephews. I had the upstairs bathroom window open when I heard an extension ladder being placed right below the window. Just as a curious head was about to peek in, I shut the window. I thought it was funny. Later that evening, I was telling Dad and he replied, "Sounds like they take after their uncle—you!"

As a freshman in 1944–1945, I began to get a little "peach fuzz" on my face. Dad would say he was going to bring an old cat in to lick cream off my face and make the hair stay down.

At the 1944 high-school Christmas party, the junior who had drawn my name gave me a sewing kit. When I opened it, I was so embarrassed since it was a "girly" thing. He just laughed and laughed. The next year, by some odd coincidence, he again drew my name. This time, he got me a shaving kit, so I figured I'd better take the hint.

This guy's girlfriend wrote a feature column for the high-school newspaper and always was very nice to this little underclassman. One of my proudest moments at the time was reading her column titled, "What we are proud of at North English Hi." She wrote, "GENE DAWSON, his personality." Mother was very happy, and Dad questioned if I was smiling at "all the girls."

On a bitterly cold night in December 1944, I went to the North English versus Conroy boys' and girls' basketball games. Since it was -15 degrees outside and snow and ice covered the roads, there was just a small crowd. I talked to senior Rita Tedrow and her brother Tommy who were seeking a ride to a dance in Victor, Iowa, about 25 miles away. They suggested that I might like to go, but I hadn't been to a dance since the Berry wedding at Dayton Hall when I was 11 years old. I knew there was no way I would be allowed to go.

After the game, they convinced a young man to drive them to Victor in his pickup truck. Some other friends joined them and had to ride in the bitterly cold back of the truck. On the way back, the driver lost control of the vehicle and plunged into a deep ditch. Everyone was badly injured, and Rita and one other passenger passed away.

On an equally cold day, Aunt Anna Agnew and I went to Rita's funeral at St. Patrick's Catholic Church in Little Creek. She was laid to rest at the age of 17 in the church cemetery. The other accident victims eventually recovered and returned to school, but the rest of the 1944–1945 school year was very gloomy.

Mother with Patrick Leo, 1945.

I loved basketball, and my brothers and I played with friends at the Swain Place when we could. This is me in 1947.

Leroy (in back), Kenny, and Bernie (in front) with horse Mabel at the Swain Place, 1947.

Uncle Johnny Agnew (in back) and his wife Rose (middle, surrounded by Dawsons) were a dynamic couple. From left in front: Bernie, Kenny, Rose, Leroy, and me.

# Chapter 4

## 1945–1949

World War II mercifully came to an end in Europe and Japan in 1945, and soon millions of American servicemen and servicewomen returned home. Many did not want to return to the farm after having seen the world. Uncle Bernard Agnew soon was married to Veronica Armstrong, and Aunt Helen Agnew's fiancé Lyle Hartzell, a Marine in the Pacific, came home. Kenny and I soon "married" them (we were altar servers) at St. Joseph's in North English, as we had Uncle Bernard and Veronica.

Now all of Grandma Agnew's surviving children were married except Aunt Anna. She never did take that step. She shared a home with Grandma Agnew and always was a kind and very thoughtful aunt to all of us.

Dad's brother Uncle Raymond Dawson had married Elisa Baldonado, a beautiful girl in New Mexico, and Aunt Marie Dawson married Navy man Raymond LaMere in Minneapolis. Uncle Jim, Aunt Catherine, and Aunt Elizabeth Dawson did not marry.

Most of the military servicepeople had been away a few years and were eager to get on with their lives. Those who did wish to farm were taking G.I. loans and seeking affordable premises to purchase. Rationing stopped, everyone wanted a new car, and housing developments surrounding the cities sprung up.

New appliances of all kinds were being manufactured. A magical "radio"—called a television—that showed a movie or live action was the most amazing item to me. Of course, we couldn't afford one. We never did have electricity at the Wagner Place, and it was not until after the end of the war that Mr. Davidson from Keswick was summoned to wire the Swain Place.

Since we didn't have electricity at the Swain Place for the first two years we were there, Dad had purchased a kerosene icebox—or refrigerator, as it was called—at a closing-out sale. A few years earlier, it had been a state-of-the-art appliance that provided cold storage for families who didn't have electricity. It worked well and kerosene was economical to use, so we kept the well-performing cold box instead of using hard-earned money on an expensive electric refrigerator. Later on, in 1955, that cold box would be instrumental in the first great tragedy of our Dawson family.

Leroy and I liked to play on the telephone. After school while Mother went out to gather eggs, we dashed to the wall phone, climbed up on chairs, and proceeded to call our friends and relatives. Sometimes we would disguise our voices and say what we considered to be very bold things and ask some obscene questions.

I usually watched for Mother and Dad while Leroy did the calling—I would get a huge charge out of his way with words and ad-libbing. Once in awhile, a neighbor woman would chime in and threaten to tell our parents if we didn't get off the party line (we shared the phone line with neighbors who could listen in on our calls, as we could theirs).

I can't recall Kenny getting involved in the phone games, but when cousin Eddie Harris came to stay a few days during the 1945 threshing season, he and Leroy climbed up to the phone as Mother was out picking strawberries. They called several neighbor women proclaiming to be "Toe" Rowe (he was given the nickname because he had operated a shoe-repair shop) and asked them if "he" could borrow their manure spreader. (Back then, saying "manure" to an adult was like saying "shit.") Then they went a little too far and called a neighbor who was in her 80s. They proclaimed it was Toe calling and suggested they get together for a sexual tryst.

By now, many on the party line had started to listen in and were aware of the shenanigans. Someone alerted Mr. Rowe. Leroy and Eddie told me that they glanced out the window to see Toe's gray car coming over the hill at a high rate of speed, kicking up clouds of dust. They hastily departed for the sheep shed, which was adjacent to a field of tall corn. Soon Toe and Mother were calling in loud voices for them to appear, but they were met with silence. The boys eventually emerged from the tall corn about the time I arrived home with the team of horses and hayrack I had used while helping with threshing.

They filled me in on the proceedings, much to my amazement. At least I can't be blamed for this or putting them up to it, I thought. Mother gave Dad the news when he got home, and then Mr. Rowe arrived to brief him.

I recall that Dad told Leroy and Eddie to enjoy their supper because the punishment would be after the meal. I sympathized with them and wished supper would never end. Leroy received one of the most severe beatings I had ever seen or heard about. He refused to cry and would say, "Hit me again! I'm not crying." Well, Dad would accept the challenge, and I was praying that Leroy would cry so it would stop.

When Dad finished with Leroy, Leroy went upstairs, crawled in the back of a closet, and sobbed his eyes out. Dad looked at Eddie and I held my breath, but he did not strike him. Eddie, although invited, never again stayed at our place and only visited when he was with his parents.

On one sunny afternoon after a nice rain, Leroy and I traveled barefooted to a nearby barn. One of the things I remember about this day is the brilliant flash of light we saw— this was the day a bomb was detonated at a test site in New Mexico. It truly is a wonder the world wasn't set afire during the experiments.

My second remembrance is climbing into the barn's cupola by walking the hay rope, holding onto the track, and finally swinging my way in. I was unsuccessful at catching a prized bird. As I emerged from the cupola, I put my feet on the rope and grasped the iron track firmly.

The rope gave way. It was about 30 feet to the bottom of the mow, and no new hay had yet been harvested.

"There goes the rope, and here am I," I said as I dangled in the air.

"Oh Gene! Oh Gene!" Leroy shouted and pleaded.

I had him get the low end of the rope and pull it back taut. With that, he wrapped it around a beam and pulled for dear life. Then I was able to gingerly ropewalk back to the end of the barn. Climbing down the side was a piece of cake compared to a nearly 30-foot drop. I didn't catch a pigeon, but that episode stands out in my memories.

One hot sunny Sunday afternoon when Aunt Alice, Uncle Kermie, and Donnie Herr were visiting, Leroy and I decided to go on another pigeon foray. We set out across the fields for the Harold Miller residence. Mr. Miller had just filled his mow with loose hay, and it was heating—up near the roof it probably was 110 to 120 degrees. I found a young pigeon that had just learned to fly and chased it back and forth over the hot, soft hay but never could catch it. I got so hot that it seemed cold when I got down to the ground.

Leroy and I started home but stopped midway on a hill in the pasture. I was getting a terrific, throbbing headache and when I would look one way, I would "see" a different way—my eyes had lost their focus! Finally we got to the house, and I lay down on the linoleum-covered dining-room floor. I passed out for a while, and when I came to, I went to the backhouse toilet and was violently ill, vomiting and otherwise. I was very weak, but the headache was gone and my body temperature had returned to normal.

I told Dad and Mother later that night, and Dad proclaimed that I had got "overhet," or in other words, had a heatstroke. He said he also had become "overhet" one time while making hay as a young man, and we were both fortunate to have survived. I didn't tell him how I had come to be in that state—he would have thought I was indeed foolish to nearly die chasing a pigeon on such a suffocating day.

It was here at the Swain Place that I confiscated an old brooder house that was not being used and in a high state of disrepair. I converted it into my first "pigeons-only" house. I previously had pigeons in the rafters of a corncrib, barn, scale house (where animals are weighed), henhouse, sheep shed, hog house, machine shed, and an old half-fallen-down shed. I had pigeons that were allowed to fly free in every building on the farms, other than the houses. I had caught all of the various groups, plus some from Grandma Agnew's and neighbors' farms, and confined them to their shed.

Two brothers lived near Millersburg and had the most beautiful pigeons I had ever seen. They lived in a "haunted-appearing" house, didn't have a car, and seldom went to town. They lived off the land with their garden and wild berry bushes, and they raised many beautiful chickens. The brothers were expert marksmen and ate many rabbits, squirrels, opossums, and raccoons. They reportedly had much money buried on the premises or stuffed in their mattresses because they didn't trust banks.

Kenny and I were bold enough to visit them one Sunday. After admiring the pigeons and gaining the trust of the brother who raised them, he agreed to sell me 10 at four cents each! I was elated and also purchased a setting of chicken eggs (15). Those chickens, which had Wyandotte and Cornish as well as fighting lines, crossed with our regular chickens and produced big-breasted offspring that were delicious to eat. The cocks also were brilliantly plumed.

I had the brothers' pigeons for three to four years until an invader got in one night and killed a couple dozen pigeons, leaving their bloody, headless, and mutilated bodies strewn about. When I went to check them the next day, the carnage was heartbreaking. The surviving 15 to 20 pigeons flew away, never to be seen again. After trapping the varmint and fixing the opening, I tried to raise pigeons in the shed again, but they never would stay. It seemed they sensed that a great disaster had happened there.

At that time, the deer population was practically nonexistent as early pioneers had used them for a source of protein. In 1945, Dad came in from husking corn to report he had seen a wild deer. Kenny and I were very excited and hoped to get a glimpse soon. About two to three weeks later, Dad found the skin and intestines of a deer. We were very disappointed. We agreed that a neighbor (not one of the brothers) had apprehended "Bambi." The men in that neighboring family toted their rifles about the area and were crack shots.

I never saw a wolf or heard a coyote. It just is in the last 40 years that wildlife has made a dramatic comeback in the rural United States. Today deer, wild geese, coyotes, and raccoons can be nuisances, cause fatal accidents, and do much damage.

A recreational activity, which I did alone or with my brothers, was "snoops." My cousin Eddie Harris enjoyed these adventures when he visited. These forays into the pigeon areas of neighbors' buildings usually started on foot, buggy, or horseback. If the neighbors weren't home—and since nobody locked their doors—we also would enter the house and proceed to investigate every room, closet, cupboard, basement, and the attic, if accessible. We never took anything. I recall religious pamphlets in one home, a collection of flags in a neighbor's dresser drawer, the remnants of a chicken in a pressure cooker at another house, a spotlessly clean neighbor's house, and the most delicious cakes and cookies at another neighbor's.

Although we didn't take anything else, we were unable to resist a piece of delicious cake and a cookie or two while at the last house. Thank God no one ever came home to find us! I can imagine the scandal, and Mother and Dad would have been disgraced. I don't even want to ponder it.

The closest I came to being caught was early one morning at the beginning of summer vacation. As I went to fetch the cows for the morning milking, for some reason, I climbed the fence and knocked on a neighbor's door. No one answered, and I cautiously entered and patrolled the downstairs while noticing breakfast dishes on the table. Deciding that the mother couldn't be far away and hearing the father shouting at his cows, I hastily retreated.

When I got home, the phone rang for the neighbor (the phone rang quietly when it was for someone else on the party line). Mother announced she was going to listen because the neighbor's mother was ill and she might overhear how she was progressing.

"No one will answer; she's [the mother] not home," I said.

Mother picked up the receiver, and I was stunned to hear a conversation! Mother reported that the mother and one daughter had just returned about 10 minutes earlier from picking blackberries. She wondered why I thought the mother wasn't home, and I quickly lied and said I had seen them picking berries. My heart skipped a beat as I contemplated the fact that I had just left the family's house about 15 minutes earlier.

I resolved to never go on snooping expeditions again or to be much, much more careful if I did. That was my last snoop to an occupied home. I still would enjoy "touring" abandoned houses, schools, or apartments, which I did in later years.

One day after a storm caused a telephone wire to hang low, a 10-year-old neighbor was riding her horse along the road and reached up to touch the wire. At that instant, someone rang his telephone, which sent an electrical shock along the line that traveled from the unfortunate girl's hand to the horse. Of course, the horse got four times the shock since it was grounded by its four feet. That gelding shot out from under the girl, and she released the wire ending her own shock and tumbled to the ground!

Another lesson learned—don't touch wires even if they are within reach.

I already had been the victim of an electric fence. When the fences were first available, they were powered by batteries and didn't give nearly the jolts that those from this time period gave (since they were hooked directly to an electric current). Some of the Agnew uncles and their male in-laws, including Dad, would show off their "macho-ness" by grasping a wire to see how long they could hold it and how much shock they could take. I didn't know what they were doing when Dad beckoned me to give him my hand. I was jolted by that awful shock that only can be given to an unsuspecting victim. I jerked away and let out a howl like a wounded mountain lion.

I occasionally dream that I have stumbled into a maze of electrical fence wires, and I am glad when I awaken just as it seems I'm going to get shocked by multiple wires. No wonder I have heart problems!

There was an ancient and abandoned cemetery on a roadside corner near the Swain Place. It was remarkable to see how many young mothers died while giving birth; usually the children also did not survive and were buried with their mothers. The markers revealed that some men had two or more wives who died in childbirth. I thought of Grandpa Tom Dawson's first wife, Winnie.

We disliked walking along that stretch of road after dark and would move at a brisk pace, always whistling or singing to let "them" know we were nearby. If an owl would hoot or a varmint dash out, we would "fly" down the road in a panic! It even was a little scary if we climbed the fence and trespassed there in broad daylight. I never understood how folks could enjoy secret trysts in such places and how they could concentrate on their hanky-panky.

In 1945, we raised many hogs, and Dad had several 50-gallon barrels that we used for soaking oats and corn for them. One of my jobs that summer was to keep those barrels full. The grain would swell and become soft and much tastier for the swine and chickens. It was poured in troughs with soured buttermilk, which had been delivered by Mr. Cliff Cox or his wife Mildred from the North English Creamery. The buttermilk was delivered via a large tank truck with a hose (like a gasoline truck) and stored in additional barrels with lids. The buttermilk was a by-product of the butter-making process, and the creamery owners were glad to get rid of it.

I developed amazing hand and arm strength as I could carry four full five-gallon buckets at a time from the water tank to the barrels or from the granary to the barrels, which were about 50 feet apart. I carried one in the crook of each elbow and one in each hand! Dad proclaimed this as "lazy man's work," indicating I was straining myself and would get less tired making twice as many trips, but it sure did cut down on the time.

I started my sophomore year in 1945, but I ended up going to high school for five years. I dropped back a class after I missed so much as a sophomore as I adjusted to the results of my polio. Since I did not attend kindergarten, I still turned 18 just three months prior to my graduation.

During high school, every guy thought he had to have a girlfriend; it seemed to be the "in" thing. My name—not my heart—was linked to Shirley of the Richland school; Mary Theresa and Yvonne of Millersburg; Joan, Margaret, and Kaye of Parnell; and Anne of Cedar Rapids. Our "romances" consisted mostly of writing letters and occasional meetings at sporting events. There were no actual dates.

These girls were the "aggressors" and pursued me. I hadn't shown any interest in girls. Sometimes I wondered when I would start feeling like my contemporary male friends and look at girls in a sexual way. I didn't realize at the time that I would never feel that way and it would never happen—since I was born gay.

One day, I went to Witte's Department Store in nearby Williamsburg to buy a suit. Each town had a dry-goods store that dwarfed all the other stores on the town square.

While I tried on the suits, I was introduced to my first three-way mirror. Much to my shock and consternation, a horrible-looking individual appeared in profile. My hair was uncombed in the back and stood on end and my turned-up nose looked like a Berkshire hog's nose. I was gangly, awkward-looking, and appeared very unsure of myself. I was dumbfounded when I realized this was how I appeared to others more than half the time. From then on, I tried to improve my posture, and with the help of a hand-held mirror, I combed my hair in the back, too.

On this day, I had saved up 25 cents, and I took little Bernie by the hand and entered the Star Drug store where I ordered my first strawberry malt. I asked for two straws so I could share it with Bernie. He took to that malt like a pig to slop, and I had to slurp vigorously to keep up! So we each had our very first malt together.

On June 6, 1946, 89-year-old Great-Grandma Minnie Burke Healy passed away at Great-Aunt Susie O'Brien's home, which was next door to Grandma Agnew's in North English. Grandma had moved to her house east of Main Street in early 1946 and stayed there until her own death in 1968.

Kenny and I were altar boys for Great-Grandma Healy's funeral. She joined Great-Grandpa Healy lying in peace at the Armah Cemetery. He had died in 1927.

Great-Grandma Healy had suffered from macular degeneration and had been blind for several years. She had a special comfortable chair where she sat each day praying her rosary, visiting, or being fed. She couldn't do anything for herself.

When we great-grandchildren visited her, we had to line up and stand in front of her while she felt our arms, touched our faces and hair, and exclaim how each of us had grown and were skinny, bony, tall, etc. I did not enjoy this and don't think my brothers and cousins did either, but that was her way of "seeing" through touch. I hope that I am never blind, nor that anyone else will be thus afflicted.

On Sundays, since Grandma Agnew and Aunt Anna resided about a block from St. Joseph's, they usually were already at the church when we arrived and parked in front of Grandma's house. Leroy and I would sit in the choir loft when I wasn't serving Mass and observe Mother, Dad, Grandma, and Aunt Anna in prayer. Then before Mass started, we would sneak back to Grandma's to make a quick raid on her cookie jar or look for something delectable in the fridge (This was after I had made my confession about eating before communion, and I no longer thought it was such a sin.)

As soon as we opened the refrigerator door, Leroy always reached and turned the knob to "fast freeze." I don't know why. We would hurry back to the choir loft and go behind the organ so that choir members couldn't see us. Then we would enjoy the wonderful homemade sugar cookies we took from Grandma's cookie jar.

On one of those Sunday morning forays, we raced through Grandma's dining room and into the kitchen. Leroy then turned the refrigerator's fast-freeze knob, I selected a carton of cold milk, and Leroy headed for the cookie jar. I was alarmed when I heard someone approaching the kitchen. So I dashed into the bathroom, which was right off the kitchen next to the refrigerator.

As I locked the door, I heard Aunt Marge ask Leroy what he was doing and what I was doing in the bathroom. He said he was just getting a cookie (he had at least one in his hand) and that I had to use the bathroom. I also had grabbed a chicken leg, so I snapped the meat off quickly with my teeth and flushed the bone.

"Since when does it take milk to make Gene shit?" Aunt Marge inquired as she pounded on the door. She actually didn't make too much an issue of it. She was feeling ill when she arrived for Mass so had come over to rest in Grandma's back bedroom.

(Later on, I realized that you don't flush chicken bones down a commode. Dear Grandma had to get the local plumber to unstop her toilet, which contained chicken bones of all things!)

When we attended weeklong vacation Catechism classes in North English and Grandma's icebox "jumped" to fast freeze at least daily, we overheard her lament to Aunt Anna that she was going to have to get a new fridge or have the plumber look at it.

"Now, Mom, you know that's them darn kids doing that," Aunt Anna replied.

I could hardly contain the laughter, and Leroy got a huge kick out of the exchange, too. But he did stop turning the knob to fast freeze, and I put chicken bones in my pocket instead of the commode.

We loved Grandma dearly and really didn't set out or plan to be mean. It was just such great fun to befuddle adults—if we didn't get caught!

Another new pet joined our family. Mabel was a 13-year-old strawberry roan mare that had once won the Green Valley race held each Memorial Day at its celebration east of North English. Green Valley consisted of one country roadside store at a four-corner intersection.

Mabel was very gentle, and we could play around her in her stall, as well as ride her to fetch the cows. We also would hitch her to a buggy and drive all over the neighborhood. In the summer, we drove her to North English so we could attend vacation Catechism classes and then tied her to a chain just off Main Street.

One afternoon on the way home, Mabel saw something out of the corner of her eye that frightened her. She charged down a deep roadside ditch, upsetting the buggy and scattering the occupants. Fortunately, there were only a few cuts and bruises so when Mabel stopped, we righted the buggy and went on home.

For three consecutive years, Mabel visited a nearby farm, the home of an Indian pony stallion. Indian ponies are bigger than other ponies, but smaller than a small horse and very beautiful with spots of various colors. They also are high-spirited.

Mabel gave birth to Prince, who was roan (chestnut) and white; Tony, a beautiful sorrel (brownish orange-light brown); and Beauty, the only mare, who looked like her father and had the same disposition. Prince and Tony were gentle like their mother.

Kenny loved horses and took care of them most of the time. They also were great to ride as we went on snooping, pigeon-hunting, and swimming expeditions with the three

Fuller boys. (The Fuller boys, Norman, Larry, and Dick, had taken the place of the Benders in our escapades.)

It was in 1947 or 1948 that Beauty injured Kenny's back after she threw him in the concrete-like, frozen barn lot with its many ruts and potholes. A few years later, he had to have spinal-fusion surgery at Mercy Hospital in Iowa City. He had back problems throughout his life.

That was one big hazard of horse riding, especially since lots of families could not afford saddles and most everyone rode bareback. It was not unusual to see two or three kids in the neighborhood with their arms in slings after they had fallen off or been thrown off a spirited or frightened horse.

Many things could cause a horse to shy: pheasants suddenly rising up in flight with their loud whirring wings, dogs racing out of yards ready for attack, or meeting speeding cars on old, dusty, tree- and brush-lined country roads. I recall that one of the Greene kids seemed to have a broken arm every summer. A neighbor broke his leg.

Kenny started driving at a young age, and one day Dad told him to drive the old pickup down the road to the cow pasture. I jumped in to ride along, and we were rolling merrily down the dirt road when he got too close to the side grader ditch and the slope pulled us off into the rather deep vine-engulfed, brush-covered side road ditch. We were neither one hurt, and he always was a very good and safe driver.

I never had a driver's license. Dad had me so intimidated about driving. One day, he was driving when he stopped and said, "Get over and drive." I panicked—I had no idea how to do it. He told me that I should know from watching he and Kenny. Later, when he didn't know it, I did start watching, and I eventually drove all over the nearby country roads (where I wouldn't get caught without a license). Mother also never learned because Dad had no patience for teaching her either. Leroy learned on his own—he just got into our Model A one day and started backing out the driveway. He was gone about half an hour.

After Kenny started high school, Dad acquired an old Chevy that Kenny and I took to school. I no longer stayed at Grandma Agnew's, so I was home to do chores each night and morning. Grandma Agnew was not alone, as Aunt Anna Agnew had begun staying with her each night and then walking to her housekeeping job in the mornings.

Kenny and I became more popular at school—thanks to the car, I assume.

In the summer of 1947, Mr. and Mrs. S. moved to a nearby farm. Mrs. S. had a nice garden and a beautiful patch of sweet corn right next to our overnight cow pasture. As I mentioned earlier, most fences were in high disrepair. The cows evidently sensed the golden ears were about to be snatched away, and they quietly entered the garden through a low place in the fence and proceeded to gorge themselves on the prize vittles. Not only did they eat the corn but they also laid waste to the entire garden!

It seemed our cows must have bided their time until the ears were just perfect while Mrs. S. was beaming to herself thinking of the delicious roasting ears and wonderful jars of golden-grained succulent corn that she and her husband would enjoy during a cold-winter meal.

The phone rang early the next morning, and poor Mother, upon picking up the receiver, was greeted with shouts of "shooting cows" and "notifying the sheriff." I knew I wasn't going alone to retrieve the cows, so Dad and our faithful mongrel Firpo steeled for the verbal assault. (We had acquired Firpo in 1943. Firpo was my favorite of all our dogs and accompanied me wherever I went on the farm.)

I could see that Mrs. S. was devastated and had sparked her husband into a high state of agitation. Dad was never one to back down from a fight, either verbal or physical, and did not appreciate their words and especially the mention of a monetary reimbursement they felt was due. At the height of the bickering, Dad pointed out that the cows entered an opening that was on their portion of the fence. (When a fence divided property, each party was responsible for the half-fence that is the right half as he/she faces the fence.)

While we were there, Firpo also tore into the couple's dog on his own turf and gave the slightly larger dog a thorough whipping. Firpo always was in tip-top fighting weight and shape.

(Firpo lived on what rabbits he could catch [not many], scraps from our table, and a pan of skim milk each night and morning. However, I did catch him eating buttermilk slop with the pigs and lapping up "fresh from the dispenser" baby pig and calf manure. After all, it was pure "cooked milk" [pasteurized?]. No wonder I've heard the description of a dog as a man's best friend who "chases rabbits, eats shit, and barks at the moon." Firpo would take on a groundhog, go at it with a gopher, put a coon on the run, attack a great big turtle [to no avail], kill a snake by shaking it vigorously, and crunch rats. Woe be it to the strange dog that crossed his path or entered his Firpo Dawson territory.)

Needless to say, bad blood existed between the two families after that.

A few weeks after the corn incident, I noticed a beautiful grey pigeon with a white tail, a rarity in feral pigeon flocks, at Mr. and Mrs. S.'s barn. In a very nice way, I asked Mr. S. to please help me capture that pigeon some night. I also said that Mother, Dad, and all of us really felt bad about the garden. So he agreed and I got the pigeon, a beautiful female who never laid any eggs.

I found Mr. S. to be friendly, but I never told Mother and Dad about the pigeon and I don't think he told his wife.

Before the advent of balers, and especially the ones that deliver huge round bales, haymows were filled with loose hay. If the hay was not well dried or if even a pocket of wet hay was dropped in the mow, it could heat, start smoking, and sometimes erupt in fire. Every season without fail, some rambunctious farmer would toss caution to the wind, get in a hurry, and not wait until the hay was adequately dry. A raging inferno would result.

In 1947, there was a rash of barn fires. One Sunday afternoon, Kenny and I set out on a pigeon hunt. We stopped at Jim Greene's deserted house that was being used to store small hay bales and had become a nesting place for pigeons.

The house was located across the road from Mr. Drum's farm. Suddenly there was a shout, "I've got you now—get your hands up and don't move!"

I was surprised to see Mr. Drum pointing a rifle at me and started to laugh. That ended quickly as I detected that he seriously was thinking that he had apprehended arsonists in the act. I diplomatically explained to him that we were cousins of the Greenes and clients of his own sheep-shearing enterprise. Mr. Drum finally put the rifle down and said that three barns had burned the previous night. He was convinced that man—not combustion—was the cause.

What I remember most about Mr. Drum are his very soft hands, which he coated almost daily with lanolin from sheep wool and skin. He also was an expert at using a knife to bring peas to his mouth. When I saw this, I was so fascinated that I lost interest in my plate. Bernie just stopped eating and watched in amazement. I have tried to emulate his technique but, without fail, the peas roll off the knife before they reach my mouth.

In late 1947, none of us boys were whisked away, but the overpowering Mrs. B appeared on the scene right after Thanksgiving. Therefore, I was not surprised when the sixth male Dawson child, Thomas Marion, made his appearance on December 2. He was yet another blond, curly-haired John and Mary Dawson offspring. Mother had help from the wonderful Dr. Miller of North English, who made house calls night or day, hot or cold.

All the Dawson babies were very handsome and cute except the first one who was born with no hair, with the toes next to both big toes longer—much longer—than the big toes, and google-eyed with a pinhead on which were attached two calf-sized ears. That was I! When I was born, Dad suggested calling me Oscar, much to Mother's consternation. Maybe he was suggesting I was her award for her Oscar-winning performance while delivering me? I'll go for that.

So after Thomas M.'s birth, Mrs. B and Leroy resumed their warfare as he played basketball instead of getting at his chores. She spent almost as much time monitoring him as she did caring for Mother and Thomas M.! Of course, we had delicious pies with most every meal as I continually praised her baking ability—out of Mother's hearing range.

When I told the kids at school that I had a new baby brother, some of them exclaimed that I must have really young parents—most of them weren't firstborns and didn't have little brothers or sisters. I'm so lucky—I got to greet all my brothers and be present as soon as they were born. Dad told me many years later that Mother had miscarried a boy in the years between Bernie and Patrick Leo's births. Whatever happens, "Lord let thy will be done."

On the farm, a loud, squealing, noisy job with hogs, besides castrating and spraying, was "ringing." A ring was clamped over and into the top of a hog's snout so when it tried to root up topsoil, the ring contacted the soil and caused pain. That stopped the damaging hog pastime. In their search for roots, morsels, and minerals from the soil, hogs could destroy a pasture in a short time. And if they happened to get out of their pens, they could eradicate flowerbeds and gardens and make a front yard look as if it had been plowed for planting crops.

If someone accidentally let a water tank overflow, hogs would wallow and soon have a deep, black water-filled mudhole. They would wallow in this right in front of the tank where the cows and horses came to drink, so we had to tread carefully when hauling water. Sometimes the holes would get so deep that Dad would haul in loads of gravel to fill them. Swine do not sweat, and mudhole wallowing was a way they kept cool.

I really liked hogs even though they could be very disruptive. They are very intelligent and actually a clean animal as they never soil their own sleeping quarters—they will get up and go outside. Cattle, sheep, and horses "let it go" wherever they are.

Another disruptive farm occupant was the Muscovy duck. A friend of Dad's told him about the wonderful taste of Muscovy and offered to give Dad a drake and two hen ducks. I was thrilled because I always liked our feathered friends and, to top it off, these ducks could fly! Well, the hens could. The old drake was just too top heavy as it had a huge breast, the virtue that Dad's friend considered when extolling the wonders of roast Muscovy duck. (I didn't like it; the meat was too dark and dry for me, and scalding and picking all the fine feathers and down was a nightmare.)

The first spring we had the Muscovies, one of the hens hatched 16 ducklings from a nest under our front porch. She promptly led them 2½ miles along a creek through Toe Rowe's timber to the Brown home where she took up residence. The Browns were happy to welcome their guests. A few days later, Dad and I went to the Browns' house to retrieve the mother and 16 children. A couple of days later, she set off again, but this time we left them there.

In the fall, we went back, and Mr. Brown gave us mother duck and eight of the offspring. Ma duck stayed home all winter, laid her eggs under the porch, hatched another group of babies, and returned to the Brown farm. This time we just gave up and left her there.

Meanwhile, the other hen and her children, after they started to fly, decided to take advantage of our nearly filled water-supply tank. The huge supply tank was constructed of wood staves, sat next to the windmill, and looked somewhat like a 3,000-gallon wooden barrel. When the wind was blowing briskly, we turned some knobs and filled the tank from the deep well so we would have water for the animals in case of a drought or a hot, windless day.

When the duck and her ducklings tried to get out of that tank, they became rather waterlogged and couldn't fly out. We had to get a ladder to rescue them, or they would have drowned and really fouled the water. As it was, their defecating and stirring up the water made it disgusting. We finally hauled some large planks and boards to float on the water so the ducks would have takeoff runways to get out. We eventually caught them and clipped their wings to put an end to their flying up to their "resort."

On the farm, one of our jobs was hauling water to various pig, cow, and chicken pens. A large transport tank was on a wooden slide that could be pulled by a tractor. We would dip water from the main tank, fill the transporter, pull it to various watering spots, and use buckets for filling.

On winter days, our gloves would freeze, and when we started or stopped the tractor to open gates, much of the water would splash out. Kerosene heat lamps were placed under each drinking spot to prevent freezing. Invariably, on the coldest and windiest days, the heater would go out. Then it would be an all-day job of constantly bringing teakettles full of very hot water to the tank to thaw it out and get it operational.

Cold weather certainly did not suspend the thirst of the stock—it seemed to me to increase their craving. It was a blessing when we got electrically heated waterers, had water piped to different locations, and acquired a huge tank wagon that could be pulled behind a tractor and taken to Parnell to fill from the town supply (this happened after we moved to rural Parnell in 1949). Hauling water was probably the coldest, most depressing, and most wasteful task of that time.

The "noon whistle" is another memory. At 12 noon, a tremendous blast—similar to a train whistle, only louder—emitted from North English to let all within a several-mile radius know that it was midday. Farmers would come in from the fields for their noon meals. The whistle also was used to alert area residents of a fire, tornado, or any natural or man-made calamity. It was a chilling sound to hear at any time other than noon.

When some momentous event occurred in the rural area, such as a fire, death, or weather warning, someone on the party line would crank the phone for a long extended "r-i-n-g." This was a "general" ring and summoned all parties to listen in.

We had a huge strawberry patch at the Swain Place, and Mother canned many quarts of those berries and made lots of jam. Sometimes when Mother and Dad would leave for such things as doctor appointments for Patrick Leo or Thomas M., I would get out the Bisquick and stir up some biscuits while Kenny and Leroy picked some red-ripe juicy berries. We would take out their stems, clean them, and sprinkle them with sugar.

Then into the car we would pile to go to the Dow Mason grocery store in North English. We would each order a quart of hand-dipped ice cream and return home to eat the most delicious, fresh strawberry shortcake. What fun we had! A quart of ice cream was only 50 cents, and we would gorge ourselves.

On February 18, 1949, I turned 18 years old, and Dad took me to Marengo, Iowa County's seat of government housed in a big, stately courthouse, where I registered for the draft. Registration was mandatory for all males on their 18th birthdays.

Then a few days later, March 1, was moving day; a returning veteran had purchased the Swain Place. We finally were able to buy a place of our very own located 3½ miles southeast of Parnell in Fillmore Township of Iowa County. This new house, the "Jones Place," had been vacated by its previous occupants a few days early and was available for move-in before March 1.

So Leroy and I were the only family members who stayed overnight at the Swain Place on February 28. After we milked the cows, we decided to make some homemade ice cream. I took some sugar and butter and cooked it on the old range stove until it was brown and like caramel. We then got some eggs, vanilla, cornstarch, and with fresh whole milk, we used salt and snow to make a freezer full of super-delicious, homemade, burnt-sugar, caramel ice cream. So Leroy and I had our last Swain Place "meal."

The next night we were in the Parnell area at the Jones Place—ours!

The Jones Place also was known as "Maplehurst Manor"—it was very large with five bedrooms and a bathroom upstairs, as well as a long hall, which was like a hospital corridor. Every room had a large closet, and a large storage closet was in the hallway. Stairs went up both at the back and front of the house, and the small boys were delighted to run up and down the stairs from one end of the house to the other.

Huge, old maple trees surrounded the house and provided cooling shade in the summer and a windbreak on windy winter days. We always could locate a breeze in some part of the house even on the hottest day. There was even a stairway to the attic, which was large enough for a ballroom dance! I could sit by the attic windows and survey the surrounding countryside.

This was the first house we lived in since Keswick that was electrified when we moved in and the first place that had inside plumbing with hot and cold running water, sinks, a bathtub, a commode in the bathroom, and another in the basement.

We had moved into the 20th Century, it seemed!

I selected the smallest bedroom in the far northwest corner to be my room—it even had a key to lock the door and the closet. Kenny had the west room, Leroy and Bernie shared the southeast corner bedroom, and the two youngest in the family always shared a bed with Mother or Dad. Mother and Thomas M. were in the east bedroom, and Dad and Patrick Leo had the north bedroom, which had an outside door that opened to a balcony that sat over the front lower porch.

The new abode was just unbelievably so much superior to anywhere else we ever had called home. The downstairs had a large kitchen with a walk-in pantry, dining room, living room, and large front entrance room. The living room had a beautiful, large, working fireplace. The full basement had front and back stairs and built-in cupboards for storing the hundreds of jars of fruits, vegetables, and meats that Mother canned. The house seemed like a castle—all that was lacking was a moat!

The move meant that Kenny, Leroy, and Bernie changed schools once again, this time to the Parnell Consolidated School. Mr. Jimmy Carney was paid by the school to use his personal car as a "bus"—he picked the boys up each morning and brought them home after school.

I stayed with Grandma Agnew in North English from March 1 until I graduated in May. I hadn't really grown much until I was a senior in high school (this year). Kenny and I always wore the same size from when he was two and I was four.

Graduation was uneventful, and I was happy to leave North English High School and the community behind. Parnell was 99.9 percent Irish Catholic—so much so that the Sisters of Humility, with a Mother house in Ottumwa, had a convent next to the St. Joseph's Catholic Church rectory in the northeast end of town. The nuns were hired to teach in the Parnell school.

We Dawsons became very popular with the fun-loving, friendly, Irish young people of Parnell and nearby Holbrook, about five miles to the east. Quite the opposite of the "WASPish" North English group! In fact, North English young folks referred to Parnell as "Part-hell." They considered the Irish to be rowdy.

Father Daniel Browne was the Irish-born priest of St. Joseph's large church, which had "wings" off each side of the altar with more seating to accommodate the parishioners. Miss Ann Coover was Father's housekeeper, and the Parnell kids irreverently referred to them as "Dan and Ann." I was shocked—we had never referred to a priest by his first name!

Not long after we moved to Maplehurst Manor, Father Browne called a meeting of the parish's high school-age boys, and I don't know if he or we felt more uneasy. He stuttered and stammered as we nudged one another and tried to keep straight faces and keep from snickering. The one line I do remember that just about cracked me up was when he proclaimed a remedy to overcome arousal was to "stick it into a pan of ice water!"

Father Browne practically "ran" the entire Catholic town of Parnell. Whenever the church hosted a picnic or fund-raiser, the town's taverns and other merchants closed so everyone bought what they needed at the parish-operated beer and soda stands. The parish also sponsored Bingo and dances.

Father Browne would "edict" from the altar what movies we were not to see and that Saturday nights were to be spent at Holy Hour—only after we attended the benedictions and litanies were we permitted to go to a dance. I did not always adhere to these orders, and a great sense of guilt enveloped me.

It seemed like every town or locale had one girl who was known to be "easy." Most of the other girls at school tore her to shreds behind her back. I thought they were probably a little jealous. The boys also shunned the "easy" girl during the day and teased one another, but after dark she became very popular with most of the guys on various occasions. However, none of them would ever actually date her or, heaven forbid, consider her for marriage. These girls always ended up marrying a guy from another town.

Mother would remark how bold and unladylike any girl was who had the audacity to call Kenny, Leroy, or me on the phone, saying that the gentleman should make the first move.

If a young lady got "knocked up," as some called it, she went away to "visit" distant relatives for a few months. I always admired one girl who went on her "visit" but returned with her child. (Many girls gave up their children for adoption, which sometimes was their parents' choice and not theirs.) She cared for him and made no secret that he was hers. She was never ostracized.

After graduation, I continued to live at home and work on the farm. Dad gave me a sow of my own, which produced a litter of pigs. I had to budget my money after selling the shoats. Then I would wait for her to provide me with more offspring and more spending money for clothes and running around.

When haymaking time arrived in June 1949, Jimmy, Bernard, Ray, and Charlie Murphy, our next-door neighbors, agreed to help with the work. Dad's cousin, Gene O'Rourke, who lived in Parnell, also was hired to help.

At one point, Dad sent Jimmy, Gene, and me to the Murphys' to get a pulley so we could hoist the loose hay into the mow while the others loaded hay in the field. Jimmy and Gene suggested that we stop for a "cold one" at Tom Hannon's Tavern in Parnell before delivering the pulley.

It sounded OK to me. Of course, one led to two and so on—the other customers were very generous in ordering beers for us. Soon we forgot about pulleys, hay, and consequences and were having a jolly good time.

I didn't have one cent on me, so by 7 p.m., I felt a little guilty about not buying a round. So I called Tom aside and got permission to run a tab. As I joyfully ordered a round "for the house," I glanced toward the door and saw a very red- and wild-eyed John Dawson enter the tavern. I grabbed Tom and canceled the order as Dad ordered us into Gene O'Rourke's car and followed us to our barn.

After we hadn't returned and all the racks were loaded with hay, Bernard and Ray Murphy went and got the pulley. They proceeded to unload the hay because they were afraid it was going to rain. But no one was there to "mow" it. So now Dad sent us up to mow it, but the others were so inebriated that they couldn't stand in the loose hay. I had to carry Gene down the ladder on my shoulders—the beer had made me strong!

The next day we paid for our afternoon of joy—we had hangovers and it was very hot. The hay had heated all night, and Dad had us in that hot mow very early untangling those four or five loads of loose hay (balers had not become that prominent or economical yet). From then on, Jimmy, Gene, and I were never assigned a task together.

Dad seemed to delight in working—and especially on national holidays such as Independence Day. Celebrations were held that day in most of the surrounding towns, and we would see our peers and their parents riding by on their way to an event.

July 4, it seemed, was always one of the hottest days of the year, and the sweat would run down my body like the flowing Mississippi River. I especially could feel it in the haymow of the barn when the sun was beating down on the roof and new hay was heating and curing. It seemed even the hay leaves that clung to sweat were itchier on holidays.

Bernard Murphy and I, and sometimes Gene O'Rourke, would stack the hay in the barn. On holidays, we usually had a fifth of whiskey stashed there. We took occasional nips for strength (ahem) and liquid nourishment. Of course, the alcohol actually made us hotter, and we would sweat even more. When we would leave the haymow, the 92-degree heat outside felt cool.

Jimmy, Bernard, Ray, and Charlie Murphy, as well as cousin Gene O'Rourke, who all worked with us on those days would say, "Johnny Dawson is a slave driver!" Now I look back at the summers of 1949, 1950, 1951, 1952, and 1953 as cherished memories. Those neighbors, as well as Tony Harney and Francis Jennings, worked as a team, and we all assisted one another with harvesting and other farming endeavors.

All of them could tell good stories and were a great group to be around. I can't forget Gottlieb Frehner, a Swiss immigrant neighbor, who could issue comical and witty remarks.

In the fall of 1949, I made some new friends from Williamsburg. Donnie Duffy, a cousin of the Parnell Duffys, became a friend, and through him I met Lloyd Yearian and David Fry. On a Saturday night in March 1950, a car carrying David and Lloyd, along with James Keegan, collided with a large truck near Marengo. All three were killed.

I read about the crash in *The Cedar Rapids Gazette* the following morning after Mass. I was in a state of shock all day. It's such a heartbreaking feeling of helplessness when young friends' lives are extinguished so tragically and suddenly. I took a knife and carved a remembrance to them on one of the walls in the barn.

That same fall of 1949, the North English High School football team hosted Williamsburg for a Friday night game. Since moving to Parnell the previous March, I had discovered the joy(?) of drinking and how a few sips of bad-tasting stuff could blot out my bashfulness and intense inferiority complex.

Kenny, Leroy, and I went to the game with two other guys from Parnell. We had another boy, who was in his 20s, go to the liquor store and purchase three pints of cheap whiskey for us, and one for him for being so kind. The rest of us were not 21 so didn't have a permit to buy the "hard" stuff.

During the early part of the game, I encountered two girls who had known me when I was shy and quiet as a mouse. They were amazed when I produced a bottle and invited them to share a drink. We had to buy cups of Coke from the band mothers' refreshment stand, and the mothers were shocked when we broke off tree twigs and mixed our liberating concoction!

"Look what Parnell has done to me!" I exclaimed.

"Look what Parnell has done for you!" they chimed in. I suddenly became popular and accepted by my aloof former classmates.

We enjoyed ourselves so much as the girls sat on both sides of me with arms around my neck. Soon we were unaware there was a game taking place and decided to cross to the other side of the field. Whistles blew and game officials scurried to escort us from the field as the game was temporarily halted.

When the game ended, I needed their support to navigate through the parking lot. A car backed into me, but I didn't even feel it. "Genie, are you all right?" shouted neighbor Jimmy Murphy, who always called me "Genie."

"He's fine; mind your own business," one of the girls announced. We proceeded uptown to Mahannah's Café, where the girls and I became irate and, as I reflect on it, quite obnoxious as the employees refused to serve us. In fact, they had the audacity to demand that we leave the premises in haste or the law would be summoned! With that, I got into Dad's '47 good car with my brothers and the two other Parnell boys, and we started for home.

I was in the back seat next to the window, but Leroy reported that I plunked down on him when I first climbed in. As we got out on the highway, I became exceedingly dizzy, and as I stuck my head out the window, the liquid refreshments decided to leave my body via my mouth.

"Don't puke! It will smell terrible! What will we tell Dad? He'll never let us take this car again!" Kenny shouted.

But I couldn't hold it. When we got home, I staggered around and tried to wash off the "results" to kill the secondhand sickening smell of alcoholic vomit.

The next morning, I awakened to the worst headache I had ever entertained(!) and the most nauseous feeling. After looking at a fried egg, I had to flee the kitchen to get some fresh air. My job on that muggy, sultry Saturday was to unload a truckload of fence posts. I climbed up and tried valiantly, but my eyes wouldn't even focus properly and every ounce of energy had fled my body.

I went into the house and told a sympathetic Mother, who was getting ready to go shopping with Dad and the little boys, that I had a bad case of the flu, punctuated with the most god-awful headache. Mother suggested I should rest—bless her heart! Thank goodness she wasn't aware that my malady was really my first hangover.

I took a blanket and pillow and climbed the stairs to the darkened attic—it seemed light only intensified my suffering. I crawled into a dark corner under the eaves to recuperate from my first and only whiskey-induced hangover. To this day, I cannot stand the smell of whiskey, bourbon, or Scotch. Of course, I also can't bear to drink any of them. Later I discovered vodka, and that was what I guzzled until I gave up all drinking in 1990.

We got our first new car about 1947. Patrick Leo is in front with Leroy (left), Dad, and Bernie.

My parents were finally able to purchase our own place in 1949. Maplehurst Manor near Parnell was the Dawson home for the next 36 years.

The barn at the Maplehurst Manor farmstead had two eye-catching cupolas.

Five Dawson brothers: Patrick Leo, Bernie, me, Leroy, and Kenny, in 1949.

# PART TWO:

## Transition ... and Tragedy

1950–1959

Thomas M. and Mother with our barn in the background, 1951.

Thomas M. (in front) with Mother, Aunt Marie Dawson LaMere, and Dad, 1950.

Leroy and me in front of Maplehurst Manor, 1952.

Striking a pose by the clothesline in the yard at Maplehurst Manor, 1952.

# Chapter 5

## 1950–1954

After Kenny graduated from Parnell High School in May 1950, with Dad's assistance, he and I purchased a hay baler so Kenny could do custom work for area farmers. I stayed home to care for the livestock and assist the family so he could be gone to do the baling and pay for the baler. We then split the profits.

At night, we used Dad's '47 Ford to gad about until Dad got us a Ford Model A for our gallivanting. The Ford Model A had cardboard where the back window should have been and stuffing coming out of the back seat. It seemed to smell like petroleum fumes both inside and out most of the time, but we had much fun with that car. Although if we pleaded hard enough—and usually with Mother's intercession—we would be allowed to use the "good" car, the '47 Ford.

I was 19 (1950) on one of the first occasions when I really felt grown up. I went to Uncles Emmett and Bernard Agnew's tavern in North English and ordered a 10-cent glass of beer from the innocent barmaid only to see Uncle Bernard emerge from the back living quarters. I didn't know what to do.

But Uncle Bernard came to the bar, started talking, and drew a glass of beer for him and one for me. As soon as I drained it, another appeared, and we had a really nice conversation. I recall telling him, "Don't tell Mother," and he said with a smile, "Don't you tell her." Uncle Bernard was a great guy and was in the room when Mother died—he always said she was like a second mother to him.

On a summer Saturday night, Kenny and I joined two friends and set out for the annual celebration in Victor, Iowa. After drinking beer in the Victor taverns, we decided to visit another tavern in Marengo on the way home. None of us were 21, but I had a false ID and getting beer was no problem.

Upon entering the tavern, I spotted a penny peanut machine sitting on the bar right inside the door. I instructed the other three to go to the back of the tavern and order something to divert the owner's attention so I could hoist the peanut machine and put it in the car. They did as they were told, but then they chose to order **peanuts**!

I grabbed the trophy, put it under my arm, and stepped outside. There was a throng of people on the street, so I sat down next to the door—on the peanut machine! Soon the owner stepped out, and I remarked how hot the night was. He looked up and down the street and went back inside.

"Now is the time," I thought, and dashed to the car. The windows were all down, so I just threw it in the back seat. As I was doing that, I heard a loud voice tell me, "Don't move." I was surprised to see the owner—and the sheriff, who was getting out of his car!

Kenny and our two friends emerged from the tavern. The owner retrieved his peanut machine, and we unceremoniously were carted to the second floor of the Iowa County Courthouse. We were sternly lectured with veiled threats of incarceration if we did not tell our parents about these proceedings. After two hours, the sheriff and deputy decided that since we had no prior record, we would be released and allowed to go home—minus my trophy, which I thought would have been a great addition to my room.

Of course, we did not tell Mother and Dad, but Leroy heard about it. If I offended him in any way, he threatened to "tell"—so I treated him with kid gloves. I scanned the local weekly papers and was pleased there was no mention of our (my) indiscretion. I thought we were home free until three weeks later. We attended a dance in Swisher, Iowa, on a Saturday night, and the next morning Kenny and I were rudely told by Dad that we would be sitting in front with the rest of the family during Mass. (We had asserted our freedom a few months earlier by sitting in the back row and "cutting up" with the other young Irish during Sunday Mass.)

On this Sunday, Father Browne seemed to stare a hole through me and looked as mean as a junkyard dog during the sermon. Mother had a pained expression, Dad also had the "junkyard" look, and I knew something unpleasant was about to take place. There was stony silence on the way home, except for an announcement that Father Browne would be right out for a visit.

Sure enough, his big black car rolled into the drive, and Dad and Bernie went outside. Mother, with the "little boys" Patrick Leo and Thomas M., took a seat on the daybed in the dining room while Kenny and I sat on straight-back chairs. Leroy stayed in the kitchen within hearing and observation distance.

Father Browne strode into the room and announced, "Well, boys, you know why I'm here." With that, Mother started to weep, Leroy grinned and peered into the room, and Kenny and I were very uneasy. We received a blistering lecture about the fires of hell, eternal damnation, being huge disappointments to our parents and the community, and how we were bringing a bad name about Parnell to other—especially Protestant—enclaves.

But the crowning blow was when he proclaimed, "It looks like you might be going to Eldora [state boys' reform school]!" Leroy nearly popped into the room, and Mother's sobs audibly increased.

Father Browne had given a very dramatic performance! I composed my thoughts and decided that since the peanut incident had happened almost a month earlier and the sheriff had released us, the last statement was for the "fear factor."

Seems a neighbor had overheard some young folks discussing our escapade and, thinking it was amusing, told Dad on the previous night while we were enjoying ourselves in Swisher. After conferring with Mother, Dad immediately reported the story to Father Browne.

When Father Browne left that Sunday, he made an appointment for Kenny and me to be at the rectory at 8 p.m. that night. Even though it was a Sunday, Dad sent us out on the tractors to cultivate rows of corn for the rest of that sunny, swelteringly hot day—probably letting us get a feel for how hot hell would be!

That night, we dutifully reported to Father Browne and found him to be very jolly. He gave us a tour of the rectory, and housekeeper Ann had nice refreshments set out for us. He insisted that we take several packs of cigarettes and told us repeatedly to just ask him if we needed money for cigarettes. It seems that he thought I was stealing the little machine to empty out the pennies for cigarette money—and we didn't even smoke!

Little did he know that I was just doing it for the challenge, to impress my peers, and to have a nice trophy. Is that called doing outlandish things for attention? Perhaps.

When we left the priest's residence, we headed to uptown Parnell where the guys were waiting to hear about the outcome of our meeting. Five of us then piled into the car and were off to North English with a couple of six packs saved from the night before. We never heard another word about Eldora and the boys' reform school.

The young men of Parnell made life rough for any outsider who had the audacity to venture into town to date a local girl. Some bloody fights ensued, and the invaders were repelled. It was a little easier for "strangers" to court country girls; they could sneak in via back roads. No wonder just about everyone around Parnell and Holbrook was related. So you had to be very careful about what you said and to whom you said it.

The Parnell guys ran with four (and sometimes six) young men in the Holbrook gang. Sometimes joining us were four other "auxiliary" members of the Parnell gang.

All the Parnell and Holbrook group members were Irish Catholics. Parnell kids attended St. Joseph's, of course, while the Holbrook bunch attended St. Michael's in Holbrook. Holbrook consisted of the church, cemetery, a country store, the priest's house, one or two residences, and a school for kids up to eighth grade. High-schoolers from both towns attended Parnell High.

These were hard times money-wise when I first started "running around." Sometimes we went roller-skating in nearby Keota or Conroy, but dances were the big events. In the warm months, Deep River (Fridays) and Swisher (Saturdays) had dances in open-air pavilions. Sigourney had inside dances every Tuesday, and there was a dance every night at the Danceland Ballroom in Cedar Rapids. By 1950, the Armah Dayton Hall no longer was being used.

The Millersburg American Legion occasionally sponsored a dance during 1950. Across the street from the legion hall was a large white house with an enormous garden in the back. In late summer, the owner had picked about a bushel of ripe tomatoes, which she arranged on a table near the back porch. Well, one of our friends spied the tomatoes, and he (and I may have been involved) decided to "bomb" dance-goers—mainly non-Parnell residents who we didn't particularly care for—when they emerged from the hall. A cascade of juicy tomatoes descended upon the unsuspecting victims, and we laughed uproariously at our accuracy and the stunned looks and screams. When the ammunition supply ran out, we gathered our gang and made a quick exit east toward home territory.

The Millersburg residents didn't know who had been the tomato culprits. The next day, Aunt Marge Costello was at a meeting of the Millersburg Garden Club when a matron said it was probably the bunch from Parnell. A sister of one of our friends and a member of the garden club jumped to her feet and asked the others to explain how anyone from Parnell would know there were ripe tomatoes on that back porch. She announced that it had to be local Millersburg kids and stated, in no uncertain terms, that she was tired of Parnell being blamed for every prank and "mean" act.

I acted dumbfounded when Aunt Marge told the story, and she agreed wholeheartedly that Parnell was innocent. Yea!

Our paternal grandma, Mary Greene Dawson, died of a stroke on August 26, 1950, at the age of 74. Her funeral was held at Our Lady of Lourdes, next to her home in Keswick. At the end of the funeral, her sister/our Great-Aunt Maggie Greene shouted, "Oh Mary, Oh Mary," and tried to get into the casket with her!

That was the first time I ever saw Dad cry, and it so affected Kenny and me that we immediately broke into tears. Aunt Elizabeth "Sis" went to live with Aunt Ann Dawson Conroy and her family in Ottumwa.

When I was growing up, the only meat we ever purchased was bologna sliced by the grocer. Even town residents had a few chickens, a pig or two to eat the scraps and drink the slop, and sometimes a cow, which was an "all-purpose" provider of food products. When electricity arrived in the rural areas, most farm families purchased a deep freezer to keep their meat.

In August 1950, we took a very large steer to the Williamsburg locker plant to be prepared for home freezer storage. The locker packaged and labeled the meat in sizes appropriate for the number of family members at a meal.

On a beautiful, late August day, Mother was standing at the table in the center of the kitchen with clean scalded jars, lids, various pans, and two large buckets of beautiful tomatoes she was preparing for "cold pack" (canning). A large pot was bubbling merrily on the kitchen range. Kenny, Leroy, and I were scattered around the kitchen chatting with Mother—not helping her!

Our kitchen had three exits: one to the outside back porch, one to the basement and outdoors, and the third to the dining room and onto the front door. As Mother carefully and expertly peeled the scalded skin from the red vittles, Kenny asked, "What are we going to have for dinner?" (The noon meal always was called "dinner," and the evening repast was called "supper.")

"I have a great big [beef] *heart on* [in the boiling pot]," she smilingly replied.

As she looked down to select another tomato, we three looked at one another and nearly burst into laughter as we each dashed to the nearest exit.

I was zooming through the dining room as Mother looked up in bewilderment at the empty kitchen. Then I heard her exclaim in exasperation, "You rotten kids!"

One day when little Thomas M. was not yet three years old, he was dashing about the kitchen swinging a dish towel. Someone had put a small pan of water on the stove to heat but, unfortunately, the handle was sticking out. The towel caught it, dumping the boiling water down Thomas M.'s back.

Dad and Mother rushed him to Dr. D.F. Miller in Williamsburg, who had a few rooms above his office that he used as a hospital. The poor little child was in the hospital four or five weeks in what today would be called critical condition.

Mrs. B again was summoned since Mother was with Thomas M. most of the time. Mrs. B could be insensitive. When Patrick Leo came down for breakfast the next morning, Mrs. B said, "I hope you're proud of yourself—you killed your Mother and little brother last night!" Just then Mother appeared, and Patrick Leo thought, "Mrs. B lies," and ordered four eggs for breakfast.

Since Thomas M. was so young at the time, he does not remember the incident but has some frightful scars on his back. Patrick Leo's version is that he was chasing Bernie with a feed sack and swinging it while Mother was giving Thomas M. a bath, and the scalding water also burned her arm in two places. For me, the saddest thing was that Thomas M. did not know me when he got home, and we had to get reacquainted.

In 1950, Mother had to have an "operation." When I asked what it was for, she replied, "from having all you boys." I decided it was some so-called "female problem" and asked no more questions. A local woman arrived to cook and clean as Mother was bedfast for some time. The woman brought along her young daughter.

One morning I went looking for Patrick Leo and Thomas M. and saw the girl hanging by her hands from the front-stair railing about 10 feet above the floor! Patrick Leo said he and Thomas M. just were watching and waiting. She and her mother left shortly after that, and an 18-year-old girl was hired as a live-in house laborer.

On February 18, 1951, I left the teens behind and became a 20-year-old. I still was very unsure of myself and of what would ever become of me. I wondered what the future held for a mixed-up ugly duck who just didn't seem to have any goals in life. It is a blessing that I could not foresee future events that were to unfold.

The gang now headed to bigger destinations for nocturnal pleasures and excitement. We would travel to Iowa City, with a population of about 25,000, plus University of Iowa students. There always was something going on in Iowa City, thanks to the young student population.

We also went to Cedar Rapids, which had about 70,000 residents and was home to the Danceland Ballroom. At Danceland, I saw some of the big-name entertainers of the time including Johnny Cash and Danny and the Juniors.

Cedar Rapids has a large Czech population and was home to a neighborhood where the Czech language was spoken frequently. I met a young resident of the area one night at Danceland. Before I hardly knew what was happening, she asked me to take her home. She and two girlfriends got in the car with the Holbrook gang, and we gave them a ride. She covered my face and lips with wet kisses.

When we arrived at her residence, she insisted we come in for a piece of Czech poppy-seed cake, which was quite good. She also insisted on introducing me to her father, who sat in a rocking chair looking as stern as a picture of Pope Pius XI. Needless to say, I was glad to get out of there. I didn't answer her letters and went to dances in Deep River and Swisher for some time to avoid Danceland.

Cedar Rapids also was where I "wound up" on a coon-hunting expedition that originated at Maplehurst Manor. Two friends drove out to get me—along with my supply of alcoholic beverages that I had been storing in a barn manger. I had gathered four fifths of homemade wine, along with bottles and cans of beer.

We had gathered the bottles of wine three weeks earlier—the gangs had heard of a wedding dance at a residence in Amana, about 20 miles north. We crashed the party and were treated cordially by the jolly, well-oiled assemblage. Everyone had a paper cup, and there were casks and barrels of wine.

I thought of the future, and after finding discarded whiskey, gin, and vodka bottles, we started getting cup after cup of the potent wine and filled five or six of the previously discarded bottles. So that is how Amana homemade wine ended up in the barn storage area, covered with hay.

When we left to start coon hunting, I suggested that we go to Cedar Rapids and have a few beers. Before heading there, at Louise's Tap and Grill (formerly Agnew's Tavern) in

North English, we started with a couple of Griesedieck Brothers beers, which were new to the local area. We had great fun carrying on about "greasy-dick" beers and ordering them by calling out, "Bring us three greasy dicks!"

We (I) figured a few beers would give us "energy" for trekking after baying hounds, and then we could fortify ourselves with the libations I had been saving. One thing led to another, and the hunt and dogs were forgotten. We were having a grand time—and never did see a coon.

We actually ended up in the Cedar Rapids city jail.

Police arrested one of my friends in Cedar Rapids early the next morning on a reckless driving charge when he was driving down the railroad tracks in the city. The police stated they were already looking for us before we were apprehended—we had been evicted from at least three taverns and reported to authorities. According to *The Cedar Rapids Gazette*, my other friend and I also were in the car with a loaded .22 rifle, two fifths of wine, a can of beer, and three coonhounds.

Yes, we made the newspaper.

The driver promptly went to sleep after being locked up while I began to get my story together. They questioned each of us separately. One friend said the other bought the booze for us, while that second friend said he found it in a roadside ditch. I said that I provided it from my dad's wine cellar. The police officer replied, "You mean you stole it from your dad?"

"Not really. I intended to replace it," I hastily replied.

Evidently, they believed my story because I was not charged or fined. The story was on the noon news on WMT Radio—the station that residents around Parnell had set on their dials. So that is how Mother and Dad found out why I was not home to help with cornhusking.

In traffic court, the driver was fined $100 for reckless driving. My other friend was fined $15 for drunkenness, and I was released after spending the night in jail.

After being released on that dismal cloudy day, I hung around police headquarters and waited for the others to go before the judge. I checked on the three coonhounds in the trunk (the lid was elevated so they could breathe freely) and then went to a nearby Maid-Rite to order four sandwiches—one for me and each dog. Jimmy Murphy later would tell the story over and over of how "Genie got hamburgers for the hounds," and laugh hilariously.

The parents of one of my fellow "hunters" were phoned and arrived to pay the two friends' fines. The parents followed us back to Parnell. When I glanced back, they looked mean and serious as if their world were about to explode. When one of the friends was lying on his jailhouse bunk, he sobbed, "Boo-hoo, this will take 10 years off my folks' lives." I thought of that when I heard about each of their deaths.

About three weeks later, after attending a Friday evening Holy Hour, Father Browne called to me. As Dad, Mother, and my brothers listened, he said, "Oh Gene, I was driving home from Williamsburg last night when a great big coon ran across the road in front of my car. I thought of you right away! Ha, ha, ha, ha!"

At least I didn't get threatened with Eldora!

In 1950, a new colt was born to our horse Bonnie. Bonnie was tied in her stall during the day, and as I went about the barn premises, the colt, which became as tame as a dog, took to following me everywhere.

All of our horses, most of our brood sows, and our cows had names. Some were named after the person or family from whom they had been purchased or by their appearance or personality. The names included Gertie, Charlie, Little Girl, Big Girl, Prize, Blue Ribbon, Leaky, Katie, Strawberry, Perrin, and Nellie.

In the late summer of 1951, Dad told Rete Lawler, who owned a hardware store in Parnell, that Kenny and I would unload two railroad boxcars of large chunk coal and place them on concrete slabs next to her store. Those coal cars were long, and it was at least 6 feet from the bed of the car to the top. The chunks were too large for a shovel, so we had to pick them up by hand and pitch or heave them over the sides. A slight breeze would blow the coal dust, and we were sweating profusely.

At noon, we went to the Little Chicago restaurant in Williamsburg, five miles north. We were so dirty, but the owner was kind enough to let us wash up in his private bathroom. Soap and water never felt better. For three days, we pitched coal and asked Dad to never get us into another such job.

I was so thankful for the last day of threshing in 1951—I never had been more exhausted. I was looking forward to the following day when I was planning to ride along with Jimmy and Bernard Murphy, Paul McCarty, and cousin Gene O'Rourke to the Iowa State Fair. They were going to pick me up at 4 a.m. But I was so dead to the world that at the appointed hour, I didn't hear their car horn. So they went on without me.

The day was a scorcher, and I intended to take it easy. However, some old farmer had heard that the Dawson boys were good workers and, without even asking me, Dad hired me out to him to make loose hay. That was the hardest I ever had been pushed. I had to load the rack of hay and then haymow it when it was unloaded.

The farmer didn't even offer me a drink of cold water, let alone a soda pop or a refreshing beer. And during all this time, I thought about how I could have been having a blast in Des Moines with Jimmy, Bernard, Paul, and Gene. The unkind old dude even hesitated about giving me a ride home. Plus, he didn't pay a decent wage. I made sure Dad understood that he was no longer my agent for employment purposes.

In Parnell on Halloween, it was customary to tip over outhouses. Some folks would anchor them with a large post at one corner and secure them with No. 9 wires. Tipping became quite a challenge, so I kept wire cutters with me to overcome such barriers. Some disgruntled elderly gentlemen would fire their shotguns to send us scattering and running into fences, getting cuts, and tearing good pairs of Levis!

Near Halloween of 1951, we (the Holbrook gang) were cruising around Parnell in Dad's '47 car. One of the guys had found some rotten eggs at home, so we decided to get an early start on Halloween. He was an expert marksman—usually—and as we drove, we met three other friends driving around. I noticed egg yolks streaming down their windshield, and the driver was very agitated. I asked what had happened, and the driver replied the same thing that happened to Mr. Selby's car, which was parked in front of the house where Mr. Selby boarded.

Mr. Carl Selby was Parnell's school principal!

Unbeknownst to me, my friend had launched his grenades from the back window and hit the wrong targets. Of course, the other driver told Mr. Selby, who informed Parnell Mayor J.S. O'Rourke (Dad's cousin), who promptly issued a 30-day arrest warrant to town marshal Mr. Bob O'Brien for "Gene and Kenny Dawson if they appeared in Parnell." Mr. O'Brien patrolled the streets at night and farmed during the day. He delighted in apprehending anyone thought to be an offender.

After the incident, Mr. Selby put two of the gang, who were still in school, to work thoroughly cleaning, disinfecting, and deodorizing his car. Needless to say, Kenny and I sped in and out of Parnell after that, stopping just long enough to pick up our friends. Evidently, Sundays were truce days as we were never bothered leaving Mass, but I don't think they really wanted to deal with Dad!

I decided I had to do something to get the attention off the Dawsons. So on a mild early November night in 1951, I told Dad and Mother I was going outside to check the sows since "Pinky," my favorite sow at the time, was due. But, instead, I changed my clothes on the front porch, donning old heavy overalls and a long flannel shirt. I gathered about a dozen very "ripe" rotten eggs—the kind that, when broken, stink to high heaven—plus a bag of overripe tomatoes.

I then walked 3½ miles through our neighbors' pastures and fields and arrived across the road from a door-less garage that belonged to marshal Bob O'Brien. He always backed his vehicle in so he was ready to roll if called.

A few dogs barked as I crouched in a patch of tall weeds, listened closely, and chose the right moment to stealthily cross the street, hoping I wouldn't be observed under the streetlight. I proceeded to bombard the windshield and front grillwork of his "police" car with a high-powered barrage. It certainly didn't take long. I then hightailed it back across the fields leaving a curtain of heavy stinking aroma behind.

As I dashed toward home, I stumbled a couple of times, ran into a fence, and was scared shitless when a flock of pheasants—frightened out of their slumber—rose up with whirring wings almost under my feet. When I was about a half mile away from home, I heard Dad shouting, "Gene!" at the top of his lungs.

I got to the front porch, changed into my regular clothes that I had hidden under the porch steps, and went yawning into the house. I told Dad and Mother that I had fallen asleep next to Pinky and all was well with the mother sows and babies.

When Dad returned from a trip to the Parnell grocery store the next morning, he said the town was abuzz over someone "rotten-egging" Bob O'Brien's car the night before. Dad had told the assemblage that they sure as hell couldn't blame this on his boys—he knew damn well that neither of our cars had left our place.

There was much conjecture over who was guilty of this nocturnal attack. I didn't even tell my buddies until much later. I think Kenny was aware of it. Many, many years later, I told Dad. He said he always was suspicious that it was I but would have fisticuffed anyone who accused the Dawsons.

After that, we didn't get blamed for every prank or ornery deed—even when the blame was deserved!

Directly east of Maplehurst Manor, in Iowa County's Greene Township, many of our neighbors were Amish or Mennonite. The Amish and Mennonites were good neighbors and honest, hardworking, and law-abiding.

Both groups had their German heritage in common. The Amish were very good farmers, and they often sold fresh eggs and baked goods from their homes. The Mennonites eventually even opened a church in Parnell—a town that was dominated by St. Joseph's (St. Joseph's was the only church that had ever been in Parnell).

The Mennonites were more liberal than the Old Order Amish, who disdained the modern conveniences of electricity, cars, etc. They traveled by horse and buggy, similar to what we brothers had used to get to Catechism classes in North English and for pleasure excursions while we resided at the Swain Place. Signs warning drivers to be aware of horse-drawn carriages were on the rural roads and some paved highways. The young Mennonites, however, drove cars and were some of the most reckless and speedy drivers on our rural country road and could send up clouds of dust a half-mile long.

I met a few young Amish men at a neighboring pond/swimming hole. They were very friendly and fun loving, but, of course, they did not drink, smoke, or tell risqué jokes. At the time I was residing at Maplehurst Manor, I didn't fully appreciate the unique folks and culture that was right down the road.

Raising turkeys was big business in the Amish-Mennonite communities just east of Parnell. Maplecrest Turkey Farms in Wellman, Iowa, southeast of Parnell, helped Wellman become known as the turkey capital of the world. Many folks from the surrounding towns were employed at the Maplecrest plant. After the birds were cleaned and packaged, the finished products went to stores nationwide under the "Maplecrest" label, which then was as popular as Butterball is today. This was before the evolvement of the large-breasted, white hybrid turkey that is raised in confinement today.

A family that lived southeast of Maplehurst Manor raised turkeys for processing. In the fall, they solicited neighbors to help catch the birds to be crated and then hauled to Wellman. The turkeys weighed between 12 and 18 pounds and sometimes more, so they could leave me bruised from being beaten by their strong wings. The Murphys, Gene O'Rourke, Kenny, and sometimes Leroy also helped. For our reward, each of us received a live turkey. As we caught the turkeys, we would select and put aside the best specimens. Sometimes we arrived home with three birds—for Thanksgiving, Christmas, and New Year's.

In the 1950s, the deadly chemical DDT was sprayed to kill weeds and brush. Before it was banished, many native valuable plants and vegetation were killed off. The runoff after rains contaminated streams, wells, and water supplies. Many birds died—my pigeons would hatch babies, but they soon would die of starvation after developing goiters in their throats.

Creosote, which was purchased in small metal drums, was used to preserve wood. Posts for fencing were soaked in creosote to make them last longer and prevent beetles and other insects from boring into them. We took small cans to paint the roosts in the chicken house. It killed all the lice and mites on the chickens.

Apparently, it also affected humans. By the time I would finish painting a roost with creosote, my eyes would be burning, my face would be almost blistered like I had a severe sunburn, and my arms would be red and itchy.

Dad had one tractor equipped for spraying crops for weeds and insects. After Dad finished spraying on hot and windy days, he came in from the fields completely soaked with the deadly spray. The spray mix was so powerful that even a sack that had been emptied of it and left on the ground for any length of time would kill all the vegetation underneath. Nothing, not even a weed, would grow there for many years.

Many people from the surrounding area eventually had cancer, and I am convinced that those deadly chemicals and pesticides contributed to their painful and premature deaths.

In September 1951, the Brooklyn Dodgers baseball team was scheduled to play the St. Louis Cardinals, and Aunt Catherine Dawson, who was a resident of St. Louis, obtained tickets for a midweek showdown between the bitter rivals. This was the era of Jackie Robinson and Stan Musial, who were superstars for their respective teams, the Dodgers and Cardinals. I was a die-hard Brooklyn fan, and this would be the first major-league game that I would attend.

Kenny, our friend Gene Welsh, and I boarded an afternoon Greyhound bus in Parnell and then stayed overnight in Ottumwa before proceeding south at 8 a.m. the next day. None of us were 21, but at our first stop in Macon, Missouri, we spied a liquor store adjacent to the bus terminal and made a beeline for it. No questions were asked, and we purchased several bottles of assorted spirits.

Buses did not have restrooms at that time, so we were happy to find one at our next stop in Moberly, Missouri. As we went on, I saw a sign, "Mexico 10 miles," and was alarmed thinking we got on the wrong bus! I had no idea a town in Missouri was named Mexico. We finally chugged into St. Louis—little did I know that I would be a resident there for most of my life.

We tried to phone Aunt Catherine, but I was so dumb that I didn't know I had to put coins in the phone. I had never heard of that. None of us were feeling any pain when I saw Aunt Catherine tapping on the phone-booth door. She had a room for us at the residential Northwestern Hotel where she lived, and we were her guests for three days.

We attended three ball games at the old Sportsman's Park and saw a loud and boisterous crowd in the "colored" section cheer on their hero Jackie Robinson, even though he was on the opposing team. While we were in St. Louis, we also visited the city's two cathedrals, downtown, a Chinese restaurant, a Catholic supply store, and an unimaginably large store—Famous-Barr—that covered an entire city block.

We rode streetcars and basically just about went into culture shock over the differences between St. Louis and tiny-town, friendly, all-white rural Iowa. After returning home via our first train ride, I decided that someday, hopefully, I would be able to reside in St. Louis.

Also in 1951, a friend told me about the Hurdle & Halter, a bar in the Montrose Hotel in Cedar Rapids. While my friends were at the Danceland Ballroom one Saturday night in December, I slipped away and walked to the hotel.

I was surprised by the dimness and beauty of the place. It was very quiet and elegant. A gentleman was playing soft tunes on an organ on a semi-stage, and a very handsome young man with wavy black hair was singing. I also noticed that the clientele was almost 100 percent male, except for two or three rather masculine women. Although I was not yet 21, I had my false ID and was served a glass of beer.

Some of the men engaged me in conversation, which made me both fascinated and wary. During the brief stop, I met Don S., who was 39 years old and had a very well-paying job. He definitely was not a farmer, although he owned a large farm in northeast Iowa, which he rented out on a 50-50 basis. He insisted on paying for all my drinks and managed to give me his phone number at home and work "in case you ever need anything."

Near closing time, I hurried back to the dance, wondering about the bar and individuals I had met. That was the first gay bar I ever entered.

I visited the Hurdle & Halter a couple of times more. Don S. also insisted that I have his address. He stated that I was the cutest guy he had ever seen and he had seen many men since he was in the military during World War II and had been all over the world. I was very flattered, even more wary, and thought he needed to have his eyes checked by a good optometrist! He definitely was not handsome in my estimation and much, much too old to be a buddy.

On one of my visits to the bar, I took Kenny and a friend along. Both were unimpressed—lack of girls—and probably wondered why I was drawn to the place. Don S. also seemed possessive, as he was brusque and somewhat rude, I thought, to others who tried to talk to me.

About this same time, I saw an ad in some paper for *Little Blue Books* by the Haldeman-Julius Publishing Company with a Kansas address. Needless to say, I ordered them and was astounded and amazed at their contents. They were so full of taboo information that I hid them in a compartment of the threshing machine that was in winter storage in the corncrib. I would sneak a few in to read at night in my locked bedroom—it was the only room and closet in the house that could be locked.

I shared most of this "knowledge" with Leroy. Somehow I knew that Kenny and my Parnell and Holbrook gang members should not share my secrets.

From this information, I found a listing of "controversial" books for sale and ordered *The Homosexual in America* book and some *Sexology* magazines. I felt bewildered, guilt, and shame upon reading the book and coming to the conclusion that I never was going to change and be like Kenny and my buddies and have girlfriends, a wife, and children. I would have to lead a double life and always be on guard or be ostracized by family, friends, community, and the church.

So I determined I would erase from my mind all "perverse" thoughts and force myself to be "normal"—not realizing that so-called "normal" was not normal for me. I hadn't heard the word "gay" in rural Iowa. People were labeled "odd" or "queer"—a word I detest.

"I know I am one of those, and I think you are, too," I announced to Leroy. So from then on and even actually before, Leroy and I had a common secret bond. At least we had each other for support and confidential discussions.

I was looking forward to my 21st birthday when 1952 began. In Iowa, 21 was the legal age to get a permit to buy liquor. Only beer was served in bars and taverns; to enjoy a mixed drink or cocktail, hard liquor first had to be purchased at a state-owned and controlled liquor store. Williamsburg was the only town nearby that had such an establishment. After a bar patron bought the hard liquor, he/she carried the concealed bottle into a bar or tavern, bought a Coke, 7UP, or mixer, and mixed the drink. The liquor bottle could not be displayed on the bar, table, or booth. However, in neighboring Johnson County, mixed drinks could be served as they are today.

Altering my Selective Service draft card to indicate I was of legal age had been no problem since I had turned 18 and moved to the "liberated" Parnell area. So I could always buy six-packs and quarts of beer to guzzle as I rode along to a nocturnal destination, which was usually a dance except on Sunday nights when all establishments were closed except movie theaters.

So on the cold winter evening of February 18, 1952, Kenny was at the wheel of our Ford Model A and I was collecting cash and writing down the drinks of choice for the guys who accompanied us on this exciting and great occasion. Everything went according to plan, and I returned to the car with a box of various spirits and, I'm sure, a grand time was had by all.

Unfortunately, being "legal" took some of the edge and fun out of the drinking experience. To me, things always were a bit more appealing when I had to be clever and inventive to get away with them.

Shortly after my 21st birthday, I received the expected notice from Uncle Sam that directed me to report to Des Moines, the state capital, on March 10 to assess my qualifications mentally, physically, and sexually to begin serving in the military. At that time, the United States was engaged in the Korean War.

Late in the morning about March 3, the mail carrier arrived while I was hauling manure from the huge barn with horses Bonnie and Nell. That was my job on that late winter day since no crops are planted, cultivated, or harvested at that time of the year. Dad was attending a farm sale or auction—there was one nearly every day in some nearby town. I can't recall where Kenny was, but Leroy, Bernie, and Patrick Leo were in school. Thomas M. and Mother were in the house.

Upon seeing an envelope addressed to me, I opened it to see "Greetings" from Uncle Sam. I immediately knew what it was as many of my friends already had been drafted. I was determined to keep my bout with polio to myself, blank out my sexual persuasion, and join the rest of the guys my age in defense of our country.

I, of course, had no idea what a shock it would be for me, an unworldly country hick who had only been as far as St. Louis. I had never witnessed continuous mental, physical, and racial cruelty inflicted on others.

I tied the team of horses to the barn door without even unhitching them, set the poop shovel and pitchfork aside, and told Mother that I was going to party and only do chores for the next seven days. She told Dad when he got home, and he agreed.

Kenny and I, along with the Parnell and Holbrook gangs, spent that time attending every dance in the area and visiting many taverns since I now was a "legal" 21. It got to the point that we almost needed to take a break from partying!

Aunt Helen and Uncle Lyle Hartzell hosted a goodbye dinner for me, as did Grandma Agnew. Aunt Helen and Lyle also met the group at the Danceland Ballroom where we had many drinks, and Lyle told me, "I hope and pray you don't get into the Marines." Uncle Lyle was a Marine veteran and survivor of the bloody Pacific battle of Iwo Jima against the Japanese. In 1952, the Marines were drafting and took recruits with high test scores and much physical strength. The Air Force had plenty of volunteers since lots of young guys wanted to be pilots. I didn't know the difference between the Marines, Army, and Navy—all I knew was that they all fought for our country.

Upon getting my draft notice, I decided to hide the "book" and *Sexology* magazines inside the house. I locked them in a typewriter case and set the typewriter next to it on my closet shelf.

Kenny drove me to Marengo on March 10 to board a bus for Des Moines. Mother and Dad had bid tearful farewells when I left the house. Mother was especially tearful after having lost her youngest brother, Leo Raymond, in Italy in 1944, and it only was the second time I saw Dad cry. Leroy waved from the chicken yard, and I almost would swear that I saw a tear in Firpo the dog's eye.

Before I left, I regret that I announced to all—with false bravado—that I would be pushing up daisies in Korea in a short time. I guess I liked seeing the pained expressions—I'm weird. Mother was particularly upset.

Charlie, Jimmy, Ray, and Bernard Murphy, Uncles Emmett and Bernard Agnew, Paul McCarty, and Father Browne all came to Marengo to say goodbye. Although I didn't smoke, the Murphy brothers and my uncles gave me cartons of cigarettes. They assured me that I would be smoking before long. Most of my send-off crew were veterans of World War II.

Upon arriving in Des Moines, we—about 90 young men from various Iowa locales—were examined in assembly-line fashion by a group of doctors who apparently were specialists in various medical fields. I did not reveal that I had polio in 1944; I had learned to cope with the leg and foot numbness.

The physical was a piece of cake, and I passed with flying colors. The previous year, I had sent for a Charles Atlas course and received an unmarked package of exercise instructions that I used for 12 consecutive weeks. I did not want anyone to know because fitness was not in vogue at the time, particularly in rural Iowa—farm work was the physical exercise. Beer guzzling was the main recreation since televisions were not yet affordable to most and reception was not good anyway.

By faithfully following the Charles Atlas Dynamic Tension Course, before long I had bulging biceps and a 28-inch waist. My beer belly was gone, and my willpower kicked in. I had a boiled egg, one piece of unbuttered toast, and a glass of skim milk for breakfast. At noon and in the evening, I had one small portion of everything—no seconds—and no bread. I used no butter or salt. I usually skipped any sweet except for a piece of Mother's homemade fruit pie or one of her cinnamon rolls, which I could not resist.

After the physical, we were ushered to a long table to take a written test. I was startled to come to the question, "Do you have any homosexual tendencies?" Several crude and hateful remarks were made around the table with laughter and a few nervous twitters, I'm sure, including my own.

Of course, I lied and marked "NO," having made a firm—I hoped—decision that I was going to be like "everybody else" and be 100 percent heterosexual.

Soon a classmate of mine from North English High School, a young man from Williamsburg, and a handsome guy from a nearby town with long, beautiful fingernails (I later wondered how he fared), and I were chosen for the Marine Corps. I was proud to be one of the chosen few and was sworn in.

We boarded a train for the two-day journey to Los Angeles with a final destination being the United States Marine Corps Recruit Center in San Diego. After we arrived in Los Angeles, we were packed on buses for the 120-mile trip south to the base depot.

During training, we were called every abusive name I had ever heard, plus some new ones to my big ears. There were no smiles, no courtesy. Our heads were shaved, we were rousted from bed at 2 a.m. to do hand-laundry for officers, and began our discipline and indoctrination. The M1 rifle was our constant companion. We had to be able to take it apart and reassemble it in the dark and never let any rust get on it. I had fired a rifle only one time before in my life and didn't care for guns.

"What on earth have I gotten into?" I wondered. I thought the Koreans and Chinese were the enemies to be punished—not us! I began to count the days before I could leave—my God, 728 left! We were drafted for two years.

During my downtime, I read the many letters written to me by family and friends. Some of the 15-to-18-year-old girls from Parnell and the vicinity wrote to me, too.

After four weeks, the constant marching back, forth, and sideways and duck-walking on gravel piles began to take a toll on my polio leg. Then at an inspection, I was told that rust was found on my rifle! I never did see it, but soon I was given a summary court martial and sentenced to five days on bread and water in the "brig," the base jail.

I was in a state of shock—this had to be a horribly bad dream. Those five days were some of the worst in my life. I was accused of being a "queer," almost choked to death by a crazy inmate, and beat up by the leaders of the prison hierarchy. I made a pledge to myself that I would disclose my bout with polio and its results as soon as I was released.

I was assigned back to my former platoon, and I knew that those in charge would be on my case even more because it reflected badly on them to have one of their recruits screw up—especially when it concerned our "best friend," the M1 rifle.

My request to see a doctor was granted, and I was fully scrutinized for my reaction to pain as my foot and leg were pricked with sharp objects. I had no feeling or pain as droplets of blood ran down my leg and heel. I watched, but sometimes they had me close my eyes and asked, "Do you feel that?"

"No," was my reply. They decided I must be insane and assigned me to the "psycho" ward.

It was like a breath of fresh air: a nice barracks inhabited by the "misfits" of Marine society. They were in there for bed-wetting, nervous disorders, being unable to respond to discipline, or being outright "goofy." There were a couple of guys who were on a hunger strike and refusing to eat.

At home, Mother and Dad went to the Red Cross representative in North English, and Dr. Miller's records of my polio were sent to San Diego. Mother, bless her heart, also wrote to the base chaplain and bolstered my true claim of polio.

My leg became weaker, and I was "tested" each morning. Then each weekday, I spent four hours in the Naval Records office separating papers that were in triplicate to go to various locations.

I was "invited" by two different Navy men to meet them after hours. But I declined as I was trying to ignore that inclination. They both ignored me after I failed to arrive at the "trysting" place.

In mid-May, I appeared before a judgment board of several top military doctors and brass. I sat on a chair in the center of their circle and answered several questions. One asked if I wanted to fire the M1 rifle and if I enjoyed guns. He assumed that since I grew up on a farm that I must surely be a hunter and gun enthusiast. I answered that my leg prevented me from tramping through the woods and, furthermore, I did not believe in killing innocent birds and animals and had no desire to shoot any gun! Another asked me why my boot was worn down in the front. That was a result of dragging my left foot.

Finally, they asked if I would be willing to help Dad on the farm to aid the war effort if I went home. "Yes, sir!" was my reply.

Four others also appeared before the board that afternoon and were discharged. I got a Medical Honorable Discharge without benefits since my polio didn't happen during my Marine service. I signed papers saying I would not pursue any monetary pension or reimbursements. Dad had told me via letter to not sign any papers, but I didn't really care. I was just glad I was going home.

Lon, one of my new friends from the psych ward, and I made plans to take the same bus back as far as Cedar Rapids with a stop in Las Vegas on the way. We were advised that our conduct must be proper—no trouble—as we still were considered Marines until we returned home. On May 19, we were taken to the main base gate and given our pay and some coupons to exchange for civilian clothes in downtown San Diego.

Lo and behold, as I was ready to leave, the officer in charge called me aside and said, "Your uncle is here to see you." I was shocked and led to the adjoining room.

There sat retired Major Don S.! He had told them that he was my uncle. I don't know what led him to California on vacation, but on a whim and knowing I had been drafted, he decided to check the Marine base to see if I might be there.

He also was shocked when I told him I had been discharged earlier that day.

"Great," he said. "You can go with me on the rest of my vacation, and I'll give you a ride back to Iowa." I already had made plans with Lon, so Don S. invited him to come along.

After Lon and I exchanged clothes downtown, we all decided to get a motel and then visit the city's sights that night. After checking in, Don S. wondered what the sleeping arrangements would be for the two beds. But before he got the words out of his mouth, Lon said, "I guess I can put up with him [me]."

I sensed tension and thought, "Am I some kind of pawn?" I had suspected Lon was gay but didn't know for sure.

That night, we went to a bar high up in the El Cortez Hotel. The next night, our travels took us to the Golden Carp in Hollywood. I immediately knew it was a gay bar—the patrons were the most handsome young men I had ever seen. I wondered what Lon would think, but he fit right in and even disappeared a couple of times. I collected a few names and phone numbers, and the bartender "tendered" several free drinks.

We kept the same sleeping arrangements at a motel in Los Angeles as we had the night before in San Diego. After returning to our quarters, getting into bed, and falling asleep, I was awakened by Lon, who was trying to fondle me. I quickly turned and rolled to the far side of the bed. I heard him mutter, "You will never get any place in this life."

But for the rest of the trip, he stayed on his side of the bed. Poor Don S. became nervous, ill, and could hardly eat. He thought for sure Lon and I were carrying on an affair right in front of his eyes.

We visited places in California and Utah, where we had great pan-fried trout. In Las

Vegas, I stayed out all night. At that time, it was small with only a few hotels, but I thought the neon lights were bright as day. Don S. gave me some money that I lost in the nickel slots.

In Denver, Don S. went to bed early fretting over my imagined affair with Lon, who had disappeared for the night. I was left to have a "whee" of a time with guys who were intrigued with my crew-cut hair and that I was just released from the military. I also had my first drink of champagne, and a handsome young guy even drank some from one of my shoes! Thank goodness, I had only had them three or four days.

Near Omaha, we stopped at the first Dairy Queen I had ever seen, and I marveled at the smooth and delicious ice cream. It was the nearest to homemade ice cream I had ever tasted. In Omaha, I walked the streets until nearly sunup and was approached by several men in slow-moving vehicles. I declined the invitations to "go for a ride."

As we entered Iowa, I realized I was arriving back just in time for the really hard-work season. I was hoping that everything would fall right back into place. Great changes can— and do—occur in 2½ months. I felt I had let down my family and community by being medically discharged while my contemporaries were in Korea fighting for their country with some being killed and others injured.

Upon arriving in Cedar Rapids, Lon caught a bus, Don S. went home, and Kenny met me at the Montrose Hotel lobby. As Kenny drove down Highway 149 about midway to Parnell, he mentioned that a neighbor had asked to borrow my typewriter a few days earlier. When Mother went to get the typewriter, she did not notice that it was sitting on the closet shelf. So Mother gave her the typewriter case—which was filled with my secret books.

Shortly after that, Kenny reported that the neighbor returned the empty case (she got it open with a hairpin) and the books. Mother was so shocked, surprised, disgusted, and perplexed by the books that she took them to the fiery coal furnace and pitched them in the devouring flames!

I had the urge to open the car door and hurl myself on the pavement as we sped along at 60 to 65 miles per hour. I restrained the suicidal move and began to formulate plans of what to do and concoct answers for the many questions I assumed would be asked. Should I be frank or act extremely dumb as if I had not read or understood the meaning of the books? Or should I just play it by ear and instinct?

A few days after I returned home—and after I received many curious looks—Mother announced that she had, indeed, burned the terrible books. I shrugged and said I had never read them, and they were never mentioned again.

The times were changing, and I knew I should start formulating plans to leave Parnell, the family, and farm. I knew that I did not "fit in" in rural Iowa and decided I would move to a large city in the near future. Chicago kept coming to mind.

Our Parnell and Holbrook gangs were no more. Kenny was dating the gorgeous Marlene Shannahan of Holbrook; she would become his wife in 1956. My best friend was attending college in another part of Iowa. Several other friends had steady girlfriends or had obtained automobiles and preferred to travel alone.

I was determined that I would not resume visiting the gay bar in Cedar Rapids. I started to save every penny from my share of the baling operation that Kenny and I still owned. I stopped going out at night, except I would accompany Kenny and Marlene on their dates to Iowa City once in awhile.

In August 1952, Aunt Marie and Uncle Ray LaMere arrived for a week's visit. Leroy and I then accepted their invitation to accompany them back to their home in suburban Minneapolis.

Upon arriving in the northern city, we decided to visit downtown Minneapolis to try to find a gay bar, which, I had heard, you could count on tracking down in a metropolitan area. Since neither of us knew how to ride a city bus or streetcar, we set out on foot from the LaMeres' suburban home. It seemed we would never get to the "promised land." It was hot and humid and took at least two hours to arrive at our "finish line."

I proceeded to visit many bars on Hennepin Avenue, one of the city's main thorough-fares, while 17-year-old Leroy walked the streets nearby or rested in hotel lobbies. Finally, a 40ish gentleman approached me. He eventually took me to "Herb's," a dimly lit tavern full of young male patrons. I knew I had found the place!

A recently discharged 23-year-old Navy veteran made my acquaintance and, to con-dense events, returned Leroy and me to the LaMere residence about 8 a.m. the next morning. Ray was highly agitated and pacing around. He shouted, "Get your clothes and get out!"

Aunt Marie was calmer and gave us a quick dish of Jell-O with pickles in it (she always liked sour things and would drink vinegar from a bottle). When she asked Ray if he would give us a ride to the bus station, he shouted, "Hell no! They found their way downtown last night."

Aunt Marie quietly told us how to board and pay fare on a city bus, so we boarded one near their home. As we rode along, I told Leroy that we were going to stay in Minneapolis for a few days. I had more than $80, which was quite a lot for 1952. We got a room at the YMCA and enjoyed three more "enlightening" days in the Twin Cities.

The young Navy veteran, who proclaimed he had fallen in love with me, was our guide. He worked in advertising and had a red convertible. I was startled as its windows opened and closed with the touch of a button and water sprayed mysteriously on the windshield for a quick wash job. When he first pushed the window control, Leroy and I both jumped. I was amazed but tried to not act too "backward."

For nearly a year after this, my Navy man made monthly trips to Cedar Rapids, and we would spend Saturday nights and Sundays at the Montrose Hotel there and visit Iowa City's gay clubs where most of the patrons were University of Iowa students. The rela-tionship ended when my Navy guy wanted me to move to Florida with him, but I was not in love and declined.

In the fall of 1952, Leroy started his senior year at Parnell High School, and he and I decided we would save all the money we could so we could move to a large city when he graduated. In addition to Chicago, we considered Minneapolis and St. Louis.

I had liked St. Louis since Kenny, Gene Welsh, and I visited there in September 1951. Also, a friend from the Iowa City gay scene told me the names of two "wild" gay bars in the Missouri city. Aunt Catherine Dawson had moved to Chicago from St. Louis, so we wouldn't have to hide from her or anyone there. We could be free to live our lives more openly.

However, there were some huge obstacles: the Holy Roman Catholic Church and some passages in the Old Testament of the Bible.

All through the rest of 1952 and until September 1953, I struggled with the "problem." I would determine through willpower that I would wipe out all aspects of so-called homosexuality in myself, get married, and be like the rest of the "normal" folks in the family and community.

Of course, I would falter because I couldn't banish the temptation of same-sex attraction from my mind. I even would awaken in the dead of night with crushing thoughts of endless days working as a farmer and being married.

According to the Old Testament, I was forever damned to eternal fire. I was puzzled and perplexed as to why I was among the ones destined for Satan's inferno.

May 1953 was graduation month for Leroy's Parnell class. The class had sponsored bake sales and other events to raise money for a group trip to Chicago. However, Leroy took his share, and he and I boarded a bus to St. Louis. We stayed at the Baltimore Hotel and had a grand time. We found the Entre Nous Lounge on Pine Street and Uncle John's Lounge nearby. Leroy was too young to be served alcoholic beverages in the bars, but the owners were kind enough to let him in the premises.

After the Missouri bars closed, we crossed the Mississippi River and enjoyed the Old English Inn in East St. Louis, Illinois, an elegant lounge that was open 24 hours a day. We met many, many friendly and kind people and several gay airmen stationed at nearby Scott Air Force Base. A few of the fellows became lifelong friends. Ms. Clarissa (Norman) was one of my most endearing friendships.

One night, I drank too much and invited four Scott airmen to my room. The next thing I remember was awakening in the bed the next morning—stark naked with the hotel door wide open. Naturally, the flyboys had long "flown" away, and I never saw them again.

When Leroy and I arrived back home, we resolved to make our move to St. Louis as soon as possible. We chose St. Louis over Minneapolis so we would not worry that Aunt Marie and Uncle Ray would interfere with our "freedom."

Meanwhile, the thought of going to confession was just unthinkable. Dad and Mother—especially Mother—were quite perturbed that I didn't receive Holy Communion at Mass and kept at me to go to confession.

How to confess to same-sex relations was a mystery to me, but Mother's persistent reminders of hell and my own conscience finally overcame me. So on a Saturday in August 1953, I entered the confessional. I talked very low and tried to alter my voice. The confessional definitely was not soundproof; it mainly consisted of one purple curtain that I pushed aside to enter.

Father Browne could not see me as I knelt and spoke to him through a cloth-covered screen. I proceeded to confess my sins and revealed that I had broken the Sixth Commandment with five men.

"Young lady, you have not been leading a Catholic life!" Father Browne shouted in response. He berated me as my ears burned, and I could feel the hot blood of embarrassment on my red face and ears.

"For your penance, say the beads of the rosary," he demanded in an equally loud tone of voice. I opened the curtain and quickly retreated to the outside front door. A fleeting glance caught the image of three local girls standing in line for confession with their open-mouth looks of bewilderment that I was the "young lady" so harshly admonished.

I never again went to confession at St. Joseph's in Parnell and still dislike going to the Sacrament of Reconciliation to this day. For many years, although I attended Mass occasionally, I never went to confession or received Holy Communion. I figured I was doomed but could not break from the church.

But that eventually changed, praise the Lord. The Holy Spirit was looking out for me.

In early September 1953, Leroy boarded a Greyhound bus bound for St. Louis. After buying his ticket, he had only a few clothes in a battered suitcase and $38 to his name. Within two days of arriving, he had acquired jobs at Scruggs, Vandervoort & Barney, a city-block-size department store, and at the Missouri Pacific Railroad headquarters at Union Station. Soon he also was working at Alexian Brothers Hospital in south St. Louis.

Back in Iowa, I gathered the money I had earned from baling and from selling my six hogs and whatever else I could sell, which included my desk that Kenny bought. I took $1,000 to the bank and received traveler's checks in $20 denominations.

I had stayed in contact with Don S. since our first meeting at the Hurdle & Halter in 1951, and he invited me to go on vacation with him to Miami in September 1953. It would cost me nothing—he just wanted my company. I would have him drop me off in St. Louis on the way back.

I wasn't even reluctant to leave my pigeons behind—they lived in the barn loft and cattle shed and could take care of themselves. So I said goodbye to dear Mother, Dad, and my wonderful brothers—little Thomas M. had just started school. I took the three suitcases that held all the possessions I owned, and Kenny drove me to Cedar Rapids.

I was overjoyed to be through with farm labor and thought, "I'll never have to make hay or fence or lift another bale again!"

Little did I know.

Don S. and I spent our first night in Dubuque, Iowa, and then it was on to Chicago and the gay clubs on Clark and Division Streets. In Cleveland, I saw my first drag (female impersonator) show and was thrilled to meet the performers who, to me, were like movie stars.

Our stop in Buffalo, New York, was uneventful, and I was not impressed with Niagara Falls. It reminded me of flushing a huge toilet with the water cascading and tumbling down the falls. To heck with scenery, I wanted to get to where there was "action"!

I found it in Greenwich Village and New York City, which seemed so open and tolerant. There were such interesting and confident people there—more than even Chicago and certainly more than St. Louis. Then we headed down the East Coast but didn't visit any more metropolitan areas until we reached Miami. For a week, we enjoyed Miami's beaches and explored the nightspots.

I met many beautiful suntanned guys in Miami, and I managed to have a tryst with a handsome lifeguard from Fort Lauderdale. The only impediment to a wildly wonderful time was that Don S. stuck to me like glue. I could never be out of his sight, it seemed.

He was paying for everything—anytime I spied a shirt or some accessory that I fancied, it would be presented to me. However, it is no fun to be a caged bird—even if the

At Jackson Square, New Orleans, 1953.

Sitting at the edge of Lake Pontchartrain in Louisiana (in male beach attire), 1953.

In St. Augustine, Florida, 1953.

cage is gilded. It seemed similar to being a chained dog because I could only go so far.

In Miami, we went to the post office for general-delivery mail, and I received an interesting letter from Leroy. He told me about his early experiences in St. Louis, including finding a rental room and securing employment.

Our next stop was New Orleans and the marvelous, exotic French Quarter where we met some Tulane University students and an extremely handsome young man, probably Creole, with snapping black eyes and black wavy hair. He "threatened" to "kidnap" me and lock me in a room just for himself forever. I was "saved" by Don S. and the students, who thought I was much too flirtatious.

On the second night in New Orleans, we went to my second drag show at a club outside the city near Lake Pontchartrain. After paying a cover charge, we were given a front-row table, and I met the performers who sat at our table between shows. I thought they were very bold as they ordered drinks and assumed Don S. would pay for them. To be beautiful, bold, and self-confident would be a dream come true, I thought.

As we entered southeast Missouri near Cape Girardeau, I broke the news to Don S. that when we got to St. Louis, I would be staying there. He was stunned and wept openly as we approached the city. It was a very fretful two hours for both of us. He mentioned that he just might plunge us into a fatal auto accident because he did not want to live without me.

I prayed that calmness would return to his mind and was relieved when we got to St. Louis where Leroy greeted us. Don S. left after I promised to return to Iowa when I was ready and done "sowing my wild oats."

I rented a room from a couple in suburban University City, Missouri. It was near Leroy's living quarters, which was a room in the home of my landlord's sister. I would raid my landlords' refrigerator while they were at work. Having to buy my own food was a great shock to me since I always lived at home or was in the Marines.

Soon Leroy and I found an apartment together on Lindell Boulevard near the Cathedral Basilica of St. Louis, or the "New Cathedral" as it was called at the time. Leroy worked at his jobs, but since I had $1,000 and rent was $10 a week ($5 for my share), I was in no hurry to work. I actually wasn't qualified for anything.

So I went to the bars every day with a few other unemployed queens (gay, effeminate, young men). I would meet gentlemen who paid for most of my drinks, and I hardly ever enjoyed food. I now had a 26- to 28-inch waist and had perfected wearing makeup. I bleached my hair platinum blond—Jean Harlow was my idol—and plucked my eyebrows à la Marlene Dietrich or Greta Garbo.

I had one young (unemployed) admirer who was very blond and handsome, but, unfortunately, I liked him more than he liked me. He was unfaithful, which is something I just wouldn't tolerate.

We were to have no overnight visitors at the apartment, so I would sneak friends in and we would take each step at the same time and tread softly by the landlord's room. One cute young fellow from West Virginia would climb in the window (we were on the first floor) and then snuggle between Leroy and me. Neither of us was interested in him sexually (after the first time for me), but he was homeless, near our ages, and a fun person.

Ms. Clarissa would raid her family's freezer and bring frozen pies and meat to Leroy and me. Clarissa was a good cook and the motherly type. He was 30 years old and had attended college, taught school, and managed businesses. But he had a "nervous" problem and, as he explained, just couldn't take the stress of holding a regular job.

Clarissa also was good at ironing, hanging up our clothes, making the bed, and lots of other things Mother had done for us that Leroy and I had taken for granted. Ms. Clarissa drank very little alcohol, was very witty, and enjoyed friendship and laughter. "She" also was somewhat like a gentle bodyguard as I fortified myself with plenty of booze to eliminate my inferiority complex. Then I could let loose and be daring, outrageous, and the life of the party (I thought).

Drinking also enhanced my perception of myself as a beautiful, desirable, irresistible queen. The next morning, a glimpse in the mirror brought me back to reality.

On one occasion as I sat in Uncle John's bar, an admirer who did not interest me managed to unfasten and take off my belt and then dashed off with it to keep as a souvenir! Ms. Clarissa ran down Pine Street in hot pursuit, retrieved the belt, and chastised me for letting people "put their hands all over you."

Steve, a 40ish foreman at a plant in a nearby suburb, tried to give me an expensive ring—I suppose he intended it for engagement or marriage—but I refused, which sent him into a depressed state of mind. He soon recovered enough to do my laundry, buy groceries for Leroy and me, and pay my rent.

Steve also arranged for us to get a better apartment away from our prying landlady who constantly inquired about where I worked and at what odd hours. She thought we made too much noise with our late-night gatherings. It seemed a little odd to her that of the eight to 10 phone calls that came in each day for me, all were from men! I had the audacity to give her phone number to various "people of interest" whom I had met. Leroy and I didn't have a phone because we thought we weren't there enough to need one.

I had told the landlady that I worked at a certain factory, even though I didn't know where it was located. I was stunned a couple of weeks later when she asked if I would still receive the free turkey the company was giving employees for Thanksgiving since the employees were on strike! Of course, this was the first I heard about the strike. She asked me to get a turkey for her since Leroy and I were going to Iowa.

Oh, my! I lied again and said the turkeys were all gone by the time I got to the distribution point. She blinked her eyes, shrugged, and strode away.

So, in November, Leroy and I took the bus back to Parnell to celebrate Thanksgiving with our loving family. It had been less than three months since I had left, but it seemed longer. Dad invited the Murphy boys and cousin Gene O'Rourke to play cards and see the "prodigal" boys. Mother fixed the usual Thanksgiving feast.

I had tinted my hair back to its original color and painted on masculine eyebrows. I was kept busy keeping my lies in order—this included a story that I had a job doing paperwork in an office located in a tall building (fifth floor). I had to repeat this over and over to Mother, Dad, Kenny, Grandma, Aunt Anna, and others.

I spent New Year's Eve at Steve's cabin along the Cuivre River near Moscow Mills, Missouri. It was very cold, and he had a fire roaring in the big heating stove. Also attending were seven others including Ms. Clarissa and friend Joe "Ms. Jennie," who was in complete drag from head to toe.

New Year's Day is a Catholic Holy Day, and Steve was Catholic. Ms. Clarissa suggested

I go to Mass, but I decided not to since Ms. Jennie, still in complete drag, was going even though he was not Catholic. So Ms. Jennie, Steve, and two of the other attendees left for a nearby church. I was appalled when Ms. Jennie came back and reported, "Kid, I took communion for you!" On top of being in complete drag, he was as high as a kite, hadn't slept in two nights, and had an emerging dark beard.

I thought for sure that Satan had grabbed all of us with his pitchfork.

As 1954 began, my money supply was on the verge of being exhausted, so I went to work at a factory in a north St. Louis suburb. Steve, who hired me, was kind of like a "St. Louis Don S." He was "someone you could count on," some would say about our "friendship"; others would say "someone you used."

I was hired at the same time as "Ms. Pierre," a very effeminate, 125-pound refugee from war-torn Belgium. We lived in the same apartment building and rode the same streetcar and bus to and from work. Ms. Pierre lived with Gus, the best bartender I ever encountered. He was Ms. Pierre's "husband," and he was tall, dark, and handsome.

Ms. Pierre and I both wore makeup to work every day and got along very well with the 12 older female employees who did "piece work" or, in other words, were paid by how much they produced. They bagged various goods for stores nationwide, while Ms. Pierre and I kept the goods on hand so they could work fast. I had to join the union and felt completely out of place at a meeting I was forced to attend.

In 1954, temperatures soared in St. Louis, and the spring heat was nearly unbearable with no air conditioning. Ms. Pierre was laid off, but I was retained because I was Steve's favorite. Each night after work, I would head to the bar to cool off.

On several occasions, I failed to go to work knowing that Steve would not fire me. I never bothered to call in, so the union wouldn't be able to save my job. Finally, though, even Steve reached the end of his rope. He told me I would have to bring in a written doctor's excuse if I missed one more day.

Of course, I did miss another day after drinking the night before with Ms. Pierre, Ms. Jennie, and a very handsome 24-year-old ex-con named Tony, who had wandered into the bar and accompanied me home.

When I did go back to work, I barely made it in the door—late at that—when I was rudely told to get back on the bus and leave. I barely had enough change for the bus ride back to St. Louis. I was really feeling low and didn't know what I would do. I stopped at a hotel in midtown and considered asking if I could work there—it was well known for male prostitution.

But I went back to my apartment at 3910 Westminster Place. (Leroy had moved to a private room as my antics and hours became too much for him while he was holding three jobs.) I had two pounds of potatoes and $1.35 to my name. I was frying the potatoes and sitting in the 90-degree-plus kitchen when Ms. Pierre and Ms. Jennie came calling. Ms. Jennie, upon hearing of my predicament, said he was losing his roommate because the roommate was moving back to his parents' home.

So Ms. Jennie, whose only possessions were a beautiful makeup case full of the most wonderful John Robert Powers and Max Factor cosmetics, a few women's clothes and shoes, and some t-shirts and jeans, moved in with me. Ms. Jennie got a $25-a-week allowance from his father, so he was able to pay his share of the rent of $7.50 a week.

There was no landlord onsite at the Westminster apartment, and an elderly deaf woman occupied the only other apartment. In the hall outside the entry to my apartment, there was a pay phone that we "annexed" and gave out the number as our own. Ms. Jennie was very "talented" and knew how to use the phone without parting with any coins.

My claim for unemployment was rejected. The factory fought it; its officials said I brought on my own dismissal. For six weeks, I was unemployed and often we lived on bouillon-cube soup and an occasional saltine cracker.

In early May, I received a letter from Don S., who wrote that he was going to New Orleans on vacation. He suggested that I ask for a leave of absence from work so I could accompany him. Of course, he did not know I was unemployed, and I lied—again—and told him it had been granted and that I could go.

He was totally surprised to see my transformation from eight months earlier when I was a healthy, tanned, muscular "farm boy." I now was a skinny (26-inch waist), bleached-blond, eyebrow-painted trollop with long silver ("the" color at the time) painted fingernails!

Evidently, he didn't mind, and soon we were heading south for Dallas. When we entered a plush piano bar there, everyone stared in disbelief that one—me—could be so bold. A few nips of straight-from-the-bottle vodka soon—as always—helped buoy my spirits. Finally someone almost whispered, "You must be from New Orleans." Most, however, were very unfriendly in very conservative Dallas.

Of course, in that time period of paranoia and McCarthyism, it was not uncommon for authorities to raid known gay bars and haul its patrons off to jail. Some bars would not serve very effeminate guys who wore makeup. So I could understand their looks, as the Dallas bars had probably had a round of police raids.

The next night we were in Houston, and Don S. went to a bar in the warehouse district that we heard was a gay hangout. There was no sign, and it sat among vacant buildings. He entered and ordered a drink, but the bartenders soon suggested that he probably was in the wrong place. Don S. had not one iota of homosexuality about his appearance, carriage, or speech.

My all-white outfit was trimmed in red with many rhinestones. I was completely made up, and my hair was the same color as Marilyn Monroe's. As Don S. reentered with me at his side, the bar became completely silent and all eyes closed in on us. Then a huge roar erupted as the patrons crowded around us, vying to buy our libations.

Some suggested that I certainly must be Christine (originally George) Jorgensen who had undergone a sex reassignment. Her surgeries in the early 1950s had made headlines around the world—even in the staid *Chicago Daily Drovers Journal*, the only newspaper our family received. (At the time, Mother had read the story and asked if I had seen it. I was completely surprised that something so drastic had happened that I never dreamed could be done. Mother did not seem offended but slightly amused.)

Back in Houston, some really did think I was Ms. Jorgensen and praised me for being bold and carefree—not knowing the "real" me needed much fortification via alcohol. So our visit to Houston was very enjoyable before we set out for New Orleans.

It had been eight months since my last visit to "The Big Easy," and we were soon on a nighttime tour of the gay-bar scene in the French Quarter. My appearance was no shock to New Orleans natives, and there were many beautiful people there.

At one bar, a very handsome, tanned, blond young man was sitting alone and staring intently at me. He had a drink sent to me and soon moved his way up the bar next to me. Don S. let him know that I was with him. But the young guy had such a terrific personality that they soon were talking.

The young man was a professional baseball player. I was a baseball fan, and he was astounded that I knew his batting average, home-run total, and other statistics. Soon I was sitting on his lap, as he told me I was the most beautiful blond person he had ever seen and reminded him of his first wife. He kissed and nibbled on my ear, much to Don S.'s consternation. I felt like I was in heaven.

This meeting started a correspondence between the player and me that continued for a few years. Don S. and I eventually gave him and another ballplayer a ride to their downtown hotel that night. When I got back to St. Louis, a letter from the player awaited me. He wrote that New Orleans was definitely his high spot for 1954.

But before I returned to St. Louis, I decided to pay a surprise visit to my loving family—a very dumb decision.

I did know I couldn't suddenly appear with platinum hair, so Don S. purchased some brown hair rinse at a drug store in Bloomfield, Iowa. I proceeded to put it on but didn't realize that bleached-out hair is very porous. When the rinse grabbed hold and my hair dried, it was blue-black. No amount of shampooing could remove the color, and I definitely looked weird. For sure, it looked like the cheapest of clown wigs!

It was 11 p.m. when Don S. dropped me off at Maplehurst Manor and then drove on to Cedar Rapids. All the Dawsons were asleep, so I carefully made my way to the south room upstairs where the moonlight identified Bernie sleeping peacefully—until I flicked on the light and told him to "get over" as I crawled into bed. He was horrified by my appearance and probably thought he was having a terrible nightmare!

Five hours later, Dad shook me and demanded to know who I was. Then he stepped back in complete disgust and asked, "What the hell? Are you completely out of your mind?"

Mother seemed to take my appearance in stride, as I made up—lies again—some preposterous story. Patrick Leo and Thomas M., the "little boys," gawked silently.

Dad was in the midst of planting corn and, just like every other year, he was in a frenzy to get done before the rains came. This time, it seemed that I added to his troubles as his eyes—red from lack of sleep and, I'm sure, allergies—were even more inflamed.

Dad told me to carry out a sack of 50-pound seed corn. I was weak from a week of partying and not eating, so I struggled across the field with the half-hundred burden. He took one look at me and told me to get in the house and "don't let any neighbors see you."

I gladly complied and knew I had to do something about my hair. While Mother washed clothes in the basement using the double-tub Maytag, I searched through the pantry and found some Lux soap flakes and a bottle of ammonia. I mixed the two and soon had my hair and scalp slathered with the pure-white concoction. Lo and behold, within a half hour and after the rinse was removed, my hair was the beautiful yellow of a pale sunflower.

I called Don S. and asked him to convey me to the Iowa City bus depot that evening. At noon, Dad came in to see that I was now sun blond. I stayed out of his sight after that and was overjoyed when Don S. arrived around 7 p.m.

Kenney's was our first destination in Iowa City. By this time, I had my own makeup kit, which I carried almost everywhere just like Ms. Jennie. I put on my full makeup for Iowa City and had a light yellow outfit that matched my hair perfectly. My entrance to the bar created almost the same stir as it did in Houston, and we were invited to many parties. I knew some of the Iowa City crowd, and they were amazed at the changes in my appearance. There was so much commotion that the owner didn't even turn on the closing-time lights.

The next day, I boarded a bus for my return trip to St. Louis.

After returning and dyeing my hair light brownish-blond, I finally mustered up enough courage to go to the state employment office to seek a job. There were probably 35 to 40 job seekers ahead of me when I arrived, but I no sooner had taken a seat before I was summoned to the front desk.

A baldish little man beckoned me to sit, squinted at me behind thick glasses, and said, "You sweet young thing, I think I have a job for you." He was an older gay man I had seen at the bars but had never met. He gave me a piece of paper and directed me to Dunbar Pattern Company that was in the heart of the city's shoe-production district, which was one of the largest in the world at the time. The job was making shoe patterns for the many factories in the area.

When I arrived at Dunbar, Mr. W. looked me over and asked, "When can you come to work?"

"Right now," I said, which evidently was the right answer. He said to report Monday at 7 a.m. This happened on a Thursday, and I was elated and a little frightened at the prospect of again joining the workforce.

I took the signed paper back to the nice little man and, as I left and entered the street, a nicely dressed gentleman asked if he could take me out for a drink. What a great way to celebrate my new job! We ended up at his lovely home in a north suburb where I spent the night.

At noon the next day, I returned to 3910 Westminster and told Ms. Pierre and Ms. Jennie about my new job and then planned a wonderful weekend with my $25 gift from the suburban gentleman.

I had been introduced to the Stork Club on the outskirts of East St. Louis, where I knew the performers. They were female impersonators with names such as Georgia White, Gaye Dawn, Stormy Day, and Sunny Day. After the shows, the "girls" (impersonators) and their boyfriends, who were extremely handsome in my estimation, would go to the Blue Flame and the Ritz, two clubs that were not in the best areas. Gaye Dawn was very jealous of me, and I was not allowed to sit anywhere near her guy. (She didn't need to worry because I was never one to be known as a home-wrecker—I didn't want it done to me and it had been.)

We were some of the very few Caucasians who ventured into these areas—this was during the time of segregation. For example, Sportsman's Park, then-home of the St. Louis Cardinals baseball team, had segregated seating and facilities. In this era and place, few black people would want to be in a "white" area after dark.

But at the clubs in East St. Louis, the black bars' owners and patrons treated us as celebrities. They had great music and talented acts from the Harlem Club in Brooklyn,

Illinois. There was open gambling, dice, betting, and games in the back rooms. Some of the gentlemen occasionally would ask me to touch or pitch the dice for them. I had no idea what was a "good" number.

It got to the point that I would hitch a ride or walk across the Mississippi River bridge to get to East St. Louis to drink and play at the black clubs. Some of the white guys began calling me the "African Queen," the name of a movie from a few years earlier. Of course, it was said haughtily and derisively, as most of them were highly prejudiced. Even Ms. Jennie, Ms. Pierre, and Chuck, another friend, thought I was going a little too far when I ventured to these areas alone.

There were two Caucasian detectives on the East St. Louis police force who hated gays and blacks. If they spied us in a black bistro, they would arrest us and take us in for a terrific amount of harassment and outright obscene suggestions of what arts we were supposedly performing with "n*****s"—their word, not mine. We were berated and called the lowest of the low—even beneath whale shit, which is at the bottom of the ocean. We eventually would be released and told not to come back to East St. Louis.

Of course, we went back, and on a Saturday night in spring 1954, Ms. Jennie, Chuck, "Ms." David, Ms. Pierre, and I were arrested and lodged in the black women's section of the East St. Louis jail. The next morning, a Salvation Army woman tried to preach to us on our "lowliness" but was shouted down. That evening, with no money, we were released to find our way back across the Mississippi River. The detectives had confiscated all of our money.

Later, on a very hot Friday night in July, I got a ride to the Ritz. Swirling, pitch-black storm clouds began to gather as I stood in the doorway, which was open, of course, since there were no air-conditioned slum bars. I was dressed in all "summer white" with my expertly done—at least in my opinion—platinum hair.

I then spied the abusive detectives approaching. I could always spot them as they were clad in dark suits, ties, and hats, plus there is an extra sense that gay people and folks who live "on the edge" seem to possess.

As I made a lightning-quick decision to depart in haste, the wind and rains came as I ran through alleys and backyards with dogs barking. The streetlights had not come on, and lightning flashes were the only mode of illumination. I ran into fences, snagging my clothes, and sprinted through mud and puddles of water. I was completely soaked to the skin with my hair matted to my head in a combination of much hair spray and the pelting precipitation.

Finally, I arrived at the East St. Louis station where buses left for St. Louis every 20 minutes. I had escaped. Who knows what they would have done to me alone—especially after being warned and threatened with dire consequences if I were again found on the Illinois side of the river.

That was enough—even for me. I no longer went to the forbidden places of danger and great excitement. We did, however, still go to impersonator shows at the Stork Club. It was located in St. Clair County, Illinois, out of the evil detectives' jurisdiction.

Overall, the year 1954 and into June 1955 was a very fun time for Ms. Jennie and me. In full drag, we ventured to straight bars accompanied by cabdrivers Mac (with Jennie) and Tom with me, although Tom was not one of my favorite dates.

One evening, we met two handsome gentlemen from The Hill, an Italian neighborhood in St. Louis. "My" Italian gentleman was 100 percent different from cabdriver Tom—he was romantic.

I met another boyfriend who was stationed at Scott Air Force Base. He had wandered into the Stork Club. All these fellows were straight.

When Halloween arrived, I went to the Stork Club in full drag. It was the first time I appeared in full drag in the St. Louis area without the fear of being arrested (since it was Halloween). That night, a henchman of an ex-con tried to force me on stage for the "Miss Stork Club" competition. But I had not come to compete. I braced my high heels and refused to go on stage. It was only later that I learned I had defied a criminal gang!

Most queens are given or select the name of a woman they consider beautiful or that they admire for their moniker. When I first appeared on the gay scene in 1950–1951 in Iowa, I was Miss Jean. Then in St. Louis, I was either Miss Jean or Miss Gina after the beautiful Italian actress Gina Lollobrigida. Ms. Jennie added O'Hara as a last name because he said I reminded him of Maureen O'Hara, an Irish actress.

Leroy's third job in 1954 was at the Foot Long Hot Dog Company at 1217 North Kingshighway. Its menu featured A&W Root Beer and Coney Islands, along with delicious custard cones and shakes. Leroy started as a carhop and soon was working in the kitchen and at the inside counter.

Leroy's employers, who lived in and owned a three-story house nearby on Maple Avenue, were Buddy Banderet and his sister Peggy. They took such a liking to Leroy that he often was allowed to drive Buddy's late-model convertible. Buddy often had Clara, a businesswoman from Kentucky, at his side.

Since Leroy spoke of me often, Buddy, Peggy, and Clara wanted to meet me and decided to invite me to dinner. When I informed Ms. Jennie, who was sharing an apartment with me, about the dinner, "she" was very offended because he was not invited. I had noticed that Jennie tried to keep Leroy and me apart—I assumed he was jealous because he didn't have a sibling.

At 6 p.m. on a Thursday night, Leroy arrived to pick me up. I had to be back at Dunbar Pattern at 7 a.m. the next day, so I vowed to myself that I would be on my best behavior. My makeup never looked better, and I dressed in black with pink trim. The only flaw was that my silk hose had a hole in one big toe, and the painted toenail showed prominently. But who would see my toe? No problem.

Upon my arrival, I was greeted by people who were all new to me—so-called "piss-elegant" homosexuals who would not be caught dead in a gay bar but met in one another's homes under private circumstances. After all, this was the 1950s—the era of McCarthyism, fear of Communism, the bomb, and crew cuts. Raids on gay bars were not uncommon, and to be caught in drag in public was a crime.

Soon I was drinking martinis with Clara, the "life-of-the-party" businesswoman, and a young pleasant queen who always had a fresh drink ready for me. As I began to loosen up, I was discussing various "fish"—in gay lexicon, a woman is known as a "fish."

Clara demanded to know, "Well, what am I?"

"Oh honey, you are the biggest fish of all—a whale!" I replied. Everyone laughed loudly, although Buddy and Leroy appeared slightly nervous. But Clara accepted it as a "whale" of a compliment and wanted to be known as "the whale" from that moment on.

When the 8 p.m. dinner, which Peggy had lovingly prepared, was ready, I took my place at the table of 12. But I announced that I would only have another martini—eating always spoiled my alcoholic buzz. I was seated next to Martha, a blond who was with her partner.

During dinner, I reached across Martha and placed my hand on Buddy's knee, knowing he was beginning to have doubts about inviting me. He jumped and was a nervous wreck, so I quit picking on him and suggested that Martha and her partner were lovers, much to their consternation (it was not exactly proper dinner conversation).

At this point, Peggy proposed that she show me her new bedroom suite upstairs. After seeing it, I told her we had to get back downstairs because I needed a fresh martini. So I picked Peggy up to carry her down the steps; we made it about midway then tumbled the rest of the way down. Peggy had a couple of bruises, but I felt no pain since I was thoroughly saturated with gin.

By now, Buddy and Leroy were having furtive conversational exchanges. I joined the others in the kitchen where Martha was washing dishes. I noticed that her feet were about the same size as mine, so I asked if I could try on her shoes. She agreed, so I removed my shoe and a big red-painted toenail appeared. I was quite embarrassed, as I had forgotten about the hole in my hose.

About this time, Leroy appeared in the kitchen doorway after Buddy told him, "Get him out of here now!"

Leroy suggested that he take two of the other guests and me on a tour of the bus station, a well-known place to pick up tricks at any hour, day or night. My reply was that I was having fun and that he just wanted to go to the station "to get a big fat peter and suck on it!"

I looked up from adjusting Martha's shoe to see that the kitchen, which had been packed with people, was empty. Everyone had fled the room.

The next thing I remember is that Leroy and another individual helped me into the car and then later politely ejected me from the vehicle at 3910 Westminster. It was probably 10 to 10:30 p.m. I crawled up the steps to my second-floor apartment—the last I remember of that night.

At 5:30 the next morning, I awoke to martini vomit on the floor, which I apparently had slipped on before falling into bed, and a wave of destruction in the apartment. As I staggered to the kitchen, I saw several smashed chairs, dishes, and end tables. I was perplexed as I entered the bathroom and saw that the window had been broken and a jar of expensive John Robert Powers liquid makeup was splattered on the outside of the next-door apartment building across from the glass-less window.

I left for work wondering what had happened and where I had been the night before. The powerful drinks had stripped my memory of the disastrous dinner party. I didn't even recall Leroy driving me to it.

This hangover felt even worse than the one after the North English football game a few years earlier, so I struggled through the morning work at Dunbar. At lunchtime, I went to a neighboring tavern and had four very hot cups of coffee. I was still puzzled about what happened the previous night.

When I got home after work, Ms. Jennie was sitting on the front steps puffing on a cigarette. I walked up the steps to see the apartment was clean and in order. The atmosphere was tense for some time, and then he apologized for going on a rampage and our lives returned to "normal."

About three days later, Leroy called to inform me that Buddy's desire was to never see me again. However, Peggy and "The Whale" were not angry. Leroy told me all the things I had done and said, and I could tell that he was disappointed in my performance. I didn't return to that house on Maple Avenue until June 1963, when I moved into it (not with Buddy!).

Shortly after my 21st birthday in 1952, I received my mailed notice to report to assess my qualifications for the military.

In San Diego right after being discharged from the Marines, 1952.

Leroy in St. Louis, 1954.

I even wore jewelry over gloves for Halloween 1954.

Having a drink before going out in St. Louis in 1954. I had done my own hair.

Ready for a night out in my sleeveless dress, 1954. I had curled my hair just perfectly.

# My Mother

*You are wonderful and young*
*Like dance music*
*Played on a violin,*
*Or like a bubbling stream*
*Of the great mountain range.*
*In your eyes*
*Sparkles the dew on the grass.*
*To be in your presence*
*Is like a trip to paradise.*
*Your mellow voice delights me,*
*And I grow statue-like*
*looking at you.*
*I am pleased to be your son.*
*I hope that you will*
*Always be pleased with me.*

1949   Gene Dawson

# Chapter 6

## 1955–1959

On February 24, 1955, Mother called me at work to tell me that Uncle Johnny Agnew had died. His death began a period of great stress for me that lasted until almost the middle of 1963.

The management at Dunbar Pattern was pleased with my work so had given me a raise. I was making $60 a week, which was not bad for 1955. I worked from 7 a.m. to 4 p.m., with an hour off for lunch. By 8:30 every morning, I would think I had been there eight hours—the work was very boring.

Some of my coworkers asked Mr. W. to tell me that my cologne was too strong and was making them ill. I didn't even wear cologne, but I did apply scented moisturizer each morning before work. I reluctantly stopped using it.

The older men, most of whom had been employed there at least 40 years, were perplexed by this newcomer who wore his hair so thick and long—I had to use egg whites to "tame" it and slick it down to go to work. I was known as "Curly John" in the Eisenhower era of crew cuts.

Since I kept my eyebrows nearly shaved off, before work I had to skillfully use my eyebrow pencil to appear to have natural eyebrows. On some days, my pencil-created eyebrows would become shiny with body oils and the egg whites on my hair would dry out. By 4 p.m., my hair would be popping and poofing like bread rising! What a dilemma! I had to keep my hair long for weekend drag, and I had to have some semblance of eyebrows.

On a warm April day in 1955, as the sun shined from outside the 16th floor of the Dunbar building directly to my forehead, Mr. W. approached me and exclaimed, "Curly John, you have eyebrow pencil on!" I said I had to have something for my eyebrows and proceeded to make up a horrible lie. I told him that I was scalded on my forehead while butchering hogs and my eyebrows never grew back.

He huffed and puffed and said, matter-of-factly, "That's feminine," and walked away. He most certainly must have liked me or my work was exceptional because he didn't fire me. I cut off a little of my hair and tried to keep a low profile from then on.

Ms. Jennie and I now had an income of $60 a week from me and $25 from her dad. We could afford to buy good moisturizers, makeup, and feminine clothing.

We had boyfriends who were not gay appearing or acting. We had the two Italian guys from The Hill, Mac and Tom (the cabdrivers), Jim and Walt were in the Air Force based at Scott, and I was planning to meet the baseball player for a weekend in New Orleans when his team played there.

June arrived and my life seemed to have regained a little stability. Leroy visited occasionally but had little free time since he worked three jobs and nearly all weekends. He was not yet 21 and hardly ever drank—he didn't have time. I also kept in touch with Don S. in Cedar Rapids, who held out hope that I would return to Iowa.

Ever since I was a small child, I always prayed that I would be the first to die in our immediate and extended family. I just didn't think I could bear to lose a parent or one of my brothers. Uncle Leo Agnew's death was very devastating, but it wasn't completely shocking because we knew he was in danger each moment.

Mother, Grandma Agnew, and Aunt Anna Agnew wrote to me regularly. I'm sorry to say I neglected my end of the correspondence. Long-distance calls were very costly and had to be made at the telephone office. When I received a call and heard an operator announce, "Long distance from Parnell [or wherever]," I (like most everyone) would assume the message would not be pleasant. When I heard those words, all kinds of horrible thoughts would dash through my head because it seemed like these calls were messages of sorrow and tragedy 99 percent of the time.

At 5:10 p.m. on June 14, 1955, I had just returned to my apartment after work when the phone rang and the operator announced a long-distance call. It was Kenny, and I was totally unprepared for his words.

I thought he said Mother had been burned to death, but he repeated his words and said Mother had been burned and was barely alive. She was at Mercy Hospital in Iowa City.

I said I would contact Leroy. He and I hastily packed a couple of suitcases and made arrangements to take the 11:13 p.m. train to Burlington, Iowa. As I threw a few articles into my suitcase, I had no idea that I would not return to my apartment for 3½ months.

The last time I had seen Mother was the previous December. Leroy and I had taken the train to Cedar Rapids on December 23, and Don S. drove us to Parnell. We enjoyed Mother's delicious dressing—she made the best I've ever had—and all the holiday trimmings. She seemed very happy and had gained a little weight (she had anemia so always had been almost too thin). She also had her hair cut so it lay in natural waves, which was the way I remembered her from when I was little before she had her first permanent. To me, her natural waves were much prettier. That Christmas was the last image I have of her as happy and beautiful, and I carry it with me to this day.

Don S. met Leroy and me in Burlington and took us to the Iowa City hospital. Nothing could have prepared me for the sight I beheld as I entered her room.

It was like being hit in the face with a shovel. I had never been to an intensive-care burn unit, of course, and the sight of the various monitors and all the bottles and lines hanging above her was overwhelming.

But even more overwhelming was seeing that Mother had only two holes where her nose had been, only holes for ears, and her hair was completely burned off. She was full of pain suppressants, and her beautiful, large blue eyes looked even bigger and clearer than I had ever seen, or so it seemed.

It was a sight I never could have envisioned.

"I wish I could get comfortable so we can have a nice chat," she said.

The nurse came in then and told Leroy and me to leave the room. Dad was outside, very distraught of course, and the first thing he said was, "Do you have any money? This is going to cost a lot."

When I replied that I didn't, he gave me a very disgusted look and implied that this would not have happened if I had not moved to St. Louis. I immediately felt great guilt that continued until Father Browne and Grandma Agnew assured me that the fire was "God's will" and I had in no way caused it.

Mother had been burned at home. Our family had kept the kerosene-fueled refrigerator that performed as well as its electric counterpart, even though we had electricity at Maplehurst Manor. A small can with a lid and spout was used to convey kerosene from an outside barrel to a burner under the appliance.

On the afternoon of June 14, Mother decided to replenish the refrigerator's kerosene supply—unaware that someone had used the small can to carry gasoline, which is very combustible and a deadly combination when mixed with kerosene. The appliance had been hot, and fumes exploded as she started to fill the burner. Disregarding her own safety, she fought and extinguished the fire.

Patrick Leo was playing in the sandpile near the back door when Mother emerged on fire. She called for him to help her, as she tried to roll to smother the flames. He ran to get water and was successful in stopping the fire.

Thomas M. and Bernie sprinted to the field to tell Dad. Dad carried Mother to the dining room and placed her on a rollaway bed that we used as a couch. She was praying fervently with her rosary beads, which she carried at all times. Dr. Miller from North English was summoned.

Someone also alerted Father Browne. Her clothes were burned off and large pieces of skin were falling off her body, so she asked for a sheet saying that she felt naked. Father Browne was trying to comfort her, and she said, "Are you going to hear my confession or just make small talk?" Everyone left the room, and he heard her confession.

Then she was taken by ambulance to Iowa City, 30 miles away. Little Thomas M. and Patrick Leo never saw Mother again.

Mother "lived" or "slowly died" for 44 days. Her moans and groans could be heard throughout the hospital. She suffered the most awful pain, and she told me that she felt like she was in a "red hot skillet." Gangrene set in her leg burns, and she had awful bedsores. When her hair started to grow back in, it was totally snow white—the shock had changed her hair color, which had been brown with sprinklings of gray.

When I came back to the house after first visiting Mother, I couldn't even tell there had been a fire. The only difference was that the refrigerator was gone from the kitchen. Some neighbors had taken it away, and Rete Lawler had come to the house and cleaned.

During Mother's 44 days in the hospital, Bernie, who had just turned 15 in April, stayed on the farm and was the No. 1 laborer. The cows still had to be milked, and all the other chores had to be done. His work ethic always came naturally.

Patrick Leo and Thomas M. spent the six weeks at the homes of aunts and uncles. They spent some time with Uncle Bernard and Aunt Veronica Agnew and their son Bob, who was near their ages, and with Uncle Leo and Aunt Theresa O'Rourke, as some of their boys also were near their ages. But they spent most of that sad time at Uncle Harry and Aunt Mary Agnew's residence near Armah and played with their kids. Uncle Harry and Aunt Mary provided clean clothes, food, and shelter for them.

Just two days after Mother was burned, Great-Aunt Susie O'Brien (Grandma Agnew's sister) died at Mercy Hospital. Mother had visited her just days before. Then on June 21, Uncle Leo Costello died suddenly of a heart attack, and Aunt Marge was left with two children who were just seven and four.

But despite her husband's death, Aunt Marge, with Uncle Harry Agnew, took Patrick

Leo and Thomas M. to the hospital twice, but they were not allowed to go to Mother's room. Small children were not permitted to visit the intensive-care burn unit. Bernie was able to visit Mother a number of times.

Leroy was summoned to the hospital almost weekly when we thought Mother would not survive. Then, remarkably, she would stabilize. So he was flying back and forth between the airports in St. Louis and Cedar Rapids. By the end of the six weeks, his once-full head of blond hair was no more. Most all of his hair on top and at the crown fell out due to the stress, and he was bald for the rest of his life.

Kenny had his faithful Marlene to lean on. She washed his clothes, and she and her family were firm rocks of support and consolation.

One of us sat with Mother day and night. A few days before she died, she said, "It looks like it will be up to you and your Dad to take care of the little boys."

I told her she was going to get well, and she looked at me like "you know better than that." I really did but did not want to believe it.

I promised I would do whatever she wished, and I knew then that I would not return to my job in St. Louis.

Near midnight on July 28, 1955, the nurse announced, "Her breathing has stopped."

I was in the room with Dad, Kenny, Leroy, Uncle Bernard Agnew, the brother she had been a "mother" to for the first six weeks of his life, and Aunt Rose Agnew, who led prayers for the dying.

And then we departed for home.

The funeral was held August 1, 1955, at St. Joseph's in Parnell. It was said that it was the most well-attended funeral in the area up until that time. The church was packed, and there were people standing outside. After the funeral, the line of cars with people going from Parnell to Mother's burial at Armah Cemetery was many miles long.

The outpouring of sympathy and kindness enveloped us. Many people donated blood to replenish the supply at Mercy Hospital as Mother had many transfusions.

Unfortunately, our hospital insurance had not been paid and was two days past the grace period, so insurance covered nothing. Leroy had saved $1,400 from all his hard work at his jobs in St. Louis, and he gave it all to Dad, who was very, very hard up. Aunt Rose Agnew, who also was newly widowed, gave $500 to Dad.

The people of Parnell, Keswick, North English, Millersburg, and the surrounding communities arranged a drive and collected enough money to pay the hospital bill. Men used their farm machinery to harvest our oats, make our hay, and pick our corn. They helped with our chores, and the women sent large amounts of food.

I can never forget the outpouring of love, kindness, and sympathy from the community and from our immediate and extended families. And I can't forget all the prayers and expressions of sincere sympathy.

The very heart of our family had been ripped out, and the lives of John Dawson and his six sons had been drastically altered in the space of 44 agonizing days.

Thomas M. was seven years old when Mother died. He wondered, "Who will make our birthday cakes now?" He apparently remembered the good days and not the previous six weeks.

I would not be going back to Dunbar Shoe Pattern Company and my independent life in St. Louis. I did what any oldest child would do and honored Mother's request. I again would live at Maplehurst Manor, and I would help care for the younger boys.

I sent a letter to Dunbar, along with a copy of Mother's obituary. Mr. W. wrote back that the guys at work got a big kick out of hearing about me canning tomatoes. I had canned tomatoes with Grandma Agnew and a neighbor to preserve more than 100 quarts from Mother's huge and productive garden.

The letter from Mr. W. was accompanied by $33 to be used for masses for Mother. He also wrote that I could have my job back whenever I returned and to take as much time as I needed. Of course, I never went back to Dunbar. It would be eight years before I again would live in my favorite city.

So, overnight, I had been practically plucked from my free and independent existence and sent back to the farm. I felt like a tree transplanted from Canada to Panama—it was culture shock and such an abrupt change.

I again was an unpaid family worker, but my main focus was providing for Dad and the boys by running the house. My "nightlife" now consisted of ironing clothes (this was before wash and wear), deciding what to cook, and doing all the other duties required to do my best to raise three brothers.

Right after Mother died, I had to get the boys ready for the new school year. August 15, the Feast of the Assumption, was the traditional day that we and many other Catholic families would go to Mass and then to Cedar Rapids to purchase school clothes and supplies. J.C. Penney, Woolworths, Montgomery Ward, Kresge's, and Killian's enticed us with promises of terrific bargains on all things. Dad now had to buy clothes for the boys; Mother had been an excellent seamstress and made most of the boys' shirts, underwear, and other clothing.

After Mother's death, poor Dad was left completely rudder-less and fell into a deep depression. He withdrew and cried constantly. My feeble attempts at consoling words were rejected, and he turned against me.

"This would never have happened if you hadn't left the farm and moved to St. Louis," he would say.

Evidently, he was feeling great pangs of guilt because our family still had been using a kerosene-based refrigerator while everyone else we knew now had electrical appliances. So he transferred the blame to me. Because Grandma Agnew continued to insist that I had done no wrong and Father Browne consoled me and said Mother's death was God's will, I felt less guilt.

But Dad still blamed me. It got to the point that Dad would put his hands over his eyes to avoid glancing at me. So I no longer sat at the table during meals. I would just put everything on the table and go to another room.

If Dad wanted to convey something to me, he did it through my brothers. He would direct them to tell "him"—he never said my name—what he wished to convey, such as there would be extra farm helpers so I should cook enough for everyone.

As an aside, I received many compliments from the neighbors and farm helpers who ate my noon meals during these years. They were nice to hear. One often-made remark was that my meals were "as good or better than a woman could make." Often those who were the most vocal in their praise were those who I thought would consider housework with disdain or consider me a "sissy." I guess they were surprised.

Dad also expected me to take an active role as a laborer on the farm. We clashed on this point. I had told Mother I would care for my little brothers, not be an unpaid farm laborer. Dad barely eked out a living, and I expected no financial assistance.

At home, it was an unhappy time for everyone, but my three youngest brothers most certainly suffered greatly as they were caught in the middle and had just lost their beloved Mother. I could see Dad's intensely sad and forlorn look of almost hopelessness. I just didn't know what to do.

Dad was hospitalized for depression on two occasions: once in Cedar Rapids and the other time at Mercy in Iowa City. He also began getting terrible headaches and complained constantly of a buzzing in his ears and head, which persisted until his death in 1985.

My poor Dad—how he suffered.

I tried to cope, but I lost what little self-confidence I had and could not stand to be in a crowd of even five or six people. I would feel dizzy, and before fainting, I would break into a cold sweat.

It even was nerve-wracking to attend Mass, so I started to sit apart from Dad and my brothers. I moved to a seat in the east wing of St. Joseph's. The wing had very few occupants and was out of view from the other parishioners sitting in the church's main body.

Don S., my "knight in not-so-shining armor," entered the picture once again. Starting that October after Mother's death, he arrived at the farm at 9 p.m. every other Saturday to pick me up. We would be back at Harold's Klub in Cedar Rapids by 10 p.m. I would have two hours there before it closed, and Don S. would drive me back to the farmstead after that.

Don S. bought me the few clothes I needed since I didn't go anywhere. He also gave me $30 to $50 every month—he said to use it to buy candy or something for the kids.

Don S. transported me back and forth for the almost four years I again lived at Maplehurst Manor. With the little money he gave me, I saved enough to visit Leroy and Ms. Jennie in St. Louis for a week or two each year.

On Mother's Day 1956, a group of my gay friends from Cedar Rapids sent me a card and a bottle of White Shoulders perfume. I felt uneasy about the card and gift because nobody could take the place of Mother, but they persisted. They said I was doing my very best to be a "mother figure" to my two youngest brothers, ages eight and 11 at the time. Now on reflection, I think it was a very kind and thoughtful deed, and I loved the fragrance of the perfume.

Grandma Agnew and Aunt Anna Agnew made sure that Patrick Leo and Thomas M. had birthday cakes, and after I left, Kenny and Marlene had birthday parties for them.

Kenny and Marlene were married on November 10, 1956. Leroy arrived on November 8, and we cleaned, scrubbed, and waxed the floors in all the rooms of the house. We did not have carpeting but linoleum on some floors. Aunts Marie Dawson LaMere and Catherine Dawson then arrived for the big event.

I was Kenny's best man, and Leroy was a groomsman. The rehearsal was held the night before at St. Michael's Catholic Church in Holbrook. After the rehearsal, Leroy and I took Dad's car and picked up two Parnell friends.

On this cold fall night, we proceeded to tip over some outside toilets at several rural schools and at the homes of some crabby neighbors. We all participated enthusiastically as we quashed our thirst with several six packs of beer. We wound up at the all-night diner located at the intersection of Highways 149 and 6. The four of us made plans to meet at the Danceland Ballroom in Cedar Rapids after the next day's wedding reception and then spend the night at a motel.

After our meal at the all-night diner, we arrived at the John P. Dawson residence at about 5:30 a.m., still feeling no pain. Aunt Marie greeted us as she lit the cookstove range to prepare breakfast.

Kenny descended the stairs and declared, "Thanks a lot for staying out all night on my wedding day!"

"You're welcome!" I answered merrily as he slammed the outside door on his way to milk the cows.

Dad, who was still in a deep depression, was in bed, and pleas from Aunts Marie and Catherine to get ready went unheeded. Finally, Grandma Agnew had a heart-to-heart talk with him, and he attended the wedding.

The Dawsons were so poor. Not long before the wedding, five of our best-producing cows broke out one night and indulged in bushels of soybeans in a harvest wagon. The beans expanded in their stomachs, which caused them to bloat, and they died painful deaths. When it rains, it pours—their deaths reduced our milk production and their sale value to zero. I don't think Dad had enough money to even buy a wedding gift for Kenny and Marlene.

On the day of the wedding, my hangover—of monumental proportion—began about the same time as the ceremony. During the wedding, I started to get weak and dizzy and thought, "Oh no, I just can't faint during the service!" Thankfully, instead, I broke out in a cold sweat. I made it through the Mass and was able to sign the papers required of the best man.

The wedding reception was held in a banquet room at the Montrose Hotel, which also was the home of the gay bar, the Hurdle & Halter. We Parnellians took over the bar during the afternoon. Leroy and I met a group of Afrikaners, Dutch descendants of the original European colonizers of South Africa, who were on a farm tour. The gay crowd wouldn't arrive until 9 p.m. or later.

By 4 that afternoon, the newlyweds had departed on their honeymoon, and most of the Parnell revelers headed home. After more enjoyable drinking with the very friendly foreigners, Leroy and I meandered to the Danceland Ballroom. We met some of my gay friends from the Cedar Rapids area. They included George, who originally was from a neighboring town; "Mae," who hailed from northeast Iowa; "Dina," from central Iowa; and "Inez," from eastern Iowa.

Our Parnell friends from the night before failed to appear, and I took a cab to George's home at about 10 p.m. Leroy and Mae spent most of the night with the nice Afrikaners.

Don S. took me back to Parnell on Monday night. By then, Leroy had returned to St. Louis and Bernie had taken Aunts Marie and Catherine to the bus station. So that is how I celebrated my brother Kenny's wedding weekend.

From June 14, 1955, to May 18, 1959, I learned how to plan and cook meals and bake bread, cakes, cookies, etc. However, I never did master the art of making a good piecrust.

Just like Mother, I made our laundry soap (lard or grease, 20 Mule Team Borax, and lye), ironed our clothes, polished the "little boys'" shoes, had a huge and productive garden, canned vegetables, made grape juice and jam, and did whatever had to be done. Ethel Shannahan, Kenny's mother-in-law, gave me ground cherries, which I love, and I made jam from them.

Bernie and I also raised geese on a 50-50 basis; one year we had 45 to sell at Thanksgiving time.

While in the pasture one day, I found a nest of 15 pheasant eggs. I carefully carried them to the house and placed them in an incubator that we had in the living room (which featured ornate lighting and a fireplace).

There were goose eggs also in the incubator, and I turned all the eggs each day (setting eggs have to be turned just as a bird's mother would do). I also occasionally sprinkled them with room-temperature water. A brooding goose does this with her damp feathers after her daily break to swim, eat, drink, and defecate.

I lifted the top from the incubator one morning, and 15 little pheasants leaped out and scurried for cover under chairs, the couch, and in all directions. They were very tiny and reminded me of medium-sized mice in terms of size and agility. I finally captured them and put them in a pen, which was fashioned from discarded window screens, in the grassy yard. The pheasants were so tiny that all but one managed to squeeze out and probably were eaten by a farm varmint.

"Birdie," the lone survivor, thought it was either a "Gene" or a goose or both. When I gave mash, cracked corn, and water to the goslings, Birdie dined with them but declined the urge to follow the young geese into water for a swim and instead started to follow me.

Later when she learned to fly, I would call, "Birdie, Birdie, Birdie," and then hear the whirring sound of small wings as she appeared. When I hoed the garden, Birdie was right there to devour the choice bugs and worms. As darkness descended in the evenings, I would sit on the front-porch swing and Birdie would fly up and roost alongside me. Then I would carry her to the goose shed to spend the night.

On one occasion, Birdie and I were in the front yard when Jimmy Murphy and Robert "Pug" Sheridan drove by and waved. Suddenly they stopped, backed up, and Jimmy said, "Were we imagining things or was that a pheasant following you?" I told them their minds weren't playing tricks on them and pointed out Birdie as I called her.

I had discovered that Birdie was a girl, as she had the camouflage colors of female pheasants and not the gaudy plumes and long tails of the males. I was glad—hoping she would survive hunting season. It was against the law to shoot female pheasants, but that would not deter some unethical slaughterer.

As late fall arrived, Birdie hung out with the large flock of young geese in the goose pasture. After the geese were sold to become centerpieces of Thanksgiving and other holiday feasts, I lost track of Birdie and was fearful that she could have been an easy target because of her trust for humans.

As an aside, I hated the start of hunting season (usually around November 11) and the accompanying "boom-boom" of the shotguns. I hoped the pheasants would escape the pseudo-warriors who descended on the farms from out of the county and state. Some did not even have the courtesy to ask if they could tramp in our fields and, if confronted, would have the audacity to get an attitude, considering us rural folks to be "country bumpkins," "plough boys," or "Hoosiers" (they even had the state wrong since Indiana is the "Hoosier" state). There were a few, however, who sought permission, some even ahead of time, and brought a gift of whiskey or the like, and sometimes even the game they managed to shoot.

In the late spring of the following year, I was hoeing in the garden when a mother pheasant appeared with several babies who were about a week old. She showed no fear and hung around for a few minutes. I'm convinced it was Birdie, but since all hen pheasants look alike, I can't be absolutely sure. Realistically, though, no wild bird would be so fearless. I think she was a proud mama showing off her new family.

Kenny and Marlene welcomed my first nephew, Terry, on September 15, 1957. It was the same day, I always remind him, that the mongrel female dog that Leroy had given to Patrick Leo and Thomas M. for Christmas 1956 had a litter of 15—yes 15—puppies! I tell Terry that is how I remember his birthday.

In the fall of 1957, the local 4-H clubs had their annual potluck at the Parnell school gym. I knew Dad would not go, so I prepared a nice beef roast and accompanied Thomas M. and Patrick Leo to the event (I can't remember if Bernie went). All the other adults in attendance were parents, and most of the kids had both parents there.

The only other adult who wasn't a parent was the Iowa County Extension leader from Marengo. I was sitting alone, and he was kind enough to ask if he could sit with me.

After this event, I didn't attend any more 4-H functions because I was a little uneasy with the older married couples, who also, it seemed, were not totally relaxed with me. Perhaps this was because I had worn some makeup; I thought I had applied it so skillfully that no one would notice.

During 1958 and early 1959, I could be found at Grandma Agnew's house in North English on most Thursdays, especially during the peak of garden production. I still didn't have a driver's license, but I took Dad's old 1932 Chevrolet to her home where we would can vegetables and make lots of grape jelly, courtesy of Grandma's very productive grape arbor. On a few occasions, we would purchase a fat, healthy hen and have creamed chicken on toast and can the remaining pieces for a hot soup on a wintry day.

A few times, I would arrive and suggest to Grandma that we go on a "tour." She always was willing, saying, "Let me get my coat," and off we would go. First we would go to Aunt Alice and Uncle Kermie Herr's residence near Delta, then back through Keswick to Aunt Theresa and Uncle Leo O'Rourke's abode, and then to the Armah church and cemetery.

Grandma would suggest that we arrive at Uncle Harry and Aunt Mary Agnew's at noontime. She proclaimed that they always had plenty of food to share with the "tour team" since they had several small children and Mary always had a bountiful noon meal. On one such visit, I recall Mary's ham and navy bean soup—delicious!

After this stop, we would go to Uncle Bernard and Aunt Veronica Agnew's, which also was the Agnew homestead. The last stop was at the Millersburg home of Aunt Marge Costello and her children, Rosemary and Michael.

Grandma always liked to go visiting, and I thoroughly enjoyed the trips, too. I would get back home soon after Thomas M., Patrick Leo, and Bernie returned from school. These are great memories of time spent with Grandma.

Grandma started referring to me as "she," which surprised me, and I pretended not to notice. However, Aunt Anna said, "Mom, you just called Gene 'she'!"

Grandma shrugged her shoulders and replied, "Well, he can do anything a woman can."

During my weekends in Cedar Rapids, I met twins Dan and David, who were very handsome, blond, and blue-eyed. They wandered into Harold's Klub one night and then attended an "after-bar closing" get-together at George's residence. Although I was accompanied by the ever-present Don S., I managed to get friendly with Dan. Ms. Inez was attracted to David.

Soon Mae and Inez would drive to Parnell to pick me up, and we would return to Cedar Rapids to go barhopping with the twins. The twins never seemed to have jobs—their father would slip them some pocket change. I was madly in love with Dan, but there was too much distance between us. Plus, I had to sneak around to avoid the smothering Don S. Then there was Lillian, a buxom blond who was Dan's female girlfriend.

I would be so depressed about Mother's death, Dan, and my whole situation that on some days after my brothers went to school, I would put some food out for Dad's noon lunch and then go to my northwest bedroom, lock the door, and weep for hours. I would huddle in the bed with my head under the covers. About 4 p.m., when my brothers would be returning from school, I would force myself to get up. This went on for two or three weeks, and then I resolved to overcome this depressed stage and force myself to keep occupied with cleaning, canning, gardening, and my other duties.

Neighbor Loretta (Mrs. Ray) Murphy also could cheer me up when I was down in the dumps. I would walk the quarter mile to her home where she was caring for her 10 children. She always had a smile on her face and a cheerful greeting. After 45 minutes with her, I always felt better.

One November morning in 1957 or 1958, I was surprised by a visit from cousin Jim O'Rourke and three of his friends from English Valleys High School (formerly North English High School). The foursome came through the kitchen door announcing that they were kidnapping me for the day! They were all teenagers, and I was 26 or 27 but could pass for 20 or 21. Soon we were on our way to Johnson County where we knew beer could be purchased with no questions asked if you were tall enough to stand at the bar.

Jim had buttered me up as his "handsome" cousin who was a "hood" in St. Louis and wore his hair in a duck's tail (which I did). It seemed they were all in awe of me, and I had to be on my best and most macho—very difficult—behavior.

After returning to Parnell, they were amazed by my ability and agility with the Hula Hoop! We drank large quantities of beer but had to drink some coffee, too, since they had to be back to the high-school parking lot when school was dismissed for the day.

On one of my weeklong visits to see Leroy in St. Louis between 1956 and 1959, I received my "Maudie" nickname. I rented a room at a downtown hotel near Uncle John's and Entre Nous in the sixth block of Pine Street. I couldn't stay with Leroy as he lived with Buddy Banderet and his sister Peggy who owned the Foot Long Hot Dog. I had been banned from their presence since the 1954 dinner party where I made a drunken spectacle of myself.

On the first night I went to Uncle John's, I made the acquaintance of a young Native-American man who went by the name "Indian Chuck." Indian Chuck ended up spending the night with me. He was unemployed so had nothing to do during the day, and I found it difficult to shake him but finally thought I had. But that first night after he was gone, I was enjoying a peaceful sleep when I was awakened by someone crawling through the transom window above the hotel-room door. Indian Chuck presented himself as the uninvited guest! He proclaimed that he had been searching for me and wanted to be sure I was OK.

A few nights later, as Leroy joined me for evening excursions, I met a James Dean-wannabe who could pass for the real person. (Dean had been a popular actor of the time but was killed in a car accident in September 1955.) Immediately I was smitten, and the Dean-wannabe invited me to his room at a squalid hotel near my headquarters. He handed me the key to his room and told me to arrive five minutes later. I had consumed several drinks by the time I left for his room.

Again Indian Chuck was looking for me, and this time Leroy was with him. They saw me enter "James Dean's" hotel where I went to the third floor to find his room. I thought he said 318—I didn't realize that the key, which was in my pocket, had the room number on it. How stupid!

On the lower floors, Indian Chuck was going through the hallways and corridors shouting, "Maude, Maude, Maude." He had forgotten my name, or perhaps I hadn't told him. As I was pounding on the doors on the third floor to no avail, Leroy was getting a tremendous charge out of Indian Chuck's loud shouts. Leroy started calling me "Maude" or "Maudie" often after that, and Patrick Leo still uses the nickname for me.

I don't remember how the night ended except I did not locate the phantom James Dean. When I cleaned out my pockets upon returning to Iowa, I found the key. It very plainly had "218" on it. I had been on the wrong floor.

I was still having a difficult time going to confession in Parnell with Father Browne or going to any neighboring priest. That weighed heavily on me, as I could not receive Holy Communion, which further assured Dad that I most certainly was a very bad person.

So when I heard that a visiting priest was at St. Michael's parish in Holbrook for the summer of 1958, I decided this was my opportunity to confess all to a complete stranger. I took Thomas M. with me for a little moral support, but there were no other folks in the church that Friday afternoon until a tall man came down the aisle and entered the confessional. He stared intently at me as I knelt in contemplation before I would enter the priest's cubicle and give my confession.

I thought of leaving then and there but went and opened the confessional door and was soon telling all my sins I could remember. The tall man was the visiting priest, Father Janssen. When I finished my confession, Father Janssen stunned me by requesting that I come and see him at the church rectory the next evening. I quickly told him that I was leaving for St. Louis to visit my brother and would be gone for approximately two weeks. So he told me to call him as soon as I returned. I said I would, and he gave me absolution.

In St. Louis, I stayed with Ms. Jennie at "her" tiny apartment on Westminster Place. I couldn't stay with Leroy because he now was in a sleeping room on West Pine Street that did not allow visitors. So he would come over to visit, and we went to the bars and all-night clubs in East St. Louis. I had a "whee" of a time.

The only really disturbing thing about my visit occurred on the last night. Ms. Jennie and I were sharing a bed when "she" suddenly threw "herself" on top of me. She began to kiss me passionately and declare that "she" had fallen in love with me and wanted a sexual relationship.

I was completely turned off and shocked—I always considered Ms. Jennie to be a "sister," just like a very good, nonsexual friend in the heterosexual world. That was the near-end of my friendship with Ms. Jennie.

When I arrived back at Maplehurst Manor, I silently debated for most of a day about whether to call Father Janssen. Knowing that I had promised to do so while in a confessional, I prepared myself to call. I tried twice and got no answer. I decided that if he didn't answer when I made a third call, I would have fulfilled my obligation.

But, of course, on the third ring of the third call, a male voice answered, and I asked to speak to Father Janssen. The reply was a hearty, "Speaking!" After I explained who I was and why I was calling, I asked when I should pay him a visit.

He suggested that "now" would be a great time to meet. It was around 6 p.m. when I set off for Holbrook in Dad's car after telling my little brothers that I would be back soon.

Father Janssen welcomed me and gave me a tour of the rectory (priest's residence) and St. Michael's church, which were directly across the country gravel road from each other. When we returned to the house, I was amazed when he opened the refrigerator, grabbed a milk carton, and drank directly from the carton—just like I (a "regular" non-holy individual) would do!

Then he threw a purple confessional stole around his neck and shoulders and said, "I'll hear your confession now. Just have a seat, be comfortable, and tell me all about your St. Louis trip." I did so and, evidently, whatever was sinful was forgiven. I returned home about an hour and a half later. I had told him about my friend Mae in Cedar Rapids and said "she" probably also would want him to hear "her" confession.

So it came to be that Mae would arrive in his little Volkswagen and spend the night at the farm, out of Dad's sight, of course. Then we would spend the next day in Holbrook where we listened and danced to all the latest popular records of that time. Father Janssen also had a Hula Hoop, which I loved and was very adept at using to gyrate to the music.

During one visit, Father got a call to come to Davenport, so Mae and I went to Iowa City to barhop with the gay college kids and a group from Waterloo, one of whom was a disc jockey who dedicated songs to me. We left for Iowa City a few minutes before Father Janssen started off for Davenport, and soon he passed us in a cloud of Holbrook-road gravel dust. He was speeding with the horn blaring, and he smiled and waved.

After Father Janssen's temporary summer assignment ended, I never saw him again. As I was writing the first part of this book, I was surprised to learn (via the Internet) that Father Janssen had multiple credible allegations of sexually abusing boys and that he was defrocked as a priest. I never saw anything to indicate this when I was with him. Our summer friendship was just that—friendship—he never "came on" to Mae or me.

During these four years of living at Maplehurst Manor, it would get to the point that I felt that I couldn't take it anymore because of the strain between Dad and me. On two occasions, I phoned Aunt Marge Costello and then grabbed my few pieces of clothing before she came and took me from the house. Within a day or two on both occasions, Dad dispatched Bernie to travel to Aunt Marge's house in Millersburg to request that I return and say that things would be "different." They never were, and I was just as much to blame or maybe even more so because of my stubbornness.

The second time Bernie came for me, he arrived about 10 a.m. He said that Dad said: "Please come home; there are seven hired and volunteer laborers there to help fill silo, and they will need dinner."

I don't know how I did it, but by 12:15 p.m., I had prepared a dinner of roast beef, mashed potatoes, gravy, green-bean casserole, and chocolate cake. I do remember that I cooked the two roasts, onions, and various spices on top of the stove in heavy pans in boiling water. That left the oven available for the cake and the casserole. I amazed myself!

By May 18, 1959, I had been back at the farm for a long three years and 11 months. Patrick Leo was 14½, and Thomas M. was 11½. Bernie had just turned 19 and had graduated from Parnell High School.

It was a damp, blustery day, and the hogs escaped from their pens. Unbeknownst to me, they headed for our lawn and proceeded to do what hogs do to damp, lush earth—they rooted and rooted and rooted. It looked as if parts of the lawn had been plowed for crops.

I was dusting the long upstairs hallway when I heard a very loud voice cursing me and describing me with unkind words such as "no good," "lazy," and "doesn't care about anything." I plopped down the dust mop and then put my clothes and the few plates and cups I had retrieved from my St. Louis apartment into a box. Then I placed a long-distance call to Don S. and told him to come and get me. His aged mother had died recently, and he had the house in Cedar Rapids all to himself.

"I will never come back here," I thought to myself. I wept while I thought about leaving my brothers and the turbulence in their lives caused by the strife between Dad and me.

As Bernie, Patrick Leo, and Thomas M. watched television, I told them that I was leaving and wouldn't be back. Since the three had heard this before and I always was back within a few days, Bernie and Patrick Leo barely acknowledged my announcement.

I then went to wait on the front-porch steps for my "savior" to appear. A few minutes later, Thomas M. came to the porch to say goodbye and that he hoped I would come back, but he understood. He was wise beyond his years—he had been through so much.

Soon I saw the headlights shining through the darkness. With a feeling of sadness and wondering, "what's next," I entered the car and wept for awhile as Don S. drove north. I knew that this time I would not be returning—I was out of Bernie's range for coming to retrieve me.


Forty minutes after leaving Maplehurst Manor, we arrived at the Cedar Rapids home of Don S. This mostly would be my home until I would move back to St. Louis in June of 1963.

I was an unskilled 28-year-old who had no idea of what I would do with my life. I knew that being an unpaid farm laborer staying at Maplehurst Manor was like being on a treadmill. I had not a penny to my name.

In 1955 (notice my beautiful earrings).

A pose in 1956.

At Armah Cemetery, 1956; driving without a license!

At Harold's Klub in Cedar Rapids, 1957.

Ready to go out, 1957.

Don S. proposed that I further my education, and he would pay all tuition and costs. I could live with him and not have to contribute rent or food money. I was penniless and homeless. I really had no other choice.

I thought about a Christmas card that Ms. Jennie had sent me in 1958. She had written, "Kid, I've become a capitalist!" She had attended cosmetology school in St. Louis and now had a booth at an exclusive salon in St. Louis County and was doing very well.

After pondering the situation, I realized I had a natural talent for styling and cutting, and so I visited the Paris Academy of Beauty Culture in Cedar Rapids to see about enrolling. I met Mrs. F., who was the manager, and Dr. Lamb, the owner. They interviewed me, and Dr. Lamb warned that there would be no dating of female students!

He need not have worried. I would be there for the education.

In late May, Father Browne arranged for me to come to the Parnell rectory for an afternoon. Bernie, Patrick Leo, and Thomas M. arrived. Happiness engulfed me upon seeing my little brothers!

The following Saturday, Don S. took me to Grandma and Aunt Anna's home in North English to stay overnight. After we attended Sunday Mass, Dad and my brothers arrived for Sunday dinner. Grandma and Aunt Anna were trying to promote a reconciliation. Dad and I were both uneasy but did exchange greetings when we were left alone on the front porch.

I still was determined to not visit Maplehurst Manor. However, to be obstinate or stubborn is not becoming. Thank God, we can change our minds.

The next classes at Paris Academy began in June, so I had a couple weeks to gadabout during the day while Don S. was at work. A very handsome 21-year-old named Rick would arrive at the house, and I would climb into his convertible. Rick's parents were "well-off," and he had his own boat and a light airplane that we easily could push around at the rural airport where they were stored.

Tranquil is the word to describe the peaceful flowing of the Cedar River upstream from metro Cedar Rapids. We spent beautiful days on his boat as we floated on the river.

On a slightly windy day, we pushed the plane out of the hangar and soon were airborne. I had never flown before (except the time I jumped 10 feet at the age of 11 while chasing a chicken at Uncle Leo and Aunt Theresa O'Rourke's!). The plane was very fragile, and when he turned it, it seemed the wind held us in place. When he asked me to pull up on the "steering wheel," we shot, nose up, straight up in the air! I was happy when we landed without incident. But the view of the fields and plots below was like a beautiful patchwork quilt.

Rick urged me to move away from Don S. Rick was relocating to the East Coast and declared if I were still in Cedar Rapids when he came back to visit, he would kidnap me and take me back with him. We corresponded for a few months and then lost contact.

Don S. would have been furious if he had known I was having such a good time while he worked. I always was back at his residence by 4:30 p.m.

Another day, Mae and I went to Waterloo to visit our disc-jockey friend who dedicated songs to me as "Jeannie, the sweetest of all from CR."

On other days, friend George "Georgia" and I toured the African-American bar, the

Midway Lounge on the outer edge of southeast Cedar Rapids, where we were treated royally. I again was home by 4:30 p.m. to escape the wrath of Don S.

We were welcome at the African-Americans' social gathering place, but at the downtown bars, the barmaids would often break their glasses when they finished their drinks. The beams of hatred shot from the Caucasian patrons' eyes were sad to observe.

Another incident stands out in my mind. Ms. Inez and I were in a little Volkswagen when we were chased by a gang on motorcycles. We evaded them after nearly being trapped on a dead-end street. Inez put that little car in reverse and backed out as fast as it would go as cyclists sped by going toward the end of the street. When we arrived at Inez's home, we jumped out and raced up the front-porch steps to see four young men by the portico. Thinking they were the terrifying "hoodlums" on the cycles, Inez pounded on the front door frantically screaming, "Mama, Mama, Mama!"

Inez was so nervous that he couldn't get the house key inserted into the lock. The guys looked bewildered as they left the porch, and when Inez's mother opened the door, we were told they were Inez's teenage nephew and friends. It scared the hell out of us, but we had outmaneuvered the gang!

When I revealed to Uncle Harry Agnew that I was going to beauty school, he listened and inquired, "You mean barber school, don't you?"

When I explained that I would be going to a school with about a 95 percent female enrollment to learn how to work on women's and children's hair, he replied, "Well, somebody has to do it, and you can probably make a good living." He always was ready to listen to my problems and give good and encouraging advice.

When I began classes on June 4, 1959, there were 103 girls and four males (including me) at the academy. All the guys were in my new class, along with 39 girls. Carl, who was a dancer/instructor, was in my class, along with Bob, who was from a small town about 25 miles away. Bob drove from home each day and gave me rides to and from school. He and his girlfriend later opened a shop. A young man who was married with two children was the other male in the class.

Our textbook had information about bones, structure, nerves, and circulation of the body, and included chapters on hair, electrolysis, and manicuring. I took to hairstyling like a duck to water and received 100 percent on all written tests at the end of each chapter.

After weeks of practicing on fellow students, we were sent out "on the floor" where we styled and cut the hair of the public. They received our services at very low prices because basically we were using them for our learning experience. There were six instructors who patrolled the 40-chair room and had to approve everything we did.

At Paris Academy, I continued to learn and enjoyed the friendships of my fellow students. The girls, most of whom were quite beautiful, would sign up to go on 15-minute breaks with me. Six students were allowed to go on break at a time, and I always had five girls "hanging" on me at the Butterfly Cafe. We enjoyed the breaded tenderloin (the very best I ever had) and lemonade or iced tea. The young guys who hung out at the cafe often asked me to introduce them to certain girls. At least one marriage resulted from my playing Cupid.

During the summer of 1959, a furnace-type heat hung over Cedar Rapids like a blanket. The heat was so intense that three or four girls passed out at school, and we (most of the students) thought we should be dismissed and that air conditioning should be installed.

So there was a meeting, which was led by classmate Carl, after school one day. We all agreed to go on strike the next day. So the next morning, Bob picked me up, along with Carl and four other classmates. We spent the hot day driving around town and observing Mrs. F. frantically coming in and out of the school. The school was losing money since there usually were 75 to 100 customers each day.

Back at home, I related to Don S. what we had done. He was extremely pissed—after all, he was paying for me to attend the school.

When we returned to the school the next morning, the owner was there to greet us. He and Mrs. F. said they wished to speak individually with the seven of us who had been in the car the previous day. After threatening to immediately expel us—scaring the hell out of us—they agreed that we could continue our education but had to attend 100 more hours of class.

Don S. was very strict, and I had to get home right after school. When Bob would pull up the car at Don S.'s house, I could see Don S.'s silhouette behind a lace curtain as he watched, hands on his hips, to see if I lingered in the car to chat.

Bob eventually invited me to accompany him to his home to meet his parents and girlfriend. Finally, Don S. reluctantly agreed, and I rode home with Bob on a Wednesday evening. His parents were very nice, as was his girlfriend. I recall that his mother cooked delicious Swiss steak. I met several of his buddies around his age (10 years younger than I) and too young to buy beer. Bob and I slept in separate rooms, and an innocent time was had by all.

After much discussion, it was agreed that I could invite Bob for an overnight stay. Don S. was so convinced that Bob and I were having an affair that he decided to spend the night at his aunt's nearby home. That way, he said, Bob could sleep in his bed and I in mine—no sleeping together in my room!

On the evening of Bob's overnight stay, he and I visited a friend of his who lived a few miles outside of Cedar Rapids. Bob got plastered, very sick, and practically passed out. I had to drive back to Cedar Rapids—even though I had no license and had never driven in a city. I was extremely nervous and slightly intoxicated but finally made it back to Don S.'s house.

I drug, lifted, and almost carried Bob into the house and then to the upstairs bathroom where I tried to clean his vomit-covered face. I finally got him into Don S.'s bed but forgot to turn off the water in the sink. Bob looked so cozy when I finally got him tucked in.

However, I soon heard water cascading over the sides of the sink. The bathroom floor had two to three inches of water, and it was running into the hall. To top it off, the water had soaked the bathroom floor and was dripping methodically into the kitchen from the ceiling above. No amount of towels or mopping could undo the damage, especially to the kitchen ceiling. I was fit to be tied.

Bob, who had a terrific hangover, and I went to school the next morning, and I knew the shit would hit the fan when I returned after classes were over. And it certainly did. Don S. accused me of all sorts of immoral acts and of being a drunken, unappreciative, conniving slut and other choice monikers. Of course, we were never allowed to stay overnight with each other again.

Each time I entered the kitchen, I had to see the stained ceiling that looked as if it could collapse over the kitchen table. I had many feelings of guilt.

Near Halloween, I went to an afternoon and evening costume ball at an African-American lodge. Ms. Dina, Ms. Inez, and I eagerly awaited the event. I ordered my dress from the Frederick's of Hollywood catalog, which featured the sexiest of garments. The dress was formfitting and accentuated all the places it should. I loaned my black knit dress and imitation fur stole to Inez, and Ms. Dina dressed for a garden party—big sun hat, etc.

I was taken aback to see some of the gorgeous girls who were fellow Paris Academy students in the crowd, but I only saw one from my class. A couple of my college-age clients were there with their dates. I tried to ignore them as they leaned and gawked, trying to determine if they recognized me, as their guys had said I was "Miss Jean."

Three professional female impersonators from Chicago were in attendance to judge and select the costume winner. I was escorted across the stage and did a few model poses and steps. It was exciting, as the band accompanied each of the contestants: Ms. Dina, Ms. Inez, and myself.

The prizes were to be $75 for first place, $50 for second, and $25 for third. Inez opened the second-place envelope and did not appear to be pleased. As I opened my envelope, I could understand the disappointed looks on the faces of Inez and Dina—$3 was my award, $2 went to Inez, and $1 to Dina!

Actually, the three of us hadn't even thought of being awarded anything or that we would be the only so-called contestants. Therefore, we just went on with the enjoyable evening, pretending the totals were as announced.

As I had more drinks, I relaxed and carried on, not caring what the other students or clients thought. I never saw any of them again—not even my college-girl clients. Upon reflection, they probably did not want anyone to know they had been seen with black men since interracial dating was considered taboo. The beauty salons were not yet integrated, nor were the uptown restaurants and taverns.

At cousin MaryAnn Harris and Larry Petermeier's wedding reception with Aunt Ethel Harris, Aunt Helen Hartzell, and Aunt Marge Costello, 1959.

Christmas 1959: cousins Michael Costello and Mary-Ann Harris Petermeier, Grandma Minnie Agnew, Aunt Anna Agnew, me, and cousin Charlotte Agnew (later Pingel).

In my masculine jacket, 1959.

I was dressed as a man, but my eyelashes and eyebrows certainly didn't look masculine.

# PART THREE:

## City Girl

1960–

Ready for a night out in Cedar Rapids in my fake "mink" stole, 1962.

# Chapter 7

## 1960–1964

The Paris Academy beauty course lasted approximately 11 months. Since I was part of the previous summer's "strike" at the school, the resulting 100 hours of extra classes delayed my appearance before the state board in Des Moines. But I cut some time by arriving an hour early each day and sweeping or removing snow from the sidewalk.

Aunt Helen Hartzell agreed to be my model for the finals in Des Moines. I took a bus to Madrid, Iowa, where she and Uncle Lyle resided. The next day, Uncle Lyle took us to Des Moines and later retrieved Aunt Helen. I rode back to Cedar Rapids with Bob.

When the final test results arrived, I had a grade of 99.8 percent, the highest ever in school history. All the students from Paris Academy passed with flying colors.

Now it was time to seek employment. The morning after the results came in, Mrs. F. called to ask if I would work for the Paris salon, which was owned by the school. She said that since I had the highest grades, she wanted to secure my employment before any other salon. I happily agreed, and she then said to be at the salon in an hour, as a new client wanted a permanent. Hurriedly, I caught the bus and was there in 45 minutes.

So began my career at Paris Salon of Beauty in June 1960.

My day off from the salon was Wednesday of each week. Don S. agreed that after I cleaned and dusted the house those days, I was on my own until 5 p.m.

I began each Wednesday by jumping out of bed as soon as I heard Don S. leave for work, and then I would set records for the fastest any house had ever been cleaned. I would be downtown by 10 a.m.

The very first Wednesday that I was off, I saw a very handsome, sandy-haired young man (age 26) emerge from the pool hall just next to the railroad tracks. I called out and ran to catch up with him. Before he could even say anything, I told him how handsome he was and suggested that he meet me at Harold's Klub next Wednesday at 10:15 a.m. For the next week, I wondered if he would be there.

I cleaned the house at tornado speed the following Wednesday, and I arrived at Harold's Klub at 9:45 a.m. I checked the clock nervously until he appeared an hour later. His name was Lloyd, and we drank 10-cent glasses of beer and played the jukebox. The song most popular with me at the time was *Cold, Cold Heart* by Hank Williams.

By 3:15 p.m., we had arrived at his residence. I was a little perplexed when he used a kitchen knife, which was secreted above a tall door, to open the apartment.

We entered the small apartment, and I went to the bathroom and was surprised to see women's hose and undergarments hanging from a line.

"Where is she?" I said.

Then he revealed to me that he resided with his very blond wife and told me where she was employed. It seems she was as attracted to the "bad" handsome man as I was.

From then on, Wednesday was the day of our trysts. He was so bold that he had his wife make an appointment with me to style her beautiful, natural-blond hair. I was very jealous and dare not show it.

Don S. wanted me to go to business school after I finished beauty college. He said he would pay—all I had to do was live with him and go to school. He would have kept me in school and in control over me forever, it seemed.

Within months after I started working, Don S. got word of my Wednesday meetings with Lloyd and forbade me to go out on my days off. With that announcement and since I now was getting a paycheck, I decided to get my own domicile.

I rented a tiny apartment off First Avenue in northwest Cedar Rapids. Amid pleading and threats from Don S., Ms. Inez arrived and my few belongings were loaded. After I reached my new home, I assumed I would be free to see Lloyd and have an enjoyable nightlife.

Once again, little did I know.

Cedar Rapids was not really a big enough city to lose oneself—especially when the person looking for you knows your favorite clothier, where you are employed, etc. But Don S. did not locate my new home for several weeks.

In the meantime, I went barhopping with Lloyd, and his wife was along on a couple of occasions. I was uncomfortable as the two of them shared one side of a tavern booth, and I was across from them. My eyes were probably green with jealousy.

On one of our Wednesday meetings, Lloyd and I encountered one of Mother's cousins and his wife, who worked at a bar next to the river. Another time, Sam, an old neighbor and farm helper from the North English area, was in that bar and joined Lloyd and me. Sam couldn't stop telling me how I looked like my mother and how pretty she was.

I had my makeup on and thought no one from my growing-up area knew of my secret. Now, I thought, "Oh my, Sam will tell people I'm gay."

Later, in the early 1970s when I was spending several weeks with Dad, Sam stopped by one Sunday afternoon. Dad, Sam, and I sat at the kitchen table. After gazing intently at me, Sam announced, "I've done just about everything there is to do in my life, and I want to take you out to the supper club."

As they chatted, I excused myself to go to the bathroom and went up the back stairs but did not stop. I proceeded down the front steps, went out the front door, and hot-footed it to the south pasture. Before long, I heard Sam shouting at the top of his lungs, "Gene, Gene, where are you?" over and over again.

About an hour later, I crept back to the house. Dad said, "Sam looked all over for you. He wanted to know when to pick you up." I never saw Sam again and heard that he got married.

Lloyd and I went to Parnell and Maplehurst Manor where I had vowed not to visit again. However, I decided to make some wine and knew that juice I had canned from wild grapes was at the house. Dad and Bernie were surprised to see us and not welcoming. They went on with whatever tasks they were performing.

I found the five-gallon crock I had left behind and took 12 quarts of grape juice before we headed back to Cedar Rapids. Of course, my attempt at making wine was unsuccessful. My "wine" was a very sour, bitter-tasting mess. I had used 10 quarts of grape juice and had to flush it down the commode.

By now, Dad had a lady friend, Maude Van Dee, whose husband had passed away a few years earlier. She was close to Dad's age and had four children.

I was surprised one day to observe the appointment book and see that Maude Van Dee was scheduled for me to give her a permanent wave.

Looking happier than I had seen him in a long time, Dad escorted Maude to the reception area. Maude informed me that Dad wanted me to come home and visit and that he was proud of me—which was an unexpected revelation.

While Maude's hair dried, Dad and I went to a nearby restaurant and had coffee. Our conversation was rather awkward in the beginning, guarded but friendly. He invited me home the next Saturday night and said that he and Maude would convey me back to Cedar Rapids on Sunday. That is what really broke the ice.

Thank you, Maude. Dad and I had not had a really friendly, sit-down conversation ever, and especially not since Mother's death.

After they left, I felt as if I were on Cloud 9, and my coworker Loretta said she and Dad chatted while Maude was having her hair done. Dad told her about me moving back home from St. Louis after Mother died and my caring for him and my younger brothers. His change of heart probably was a result of his heart-to-heart talks with Maude.

My cousin Jim O'Rourke had been the individual who revealed to me that Dad had a girlfriend. Jim did not like it. I explained to Jim that Dad deserved happiness and that Maude would not, could not, and didn't want to take Mother's place. I told him of my approval. Maude just wanted to be happy, too.

My three youngest brothers did not want another mother, and they felt Dad was neglecting them as he spent time with Maude. Therefore, I had to do some gentle arguing so they would think of Dad's happiness and know that everything would be OK.

The following Saturday, Mae drove me to Dad's place. Happiness to be home enshrouded me! On Sunday night, Maude joined Dad and me for the ride back to Cedar Rapids. Before we picked her up, Dad jokingly said to me, "Don't you go flirting with her—she's my girlfriend."

I sat in the back seat where I felt like the eldest of us three—they almost seemed like teenagers on a date. They had a laughing, happy time bantering back and forth. I thought, "They are so happy together that they have forgotten that I'm back here."

From that time on, I was either at Grandma Agnew's or Dad's every other weekend. While I was at Grandma and Aunt Anna's house, I would fix their hair and use Come Alive Gray rinse. Early on Sunday mornings, I would comb out their hair after removing the clips and pins. It always was enjoyable to then accompany them to Mass, and Dad and my three youngest brothers would visit at noon.

This routine continued until 1962 when Maude succumbed to stomach cancer. As far as I know, Dad never again dated any lady.

My client numbers were increasing, and I had been to so many taverns in Cedar Rapids that many of my customers were barmaids or waitresses. When I would get a new client, one of my coworkers would ask, "Where does she tend bar?"

But I also had doctors' wives, bored housewives who told me of their secret affairs, college students who it seemed had more than hair on their minds, infatuated young girls, extremely kind elderly women, Parnell friends, and Dad's girlfriend, Maude. My client list also included Aunt Mary Agnew and her daughter Suzanne, Aunt Marge Costello and her daughter Rosemary, and Jill Dunn, a Healy cousin.

My two favorite clients were Marge McNabb and Ruth Taylor; I was an usher at both of their weddings. After I moved back to St. Louis in 1963, Ruth visited me so I could give her a permanent. When I did her hair in Cedar Rapids, we would laugh so much that a few other operators would peer in my booth. She always gave me a generous tip.

One night, I went barhopping with friends Ms. "Patricia" and Ms. Inez, and we drank large quantities of beverages. When Patricia became intoxicated, he/she would become very obnoxious and sputter extremely hateful and hurtful things. As we were heading for another tavern, I was in the car's back seat when Pat turned and leaned over from the front, stuck his face toward me, and said something I must have considered just too much. My fist popped him in the nose and blood spattered. He—Irish and ready to fight—hit my eye, which later turned black.

At that moment, the police pulled Inez over. They had been directly behind us and observed the fisticuffs ensuing. Patricia and I were booked and put into a cell together where we sheepishly giggled and thought of how foolish we were. Upon appearing before a judge the next morning, we were fined $25 each. I only had $10 in my possession, and Pat graciously paid my fine. Wasn't that a true friend?

We went to my apartment and hardly could look at one another—he with a swollen nose and I with a black eye. I was missing work since I just got out of jail, but Loretta helped me come up with a story when I returned the next day. I said I had the flu and couldn't call since I didn't have a phone (the second part was true). Thanks to a cosmetic called Erase, I was able to skillfully camouflage my darkened orbs and averted a lecture and perhaps a dismissal.

One Saturday, I was 15 minutes late to work and my first appointment. My client was an upper-class matron who had moved to the area from Chicago. Knowing the matron was my first client, Loretta told me, "Go to the Butterfly Cafe and get a cup of hot coffee; you smell like a brewery. I'll go chat with Ms. Matron." Loretta had been an ally since my very first day.

Since I knew that morning that I would be late and that Ms. Matron enjoyed cooking, I brought a quart of my wild grape juice to present to her. I thought she could use the juice to make jelly. When I got to my booth, I placed the juice on the edge of the table that held my supplies. I set her hair, and everything went as planned—until I forgot where I placed the jar. As I turned the matron toward the mirror, my elbow accidentally struck the jar of purple juice.

I froze in slow motion (it seemed) as in silence I watched the jar smash to the floor with a resounding sound of breaking glass. Fragments of glass and juice shot out from beneath my booth into the drying area where a few ladies were thumbing through magazines. Amid shrieks—some thinking the juice was blood—the other operators charged from their booths. All eyes were on me as I grabbed a stack of towels to clean the mess and then crawled around soaking up grape juice and apologizing profusely to customers and coworkers.

I doubt if anyone other than Ms. Matron believed it to be grape juice. The others thought it was wine I had been guzzling at work. Normalcy commenced the rest of that Saturday, but I detected that Mrs. F. and my coworkers were observing me in a different manner. No further missteps would be tolerated was the vibe that surrounded me.

When I began work at the Paris salon, I was given a locker between the men's and women's lounges in the basement. The prior user of that particular locker was an elderly beautician who passed away some time earlier, and the space had never been cleared. A couple of common-looking dresses and a pair of black women's shoes—thick and low-heeled that a middle-aged or elderly woman would wear—were in the locker. I never removed these things, as there was more than adequate room for hanging a shirt or slacks. This would come back to haunt me.

In early 1961, my schedule was changed. I worked on Wednesdays from 1 until 8 p.m. and then locked up the salon. The other hair professionals left at 5 p.m., which had been the closing time until this change.

Soon I had appointments for my evenings. I became friends with Bessie, who laundered, dried, and folded towels during these hours so they were ready the next day for the school and salon. Two huge washers and dryers were next to the men's lounge in the basement. It never occurred to me until then that someone spent the night laundering all those towels. Bessie became a great friend, and barbecued chicken was one of the delicious treats she bestowed on me.

On Wednesdays, I would take a shirt to change into after work. Then I could dash to Harold's Klub or meet Lloyd after closing. As I was finishing my last client one Wednesday evening, I was startled to see Dean, a good-looking, married man. I had met him before briefly, and I didn't know he had even remembered me.

After I said good night to my client, Dean and I went for a beer and the evening ended at my apartment. We had a couple more trysts, but he had to hurry home to his family. I realized we never could have a future—it was the same situation with Lloyd and his wife, just as it was with Dan and his girlfriend.

Several weeks after I moved, Ms. Dina revealed to me that Don S. had purchased a gun. Dina said he was going to confront me and make me beg for mercy on my knees if I didn't move back in with him. He had found out where I lived.

I returned home from work one day and tacked to my door was an 8-by-10-inch picture of me that I had given to Don S. He had taken a knife or a blade and slashed it several times. That sent shivers down my body.

Don S. sent a package to the Paris salon for me. Of course, my female coworkers kept clamoring for me to "open it, open it." I did so reluctantly and was shocked to find a pair of beautiful women's sheer lace panties with the note: "To the hottest ass in town." I was totally embarrassed and had no explanation, as my coworkers speechlessly gave me weird and strange looks.

Several times a week, Don S. would come and lurk outside my apartment door in the middle of the night, making sure I heard him come up the stairs. When Lloyd and I went to various taverns, Don S. would be only a few minutes behind, as we went out back doors on the way to another watering hole.

About a year after I started working at the Paris salon, in May 1961, I was granted a week's vacation and made plans to visit Leroy in St. Louis. Inez and I embarked in his car on a Sunday afternoon. Inez was going to stay for a couple of days, and I would take the bus back to Cedar Rapids. We had rooms at the downtown Baltimore Hotel (which has since been demolished). Leroy would join me in the evenings.

We had a great time visiting bars in both St. Louis and in East St. Louis, where it seemed they never closed. A 21-year-old man, who I knew only as "Red," latched on to me and stayed with me at the hotel. Naturally, he was unemployed and probably homeless. But he was gifted with a terrific personality and—it appeared—devotion to me, so I was happy to be with him. We took Benzedrine (bennies) obtained from street dealers that could keep us awake and alert for hours and hours. I can testify that taking bennies with beer was quite a combination—after too much, I would pass out.

Before leaving on vacation, I asked three coworkers if they could work my clients into their busy schedules. I thought these women were all friends—especially Fran, whose booth was directly across from mine. Coworker Betty had asked me on a couple of occasions to advise her on color combinations for her clients' hair. She said she admired my ability to mix colors. Never one to be secretive or greedy, I shared my knowledge with all who asked. I considered being asked a compliment.

While I was gone, Fran and coworker Pearl claimed they had seen me leave after closing on a Wednesday night dressed in drag and made up. It was half true, as I did powder my face and put on a little eyeliner after I changed into a sexy shirt for my evening foray. While I was in St. Louis, they opened my locker—an invasion of privacy—and said the evidence was there. Indeed, those two horrible dresses and old women's shoes proved, they said, that I sallied out in those terrible garments.

No self-respecting gay queen would have been caught dead in those ugly things!

Fran and Pearl gathered an eager ally in Betty and, besides telling Mrs. F., they told each of my clients about the shattered quart of grape juice that "proved" I was a wine-head alcoholic. They painted such a horrible picture of me and were so convincing that only the barmaids and four others continued as my clients afterwards.

I was greeted with chilliness when I returned from my vacation. I was busy with appointments that had been made before I left, but around mid-afternoon, Betty said she wanted to talk to me. In the supply room, she told me—with glee, I thought—that Mrs. F. would speak with me at the 5 p.m. closing time. I had no idea that all those lies and exaggerations had been told about me while I was gone.

Mrs. F. appeared as I was told. She had a pseudo-sugary smile, the perfect example of a four-flusher. She informed me that she was letting me go because she thought I should have garnered more weekly clients and I had not met her expectations. Then she had the audacity to ask me to finish out the week as I was booked up.

Crestfallen and semi-shocked, I contemplated what I should do. I wondered if I should just say, "Hell no!"

I considered the situation and agreed to finish the week. That way, I could tell my clients that I would call them since I would be off for a while. And, at least, I would have one more paycheck. The other beauticians had left, and there were no goodbyes. Those bitches had been instrumental in this and already knew I was fired.

It was the second, but not the last, time I would be axed. The first time was the worst. I had to learn to gain strength from my roadblocks and failures in life. I resolved to be stronger.

After living just a few months in my apartment, I decided that to get some peace of mind, I would move in with Don S. again. I returned to living at his home feeling somewhat like I had been whipped. Don S. was temporarily laid off at this time because his workplace was restructuring. So the two of us collected unemployment checks and visited his farm on two or three occasions.

I would go out with Don S. on Saturday nights. But he promised that I could go out on Friday nights by myself but had to be home by 2 a.m. (the bars closed at 1:30 a.m.). On Friday nights, after I was dressed and ready to catch a 7:45 p.m. bus, he would say "come over here" and check to see if I had underwear on, my color of socks, etc. It was very humiliating and degrading.

On a few Fridays when the bar was closing, friends would encourage me to come along to a party, preaching over and over, "Don't let that old man stop you." (Don S. was 19 years older than I.)

Once in awhile, I succumbed to the temptation to stay out past 2 a.m. and would be frightened to return to Don S.'s house until I was sure he had left for the day. After creeping in around 10 a.m. on these Saturdays, a very tired me would go to bed for the rest of the day. I would be waiting and anticipating the threatening verbal assaults that I knew were coming upon Don S.'s arrival. And they did. After an assault would die down, he would tell me to get ready and look as good as I did the night before since we were going out.

Since I already would be exhausted, I would offer to spend a quiet evening, just the two of us, at home. He would have none of that. We often went to downtown Iowa City to Kenney's, the hangout of many gay university students, gays from surrounding small towns, and a Quad City group who occasionally would caravan there.

We would join a table where jovial friends and other acquaintances were holding forth, and soon Don S. would be ordering pitchers of beer. He would make sure my glass was always full, saying, "Drink up, Buster [one of his favorite names for me that didn't indicate I was a cheap hussy]. Drink with me like you did last night." It definitely was not enjoyable.

One Saturday night, as closing time approached, he asked where I had gone after bar hours Friday night. He assured me he was over his anger. Believing him, I said I had indeed gone with Inez and Dina to an after-hours club in a private home. (The after-hours clubs were unlicensed. A club usually was in a basement that had a bar with beer and mixed drinks, dim lights, booths, a jukebox, and a small dance floor.)

As soon as I divulged that I had been to an off-limits-to-me bar, he left the table, grabbed his coat and hat, and left me sitting alone. The bar was about to close. I panicked momentarily, but then I remembered that I always carried $50 hidden in my shoe for an emergency—and this was one.

I rented a room at a small hotel connected to the bus station right around the corner. After getting a peaceful sleep, I took the afternoon bus to Cedar Rapids. Upon arriving, I phoned Inez, who took me to Don S.'s house. When I entered, I could tell he had been concerned that I was not coming back and had left him. I acted as if nothing had happened but gave him the silent treatment for a couple of days. From then on, he knew I would not accompany him out of town on Saturday nights.

On Saturday nights, Don S. and I often visited Harold's Klub, and usually two friends would open their home for an after-bar-closing party. Guests brought six packs of beer or the libation they had been imbibing earlier in the evening.

Rheumatism was afflicting Don S. ferociously. He took many cortisone shots, which, he informed me, were damaging to his heart and other body organs and muscles. He was around 50 years old, and it took quite some time for him to ascend and descend steps.

"Between the cortisone and you, Buster, 20 years will be taken off my life," Don S. declared.

On a Friday night in this time period, I again overstayed the deadline and went to the Midway Lounge with Dina. It was usually he or Inez who ranted against letting that "old man run your life." But, weirdly, I also believe they enjoyed hearing about those nights when I was verbally assaulted.

On this weekend, either I was getting accustomed to Don S.'s rants and raves or he was getting worn out from them, as Saturday night at Harold's Klub was uneventful. I did not notice I had misplaced my little wallet sometime Friday night, but there was no money in it. Basically it had only my name, Don S.'s phone number, some religious medals, cards, and a couple of photos.

On Monday evening, Don S. fixed oven-baked steak, baked potatoes, peas, and rolls. He was jovial as we dined. He then told me that he had received a call from a member of the Cedar Rapids Police Department, and the police were looking to question me about an early Saturday morning robbery as my wallet had been found at the scene.

I had not told him that it was missing so that sent my heart racing, and I had all kinds of panicky thoughts that each seemed to have dire ramifications. I knew he knew many on the police force, as some had been military men and others had been classmates at his high school. He said that he had assured them he would bring me in. He told me to bring a toothbrush and a change of underwear (which I probably needed then) and handed me a paper bag.

As we entered the car, he said he hoped I would be cleared soon. He seriously inquired if I had actually been present or even committed the crime in my drunken state of mind—which he emphasized—and something about a lawyer. He told me we still had a half hour before he had to haul me in, so I slumped in despair in the car seat as he drove around Cedar Rapids.

"You just as well have one last drink before you go," he said as he pulled up to the Midway Lounge.

I was numb from the proceedings of the last hour and a half, and now this! We perched at the bar, and Don S. beamed a big smile at the bartender who, of course, greeted me amiably. I didn't want a drink or anything at all.

I looked on in amazement, as Don S. seemed to know Eddie, the bartender. Finally, Eddie asked if I was ready to "pick it up." Don S. said, "just as well," and Eddie handed me my billfold.

Relieved, I was! Everything was intact except a couple of pictures of me were missing.

It seems that the maintenance crew found my wallet when they were cleaning the bar over the weekend. Eddie called for me Monday afternoon, and Don S. took the message and said he would bring me down there that night. Therefore, he concocted that heart-skipping "police" account and carried it out. I must admit that it really got me.

As I thought about it over and over, it only made me very angry and resentful. I opened a savings account and began to save every penny I could, determined to leave for good as soon as possible. I knew it would take time and much planning.

Aunt Marge Costello occasionally would write that she, Rosemary, and Michael would be in Cedar Rapids over a Saturday night to stay with Minnie Costello, sister of her late husband, Leo. I would meet them at Sunday Mass, and we then enjoyed dinner at Minnie's little house. She fried the most delicious chicken and also served mashed potatoes, gravy, vegetables, homemade cake or pie, and always brown 'n serve rolls, a fairly new product at the time. What a comfortable, relaxing afternoon I would spend with them.

I had a painful cyst surgically removed from the roof of my mouth. It was the size of half of a lead pencil and had to be removed so it didn't grow and pass by my nose and go for the brain. Don S. paid a specialist to remove it. Thankfully, the biopsy showed no cancer.

I had a lot of pain after the removal, and I went to Dad's for three weeks to help out, recuperate, and enjoy my brothers at home and Kenny and Marlene and their children, Terry and Tammy. Tammy is the first girl in the John and Mary Agnew Dawson line and my oldest niece. It dawned on me that I was an uncle—I would rather have been an aunt—two times. I was grateful to Kenny for extending another generation to our family, knowing that Leroy and I were highly unlikely to leave descendants.

(My love for my nephews and nieces is sincere and heartfelt. Later, I would be around for the births of Patrick Leo and his wife Geneva's brood, and babysitting them gave us a wonderful bond. Kenny and Marlene's chicks would become very special to me when I visited Iowa later on; they would disembark from their school bus at Dad's place before going home later. Thomas M.'s little Esther became very dear to me. I am very blessed.)

Aunt Catherine Dawson arrived to spend a few days at Dad's during this time. I had told no one about being fired but had written the news to Leroy. Everyone at Dad's accepted that I was there for three weeks to recuperate, although there was nothing to prevent me from working. I think they were almost as happy to see me as I was to see them.

When I returned to Cedar Rapids, Don S. suggested that he buy a beauty shop for me and I could repay him after I became established. I already was depressed and that idea seemed overwhelming, as I had no knowledge about operating a business. It also would mean that I would be tied down with him indefinitely. He was in no hurry for me to rejoin the labor force since he was my sole provider.

Leroy came to Iowa to celebrate Thanksgiving with Dad and his brothers. He arrived at my place early Thanksgiving morning, and we traveled to Grandma Agnew's home in North English. Aunt Anna greeted me. "You sure do look pretty today," she said.

Then it dawned on me that my mascara, eyeliner, powder, and eyebrow pencil were still on from the previous night.

No one else said anything except for cousin Eddie Harris. He said he didn't want to walk next to me, as all the men in the family became quiet when I joined them in the room where they were smoking, playing cards, and watching a football game. From then on, Eddie would not appear in public with me.

I was still unemployed in mid-December when I received a call from a man named Loren Lundgren. He managed the Iowa Theatre Beauty Salon in the downtown building of the same name. He previously managed the most beautiful salon in Cedar Rapids, and his clients from there had stuck with him.

Loren had heard that I was dismissed from the Paris salon because of alcoholism. He heard all the exaggerations that had become part of the lies and falsehoods. Without even asking to meet me, he asked me to work for him. I can never forget Loren's faith in me and for giving me an opportunity to overcome my depression and not feel like a failure again.

At the Iowa Theatre Beauty Salon, Loren employed Nancy, a beautiful, platinum (out of a bottle) blond with movie-star good looks and an equally curvaceous body. Nancy, who loved to drink and have a good time, told me that she had seen me at a few bars. We became fast friends, and she informed Loren of my Don S. situation and my gayness.

When I called some of my former customers, I was surprised at the coolness of their voices as they informed me that they were sticking with the Paris salon. It was only because two of my clients told me about the lies that were pumped into their ears that I knew what my former coworkers said to my customers. My ex-coworkers painted me as a depraved sex maniac-alcoholic, and most of the very proper housewives believed them. My barmaid friends, however, did not desert me and never believed the lies.

Loren made an appointment with a photographer to assemble some photos of me. He selected the one he liked, and it appeared in *The Cedar Rapids Gazette* in an advertisement for the Iowa Theatre Beauty Salon. It was captioned "Mr. Gene, Hair Stylist." Soon I had many thirtyish bored housewives and young ladies who liked the photo as clients.

Not long after I started at the salon, I attended a convention of beauticians from all over eastern Iowa and western Illinois, which was held at the Roosevelt Hotel in Cedar Rapids. At the convention, I won a drawing for a case of professional hair spray. I gave it to Loren for the salon, of course, since he purchased my ticket.

Mrs. F., the four-flusher, and her group of lying bitches flashed pseudo-smiles that I accepted and beamed back at them. I wasn't bitter, although I sound as if I am. I was much better off and liked for being me.

I had learned that I was no longer dealing with gentle and 99-percent straightforward folks like the farmers and rural residents who I grew up with. I was now in a cutthroat profession.

Maude Van Dee passed away early in 1962. Dad told me he and Maude had planned to marry before stomach cancer starved her to death because she couldn't hold any food.

She had asked that I fix her hair for the wake. I agreed, and I did her hair after fortifying myself with a half pint of vodka. It was the only time I styled the hair of the dead. I was honored that she had requested that I do it.

At the Armah Cemetery, Dad walked with Maude's children behind the casket. They all liked him and vice versa. After the funeral luncheon, Dad and I had many drinks at the local Little Chicago lounge and then at Joe's Tavern, also in Williamsburg. At Joe's, a man approached me and said I was the best-looking guy he had ever seen and wondered if we could go drinking sometime. I gushed (I had drunk twice as much as Dad), "Oh, yes, yes!"

"Let's go!" Dad said quickly, and ordered a pint of vodka for the road.

My younger brothers were bewildered to see me in such condition. Maude's sons arrived about 8 p.m. to give me a return ride to Cedar Rapids. I barely remember them being there, and Dad and they decided that I was not in any condition to go anywhere. The next thing I recall is Dad and my brothers shaking me awake the next morning and seeing bloody clothes and towels in my bed. The pillow had crimson spots on it.

Apparently, after the Van Dee family departed the prior evening, I went to the bathroom and proceeded to tumble into the tub. Evidently, my head bounced like a basketball, rendering me unconscious. Dad and my brothers got me into bed after stanching the blood that was gushing from a couple of spots on my skull.

I remembered none of this. My head was messed up with deep gashes and hurt slightly. I should have known to avoid bathtubs when indulging heavily in alcoholic beverages.

All is well that ends well, and Don S. transported me back to Cedar Rapids. I was back at Loren's shop the next day.

Everything was going smoothly. I had overcome my extreme crush on Lloyd and could no longer tryst with him. On a very cold Monday, one of those sunny, but extremely cold February days when frozen snow and slush were piled by the curbside, Leroy arrived for an overnight visit. He had been at Dad's since Saturday and appeared at the salon about 2 p.m. Loren had departed since his clients had canceled due to the cold.

Leroy and Nancy hit it off immediately, and he had her in stitches. I could see by the gleam in his eyes that he was ready for some fun and barhopping. Nancy hurriedly canceled a longtime client, blaming the cold weather. I could not afford that luxury, as I had new clients and desperately needed the cash for my escape from Don S.

They weren't feeling any pain when they got back at 5:30 p.m. They laughed hilariously as they told about Leroy draping himself in Nancy's mink and then attempting to sit on the laps of bar patrons while asking, "Honey, will you buy me a drink?"

The patrons and Nancy found it extremely hilarious when Leroy took one of Nancy's cigarettes (he never smoked) and asked, "Honey, will you give me a light?" They said it was especially comical to see him puffing on a cigarette with extremely exaggerated feminine mannerisms.

I decided to join them even though I knew there would be an explosion when I returned to Don S.'s home. I didn't even consider phoning him because I knew he would raise hell immediately.

We toured two or three bars and eventually arrived at the Midway Lounge where a man named Charles was seated at the bar. He knew me, as did the bartender and most patrons, due to my forbidden excursions. Leroy, of course, fit in anywhere. He never met a stranger.

At closing time, Charles invited us to his apartment. He had purchased two six packs of beer, and we entered Leroy's car. I was carrying the canned beer in the -15 degree cold, and it felt as if it would freeze immediately. When we left Charles's apartment after more partying, we gave Nancy a ride home, and after a cheery good night, our next stop was my home in Cedar Rapids.

We had no sooner entered the house when a pajama-clad Don S. thundered down the steps. It didn't seem like arthritis was affecting him then. He started to berate me in a tirade of accusations, even as he saw Leroy sitting there. I tried to explain that it would be impossible to do the things that he accused me of while Leroy was present, and did he want to deprive me of a night out with my brother? (It was probably the first time Leroy and I drank together as Leroy was not yet 21 when Mother died. He usually didn't indulge in liquor because he was working three jobs and didn't have time to party and imbibe.)

After Don S. finally tired himself by his constant diatribe, he hobbled back up the stairs. When he was out of sight, Leroy said, "You don't have to put up with that. I didn't realize how he verbally assaulted you. Come to St. Louis. You can work at the Foot Long Hot Dog stand until you get your Missouri beautician license." He was the Foot Long's manager and in charge of the entire operation.

At that moment, I decided I would be joining Leroy in St. Louis the following spring.

On Halloween of 1962, Leroy visited Cedar Rapids. Don S. agreed that Leroy and I could go out on trick-or-treat night. I was attired in full drag with a black knit two-piece outfit, faux fur stole, silk hose with seams straight up the back, and three-inch heels. My hair was in a pageboy with bangs.

Harold's Klub was our first stop. After it closed, Leroy and I were on our way to his car when we encountered four African-American teenagers who I knew (two boys and two girls). A party was scheduled at an acquaintance's abode, and we were invited if we gave them a ride. We agreed at the same moment that a 20ish extremely handsome Caucasian man approached and asked if he could attend. Without asking the teenagers, I enthusiastically said, "Of course!"

The handsome man left his red convertible parked on the street in front of us. The teens got in the back seat of Leroy's car while the handsome man slid into the front passenger seat next to me. I was completely surprised as he began to smother me with kisses. I assumed that he knew I was not actually a woman since it was Halloween, the one day that police would not arrest a guy for impersonating a female. (I was always a little mystified why women could wear slacks, shirts, and men's shoes and have mannish haircuts, which many lesbians did, and not be harassed.)

The handsome man tried to place one of his hands under my dress, and I resisted as any decent girl would in that era (the sexual revolution was barely under way). When we arrived at the party address, Leroy and the teenagers hurried into the house, thinking the two of us were coming along with them. But the handsome man clutched me and announced that we were staying in the car.

He had become highly sexually aroused and started trying to disrobe me. "You know I'm not a real woman, don't you?" I pleaded.

"You damn well better be real—I've even kissed you," he replied in an angry voice.

Fortunately, Leroy and a couple of the teens came looking for me. The handsome man demanded to be returned downtown to his convertible. All the way back, he kept putting his hand over his face while glancing at me occasionally. He shook his head in disbelief and kept muttering, "and I kissed you."

After returning him to his vehicle, Leroy and I went back to Don S.'s house. We had enough excitement and a close call.

The anger and surprise in the handsome man's voice indicated to me that he could have issued a brutal beating or even worse, feeling he had been duped. Drag queens have been viciously murdered after unsuspecting men learned of their true identities.

The gay community had its own lexicon that I now knew well. A feminine-acting gay man is called a "queen" and may look physically very masculine or extremely feminine. A masculine man or woman is "butch." Hoodlums who seek out gays to beat them up are known as "dirt." A young man who is a receiver of oral sex as a passive partner is known as "trade." A woman, if not a friend or relative, is called a "fish" (as mentioned earlier) or "fag hag."

Thinking of my future, I took a Greyhound bus to Chicago to secure a license to practice beauty culture in Illinois. Patricia, who had moved there, and his older gay partner, Tom, met me at the bus station and then escorted me to my destination. Ms. Inez and two lesbian friends, Mary and Alice, surprised me by coming to my hotel room that afternoon. The four of us, along with Patricia and Tom, went to a few Chicagoland bars. I returned to Cedar Rapids the next day via Inez, Mary, and Alice.

Soon I had an Illinois license. I wanted to get as many state licenses as possible to impress the Missouri licensing board since it did not have reciprocity with Iowa licensing. I got licenses permitting me to practice cosmetology in New York, Louisiana, Arizona, and a couple of other states where paperwork sufficed and I did not have to appear in person, as in Illinois.

I had continued to save money and tried to gently break the news of my impending departure to Don S. When I did tell him, I thought he was going to become unglued as he alternately sobbed and made veiled threats. I revealed that I intended to leave about June 1, 1963.

In mid-April 1963, I informed Loren, Nancy, and my clients that I would be leaving soon. It was difficult to do. Soon I had letters of recommendation from Loren, owner Bill, and many of my clients.

About this time, a suave, sophisticated lady made an appointment with me to do her hair. As I was setting her hair, she invited me to lunch and disclosed that she was a representative of Seligman & Latz, which operated beauty salons throughout the country with headquarters in New York. I was flabbergasted.

She proposed that I manage and be the head beautician at a new shop the company was opening in Little Rock, Arkansas. The company would help me obtain an Arkansas license. I was not ready to suddenly make that move and accept that responsibility. Besides, my goal was to again be in St. Louis with my brother, who was my best friend.

Just prior to this, Nancy had left the Iowa Theatre Beauty Salon and had been hired by the Seligman & Latz shop inside Armstrong's department store in Cedar Rapids. I assumed that Nancy suggested to the lady that she recruit me. Just think, beauticians are sometimes recruited like athletes—isn't that something?

For three weeks in May, I was at Dad's house. I cleaned the entire house, washed and put away winter bedclothes, cooked, and baked. I visited Grandma, Aunt Anna, and my other aunts and uncles, along with Kenny, Marlene, and my nieces (they now had another daughter, Anna) and nephew.

Dad took us on long afternoon rides to the places where he grew up and those that carried pleasant memories. We traveled back roads that were familiar to him, and he continued a steady explanation and stories of the surrounding area. I felt contentment and peace those afternoons as I sat between Patrick Leo and Thomas M. in the back while Bernie was in the front passenger seat.

I laundered clothes that Patrick Leo, Thomas M., and Bernie had outgrown and gave them to Ray and Loretta Murphy, who had boys who could wear the garments. Grandma Agnew and I also took some smaller boy clothes I had laundered to Nell George, mother-in-law to Orpha George, who had died a few years earlier. Leonard George was left a widower, and he and his parents were raising his children. I gave a pigeon I had raised to one of the children. If you stop and survey the landscape, you will find that there are folks who are much worse off than you.

Three weeks of happiness was the result of my visit, and I returned to Don S. He sobbed on his knees and made hollow promises, which I would never let him attempt to fulfill. I was adamant. I was leaving.

Finally, he intoned that he would give me three months in St. Louis to get the "wildness" out of me. Then he planned to come to St. Louis to get me and bring me back to his domicile. I determined to worry about that later.

Bernie had purchased a car, and we rented a U-Haul trailer as I had one piece of furniture, a very sturdy desk that had been my Uncle Emmett's. Emmett had died while I was in beautician school. We loaded my desk at Dad's, and I said my goodbyes.

Bernie and I detoured to Iowa City to say goodbye to cousin Jim O'Rourke, who was in the University of Iowa Hospital after an industrial accident. How sad, he had been such a strong, muscular lad.

Bernie and I arrived at 5006 Maple Avenue in St. Louis around June 3 or 4, 1963. This was the same house that I had been forbidden to visit. But Buddy Banderet had died, and his sister Peggy had sold the financially profitable Foot Long Hot Dog Company.

The house was large with four bedrooms and a bath upstairs and a walk-up third-floor attic bedroom. The downstairs consisted of a large kitchen, an equally large dining room with a crystal chandelier, a living room, and a front-hall entrance with a closet.

The entire area was teeming with activity; there were many thriving businesses including a huge Sears department store. Maple Avenue intersects with North Kingshighway Boulevard, and at the time, it was one of the busiest areas for bus, car, and human transportation in the metropolitan St. Louis area. The Foot Long was at 1217 North Kingshighway.

As we unloaded Bernie's car, sisters/new neighbors Louise Golden and Nell Forest and their children waved and smiled friendly greetings. They eventually became good friends.

At dusk, after unloading my few possessions and being shown my northwest corner upstairs bedroom, I traveled 25 steps to the restaurant's back entrance. The parking lot was mostly filled with cars, and carhops scurried about taking and delivering orders. Leroy told me to just observe that night to get the hang of the place and learn the menu and prices.

There were three cooks in the small kitchen, which was extremely hot. Four waitresses and a young man patrolled the front counter area. The main food they served, of course, was a foot-long hot dog on a foot-long bun (30 cents) or a foot-long hot dog with chili, pickles, and freshly chopped onions on a bun (40 cents). The menu also included French fries, ham sandwiches, egg sandwiches, buttered-beef sandwiches, 30-cent hamburgers, and 40-cent deluxe hamburgers (10 cents more for lettuce, tomato, onions, and pickles). Malts, milkshakes, custard ice-cream cones, orange soda, grape soda, root beer, Coke, and delicious O'Connor coffee completed the menu. There was a walk-up window for street traffic.

Customers stood in rows of two or three up and down the counter that had 10 stools. One young man kept hollering, "Snowball, come out from there and wait on me." I was in the kitchen area, but he could see me. Since I couldn't wait on him yet, I got out of his view.

I did not see a single Caucasian except Leroy, who oversaw the operation. He was seemingly everywhere at once, joking and bantering with both the employees and customers.

When Leroy integrated the Foot Long, all the food and beverages were served on china or glassware. But the new owner switched to throwaway utensils, which I think was to eliminate the need for the two or three employees who washed dishes.

Upon integration, the business at least tripled since African Americans could sit and dine at the counter. There was much racial strife at the time, but color-blind was a good description of Leroy.

When I began at the Foot Long, I worked the counter, filled orders, made shakes, and got the hang of making those twisting cones of custard. I worked from 9 a.m. to 5 p.m. for the first two or three months. Then I was given Thursdays and Sundays off, as Leroy wanted me to work Saturday nights since he said I could do twice as much as the other waiters. Of course, he had laid off one of them—therefore I actually did the work of two.

Flirting and propositions were abundant, even from some women! I resisted all. On the nights I didn't work, I would go to the downtown gay bars where a lot of my friends from eight years earlier still gathered.

I reached out to Ms. Joe "Jennie," who was still working at the same beauty salon. She had purchased a little red MG, an English-made car (Ms. Jennie was of English heritage and proud of it). That was her reward to herself for being successful. Ms. Jennie now had a partner, Bill, and they lived in an apartment in the suburbs.

Ms. Jennie immediately wanted to help me secure my Missouri cosmetology license, as he had made arrangements for me to work at the salon with him. At that time, either the Iowa or Missouri cosmetology board was in upheaval over a strike or disagreement, which held me up from acquiring a Missouri license. By this time, I also was firmly entrenched at the Foot Long, and I could see that Leroy depended on me. So Jennie and I drifted apart.

Don S. made plans to visit St. Louis for the purpose of returning me to Iowa. But two days before he was to arrive, he was stricken with a heart attack that left him very weak. He was told not to drive a vehicle. It was at least a year before he returned to work on a limited basis.

That rendered it impossible for him to fulfill his threat for a September 1963 showdown with me. Thereafter, we corresponded sporadically, and we always exchanged Christmas cards and he never forgot my birthday.

I was no longer practicing my Catholic faith. I didn't attend Mass, as I worked the Saturday night shifts and sometimes the Foot Long would be open until daylight on Sunday mornings. I would tell myself, "I'll go to Mass next week."

In September, Dad, Patrick Leo, and Thomas M. arrived in St. Louis with a 10-gallon crock full of dressed chickens that Dad had raised for Leroy and me. Leroy had purchased tickets for them to attend Stan Musial's final baseball game for the St. Louis Cardinals. Up to that time and perhaps even today, Musial was one of the Cardinals' all-time, all-around greatest players, excluding pitchers.

Less than two months later, the country was devastated by the assassination of President John F. Kennedy. As I worked the noon-hour counter, one of my fellow employees distressfully said that she heard on a customer's radio that the President had been shot. We turned on the counter radio, and it was unbelievably true. All the African Americans I have ever known were fans of the Kennedys.

Just after the JFK assassination, Patrick Leo joined us in St. Louis and took a job as a daytime carhop. Patrick Leo had graduated from Williamsburg High School back home in Iowa, and Leroy previously had assured him that a job was his at the Foot Long whenever he was ready.

When I moved in with Leroy at 5006 Maple, he announced that no men or boyfriends were allowed to visit inside the house. I had happily abided.

As 1963 continued, I slowly started to wear a little makeup and then a little more. My hair was growing out. It had been very sun-bleached blond and about three inches long upon my arrival.

One night in late 1963, Leroy awakened me and said there was a very nice-looking young guy downstairs who wanted to meet me. Leroy had broken his own rule and invited Melvin, a 19-year-old neighbor, in for a drink. Leroy had just closed the Foot Long for the night and was tired and evidently bored.

Leroy was never one to listen to music or keep up with the latest popular releases. I was just the opposite. I had a portable record player purchased by Don S. and up-to-date popular records including those that featured The Miracles, The Temptations, The Supremes, Mary Wells, Sam Cooke, Jerry Butler, Marvin Gaye, Jackie Wilson, and others.

Melvin and I listened to many records and drank a few beers. At daylight, he said he had to sneak into his home where he lived with his wife and their baby.

On many an evening for the next couple of months, Melvin would observe me leaving work and knock lightly on the door at 5006 Maple within a few minutes. We would be alone for the evening as Leroy worked the night shift and would arrive at the Foot Long as I was leaving.

At first, Melvin and I would sit on the stairsteps in the entry room and sip vodka from a quart bottle while he smoked cigarettes. Sometime in February, Melvin arrived with a gray-eyed male friend who recently had moved to St. Louis. His name was Donald, and he was carrying an album by Ted Taylor, a popular blues singer.

We had several sips of vodka, and Donald said he wanted me to hear Ted Taylor and proceeded to put the album on my record player. Melvin came in, and they perched on the couch. I thought, "I'll have to get them out of here before Leroy comes to the house for a break or something." I didn't get a chance, as he came home about 10 minutes later, greeted everyone, and then left.

From that time on, the house was available for visitors.

It seemed my life was on an even keel as 1964 continued. Melvin and his family had moved from a few houses down to an apartment. Melvin's birthday was approaching, and his aunt, who knew of our involvement, and I decided to bake a cake for him. It was just a 13-by-9-inch devil's food—nothing fancy.

Naomi, Melvin's wife, threw a birthday party for him. His aunt and I carried the cake up the street to their apartment. We had consumed a few sips of vodka prior to embarking and carried a quart of vodka along to contribute to the festivities. The cake was placed on a coffee table in the center of the small living room. Soon music was playing, dancing ensued, and more drinks were consumed. I was consuming lots of vodka as I was once again in the situation of being the other woman/man—the odd person out, which I always was.

I danced with Melvin's aunt, who appeared to enjoy vodka almost as much as I. We spun around and I lost my balance, staggered backwards, and fell—making a direct hit on the cake and coffee table. I shattered the coffee table, and most of the cake was on the back of my all-wool, Italian-made jersey. I was embarrassed, and Naomi screamed and dispensed evil looks directly at me during the chaos.

Melvin's aunt and I hotfooted down the street, and I went to 5006 Maple to get out of the cake-smeared clothes. I hope Melvin had a happy birthday. That incident was the end of the Melvin infatuation.

Alligator shoes, men's silk hose, Italian wool jerseys, and jaunty hats were in style for young men in the black community. I joined the crowd (When in Rome, do as the Romans do) and wore all of those except the hat.

My hair had grown long enough to lay in waves and curls, and I dyed it a light peach blond. I wore makeup every day, as I felt very bland and almost naked unless I was discreetly made up. I didn't wear false eyelashes, exaggerated painted lips, or rouge to work though.

Around this time period, I remained calm during a situation that otherwise could have ended quite badly for me. One night around 10 p.m., I was walking with two African-American friends on Martin Luther King Drive on my way to LaDonna's bar. A car that had a light flashing on top pulled up next to us. A 30-something Caucasian male flashed a badge and ordered me—only me—into the car.

The man was intimidating with his badge, so I got in. As he drove away from my friends, he revealed that he was taking me to a farm near Labadie, Missouri, about 40 miles away! I quietly told him that my brother would miss me at home and my friends could have written down his license-plate number. Plus, people would be looking for me at my job.

Fortunately, the man's good sense prevailed, and he drove me home.

I was not as lucky on a Wednesday night in the fall. I ventured to a gay bar downtown where I met a good-looking, dark-haired, 20ish man. Naturally, he was unemployed (sound familiar?). He had a room at a cheap, rundown hotel, and I spent the night with him.

The next day (Thursday, my day off), we decided to visit some of his old haunts, which were seedy bars in an area populated by what so-called "sophisticated" whites called "Hoosiers." Hoosiers, who were known to be rough, usually were fairly new to St. Louis.

When I went barhopping during this time period, I carried lipstick, eyebrow pencil, and a compact in one pocket, and rosary beads and keys in another. Money was in various pockets and in my shoes.

We entered the "seedy" bar about 2 p.m. After a few beers, I grew bolder, so I went to the restroom to powder my face and apply a little eyebrow pencil and eyeliner. My guy was soon talking to a girl at the bar, and a very young girl (17–18) was talking with me. She was very complimentary and called me her "little sister." At the time, I had a 28-inch waist and was becoming anorexic; I probably weighed 145–148 pounds (when I graduated from high school in 1949, I weighed 165). That is probably why she called me "little" sister.

I was wearing two very large, cheap, fake diamond rings that could be ordered from ads in magazines. How they glistened and flashed in a dimly lit bar!

I met several other people, and my date disappeared. As the night wore on, I grew more emboldened and applied more eyeliner, eyebrow pencil, and lipstick. My teenage "sister" was too young to be served and was in and out of the bar. This was not a gay bar for sure.

At the closing hour, the young girl, accompanied by four young men, asked if I would like to go with them to East St. Louis where it seemed the bars never closed. Gleefully, I agreed. Fine misty rain was falling as we entered the car. I was between two fellows in the back seat, and she was in the center in the front.

As we traveled along, there were less and less streetlights and we hadn't approached a Mississippi River bridge that would take us to East St. Louis. I was very slightly concerned. Soon the vehicle stopped at a deserted area, as one of the guys said he had to urinate. I was going to stay in the car since it was misting and I didn't have to go. But I was told to get out because the driver and the girl were going to have intercourse and wanted privacy.

As soon as I left the car, one of the guys pointed away from it and asked, "What is that light over there?"

As I turned my head, I did see many lights as a fist met my eye and then more and more blows rained on me. Yes, it is true, you do see "stars" and many other assorted lights.

This truly was an encounter with serious, violent, murderous dirt—the gay language for such individuals.

As I collapsed semi-conscious, I thought I must feel like a live chicken being plucked. The rings were pulled from my fingers, and all my pockets were turned inside out as they searched for money. The shoes were yanked from my feet. I can't recall if my makeup was taken, but the rosary beads were left in my pocket.

As they tossed me in a grader ditch (not water-filled) next to the rural roadside, I heard the girl ask, "Is he dead?"

After they muttered a reply, I heard her say, "Goodbye little sister," as they drove away.

I stayed very still for an undetermined amount of time before feeling my face and jaw. I felt as if all the teeth on my left lower jaw had been knocked sideways. Warm blood flowed from my mouth and various facial abrasions. I recall moaning as the mist felt refreshingly good on my face.

Struggling to my feet, I saw a light shining in the distance. I had been deposited in a semi-rural area of south St. Louis. I approached a porch where a dog growled menacingly but, at that point, a mean dog was not going to deter me. After knocking at the door, a gentleman opened it, and I asked if he would please call a cab for me.

"Don't you mean an ambulance?" he replied. I assured him that a cab would suffice.

My next recollection is the arrival of the cab. Before the driver could ask any questions, I said, "I don't have any money. I've been robbed." I pushed the rosary beads into his hand and told him to hold them and I would pay him when I got home.

At about 3 a.m., the cabdriver dropped me off at 5006 Maple. I secured the money for him, and he returned my rosary.

Then for the first time, I could see that the front of my shirt was thoroughly saturated with blood. Blood and saliva were seeping out of my mouth and slowly running down my chin. I grabbed a few towels, wiped my face, and then proceeded up the stairs to the bed I shared with Patrick Leo, as it was in one of the two rooms with a window air conditioner (Leroy's bedroom was the other).

"Get over," I announced—mumbled actually—to Patrick Leo. My jaw was giving me terrific pain, and I had taken some aspirin as soon as the cab left. I fell into a fitful sleep, and Patrick Leo said I moaned and groaned the rest of the night.

I awakened with the hope that it was all a bad dream, but I quickly abandoned that thought because the pain was intense. I had to hold my jaw and push it up as my teeth were hitting the inside of my mouth. Leroy, who always looked out for me, insisted on taking me to a neighboring dentist. The dentist said I had a broken jaw. He proceeded to set my jaw and put braces and rubber bands in place.

Leroy conveyed me to St. Mary's Infirmary where I was confined for four days and nights, and I was introduced to morphine. I have since developed an allergic reaction to morphine but, at the time, it stifled my pain and gave me the most wonderful and peaceful sleep that I could recall.

For six weeks, I could eat no solid food. How I craved a hot dog and French fries. Patrick Leo would go to the Howard Johnson's restaurant a few blocks away and get a pint of gravy to go for me. I would drink it through a straw, as I craved the meat flavor. I grew tired of milkshakes.

The day before Thanksgiving, my braces were removed. I cooked a tremendous dinner for the holiday with everything I craved for the past six weeks. Then I could barely eat anything as my stomach had shrunk.

In the meantime, fearless Leroy gathered a few of his thuggish friends, and they went to the bar searching for the robbers. The patrons were surprised by their boldness, but Leroy did learn that several young men and a girl were peddling rings for sale and had suddenly left for their Hoosier homes in outer Missouri.

They never were brought to justice, especially since no police report was ever made. At that time, most gay-involved crimes were not reported, unless the crime was murder.

During the weeks of my recuperation and the time of my wired-shut mouth, the St. Louis Cardinals represented the National League in the 1964 World Series and played the New York Yankees of the American League. Tickets for fans who were not season-ticket holders were sold on a first-come, first-served basis.

Two days before tickets went on sale, Patrick Leo got in line. He was one of the first two to camp out to get three tickets for the home games. Leroy took food and blankets to him, and I think Patrick Leo took along reading material. He and the other early camper made the local prime-time television newscasts, and their pictures and story were in the *St. Louis Post-Dispatch*.

All three of us attended the games in St. Louis—me with my mouth wired shut. The games were held at the former Sportsman's Park at North Grand and Dodier Streets. The Cardinals won in seven games with super pitcher Bob Gibson winning pivotal games. I got to see Mickey Mantle and Roger Maris for the Yankees and Mike Shannon for the Cardinals, who later became a lead broadcaster for the team, up close. We had seats in the right-field bleachers in the small 30,500-seat ballpark.

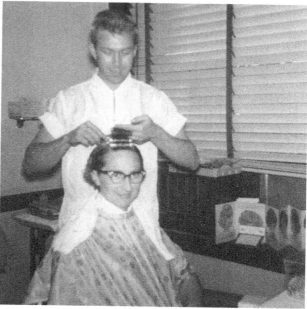

Ready for work, 1962.

With a client at the Iowa Theatre Beauty Salon, 1962.

Dressed as a man, 1962.

A night out in East St. Louis.

Standing on the porch of my Maple Avenue home in St. Louis, 1966.

Geneva and Patrick Leo, 1968.

Trying to look sultry, 1965.

# Chapter 8

## 1965–1969

Patrick Leo, knowing that he soon would be drafted, volunteered for the draft and was sent to Fort Leonard Wood in southern Missouri for basic training in July 1965.

Patrick Leo corresponded with us from his military locations; he eventually was sent to Germany. The Vietnam War was raging in the Far East, and Patrick Leo, feeling he wasn't doing anything in Germany for his country, courageously volunteered for duty in Vietnam. He arrived there in August 1966 and eventually earned a Purple Heart. I am extremely proud of him and his love of country and bravery. His harrowing experiences are for his own memories.

Not long before Patrick Leo began his military service, Dad and a friend came to visit. Their arrival was on a Friday, and I had Saturday off.

I asked neighbor/friend Louise if she would fix Sunday dinner for Dad, his friend, Patrick Leo, Leroy, and me. I told her that I would purchase whatever food she wanted to cook, including enough for her extended family. I intended to carry the food from Louise's kitchen to our house next door—at that time I had never seen interracial family dining, and I didn't know what Dad's and his friend's reactions would be.

But Louise said we should all come to her residence and I agreed. My purchases from the neighboring Kroger (one of my favorite grocery stores) consisted of several chickens, sweet potatoes, white or "Irish" potatoes as I call them, bread, margarine, and crispy fresh green beans.

Dad and his friend met everyone on Friday night. On Saturday night, Louise barbecued in her backyard just next to the Foot Long parking lot, so it was nicely lighted. Dad, his friend, and Patrick Leo all were there, and Leroy came over during his breaks.

At the sumptuous dinner that Louise served on Sunday, Dad especially liked the garden-fresh green beans. It was a delightful experience as David, Louise's longtime common-law husband, and Dad traded stories of their childhoods. David had grown up in Mississippi, and his parents were tenant cotton farmers and most definitely experienced hard work and impoverishment.

As they traded stories amid much laughter and joviality, I thought about how God's children are all alike and they just need to get to know one another. A good way is to break bread together.

At one point, neighbor/friend Nell glanced at me and said I could put my shoes under her bed anytime. Dad really enjoyed that remark and laughed hilariously. He probably wished it were true as he was always telling people he wished I had a girlfriend or would consider marrying and settling down like Kenny had.

I had given my room to Dad's friend for sleeping and thought nothing of it, but he thanked me over and over and repeated constantly what a wonderful time he was having. After returning to his home in Iowa, he often would call me to rehash the entire weekend and thank me again and again.

In early December 1966, I was in the front seat of a car owned and driven by a man whose only name I remember is "Buzz," a nickname I'm sure. It was a rainy night, and several of us had been drinking. While Buzz was driving on Kingshighway, he lost control and the car struck and knocked down a lamp pole. The car stopped abruptly and, with no seatbelts, the impact thrust me forward.

My head smashed the windshield, making a hole the size of a bowling ball and resulting in a huge, irregular zigzagged cut on my forehead and cuts on my lower-eye area and the left side of my face. My left side was bruised, there was a deep cut on my left leg, and my left knee felt as if it were out of its socket. I was never unconscious and, as the blood flowed, I was not really in pain. I was the only one of the five injured, and the rest walked away unscathed. And, I mean, literally walked away—when the police arrived, Buzz and I were the only two there.

The ambulance took me to the nearby Homer G. Phillips hospital. It was an African-American hospital before integration, which happened at a snail's pace in St. Louis. I was stitched, bandaged, and then admitted to a ward of about 20 beds where I was the only Caucasian. Evidently, I possess a very hard head, as I don't recall a headache. (I didn't even have headaches after whopping hangovers; I just would be extremely tired.)

Early the next morning, my first visitors were insurance men who wanted me to sign papers to sue Buzz. I was horrified; how could I sue a friend? I didn't realize until Leroy arrived shortly thereafter that it actually would be the insurance company that would be liable. Leroy declared, "K, you should get some money for this."

(As an aside, Leroy had started calling me Kay [K!], as he proclaimed I was very set in my ways [stubborn?], opinionated, and my diction and word selection were similar to those of our Aunt Catherine "Katie" Dawson. To this day, "K" is the name most of my nephews and nieces call me.)

I never dreamed of getting money for getting injured. Leroy took care of locating a lawyer, who would forget appointments among other foul-ups. He initially asked for $30,000 from the insurance company, but after two or three years, the final result was $1,500 for me plus the lawyer's fee. The insurance company paid for my visits to a doctor who determined if it affected my mental capacity. I wore a neck brace, but it was uncomfortable and I soon discarded it.

I had plastic surgery at Saint Louis University Hospital to eliminate the horrible facial scars, which only seemed enhanced by makeup. Thank the Lord that the plastic surgery was successful, and only I can tell where the original scars were located. Insurance also paid for this.

On a Friday night, I got ready to go to a neighborhood watering hole. My finery consisted of semi-drag clothes, makeup, and very long hair. As I set out, I decided to stop at the Foot Long to greet those on the night shift, who included manager Leroy.

A husky high-school student named Earl was seated at the counter. I had no sooner perched on another counter stool when Vernon, a 20-something resident of our block, came in the door and proceeded to grab my hair, twist my head, and try to pull me to him. Upon seeing my plight, Leroy picked up a hammer and threatened to "nail" Vernon.

Earl and I escaped to my house. A few minutes later, Vernon pounded on the back door demanding to be admitted. We cowered in the living room, and then he went to the front door and threatened to bust in.

Leroy had called the police, and Vernon told them that he had just come to visit us and no one answered the door. Fortunately, that was the one and only time I had trouble with Vernon. A few years later, I encountered Earl at a gay bar.

On the first Super Bowl Sunday in January 1967, I ventured to Nell's home to view the game. My constant friend, a quart of vodka, accompanied me.

Del, a handsome Native American/white/African man, was on hand. He was 28, which was a little old for me since my preference usually was for men in the 19-to-23-year-old age range. But he was very good looking and charming. He was separated from his wife and had a young child. He had a room near the Foot Long. And guess what? He was unemployed at this time, although he was receiving unemployment benefits. His preference for vodka was equal to mine, and we hit it off immediately.

He accompanied me to 5006 Maple and didn't leave for three days. I was still on sick leave from my Foot Long job to recuperate from my windshield event. For approximately eight months, Del was like a member of the household. I eventually went back to working day shifts plus Saturday nights. I would bring food to the house from work, and he would have an ice-cold vodka and orange soda (also from the Foot Long) ready for me as I came in the back door.

On one evening, he fixed baked beans, which were the very best I ever had eaten. His recipe consisted of an abundance (he didn't measure) of brown sugar, drained pork 'n beans, a little catsup (not much), cinnamon, nutmeg, and vanilla. That is the recipe I began using, but I add some more ingredients (honey being one) and sometimes eliminate the catsup.

One of Del's friends dropped by our house one evening. He went upstairs to use the bathroom and called down that he thought he heard something in the hall closet. I hollered back, "It's probably the ghost that lives in there." Before I had even said "in there," he was leaping down the stairs, probably three at a time, for he was terrified at the word "ghost." He beat it out the front door. He would never go upstairs again and was never at ease downstairs. His visits soon ceased.

On my days off, Del and I toured most of the taverns in the immediate area. I always had money for drinking since I had no rent or utility expenses (the Foot Long owner let us live at the Maple Avenue house so we could keep an eye on the restaurant). Although I was paid just $1.35 an hour, I had enough for my makeup, dry-cleaning charges, and other miscellaneous items. I certainly had no money to save, but I didn't consider the future with my vodka-saturated brain.

When Del and I would go out for a day of barhopping, we usually would get pretty tore up after a few hours. As we sat at a bar side by side on one occasion, it was as if we were puppets or a well-orchestrated stunt team because we fell backwards off our stools at the same instant.

We stood up at the same time, mounted the stools simultaneously, and acted as if it were an ordinary occurrence. I considered this proper bar etiquette—to act as if it didn't happen. A faller definitely should not call attention to himself/herself. I've done it a couple of times as a solo act, and it doesn't hurt at all. But I probably was immune to pain from the alcohol.

During this time, I arrived to work one morning completely inebriated after consuming vodka all night with Del. As I entered the kitchen, I asked the cook, "Where do you keep the aprons?" I had grabbed an apron hundreds of times before. I was so out of sync that my eyes would hardly focus.

The owner hastily came to the kitchen and told me to go home and take the day off. Those words were music to my ears in my condition, and I happily made my way to our back door. The owner related to Leroy that I looked like a zombie, the walking dead.

The next morning, completely sober, I entered the workplace and asked the owner if he wanted me to work. He said, "Do you think you can behave yourself?" I assured him I could. I was a very good worker when I was sober, and I knew no one could really replace me.

On one occasion when I lived on Maple, I went to a house party in the next block. The last thing I recall from the party was a piece of candy that a gentleman gave to me. My next memory is walking on Burd Avenue at least 15 blocks from the address of the party. I was dressed in an outfit that had been snow white when I started the night. It was now entirely gray and covered in dust as if I had been rolling on a dusty dirt road or had been in a dust fight.

There were many small manufacturing businesses located on Burd where I was walking, and employees were going in the doors. I walked into a business entrance with some employees who, for some reason or other, gave me odd looks. I asked the receptionist what day it was and saw from the clock on the wall that it was 8 a.m. She kindly called a cab for me, and I again had no money but my rosary was not stolen. This cabdriver also held my rosary until I paid him when I got to 5006 Maple.

It was like the movie, *The Lost Weekend*, except mine was a lost 12 hours. That time period is a complete void. It's probably best that I don't know what actually occurred, but it still haunts me.

It was probably in August 1967 when Dad arrived for a visit. By now, I definitely was anorexic. I would have periodic bouts with anorexia and sometimes bulimia for years. Dad invited me to accompany him home for a visit, and Leroy said I could take time off from work.

I said that if Del could go with me, I would go. I visualized drinking beers while looking at the peaceful pastures and hills, visiting the Parnell tavern to introduce my friend, wonderful drives through the countryside with Dad, and visiting Kenny's family, Grandma, and Aunt Anna.

In my besotted pipe-dream mind, six-packs always were on hand.

Dad appeared to agree that Del could go along. Del was looking forward to it as much as I, and he and Dad had friendly, civil conversations. When Dad told Leroy that I was planning to take Del with us, Leroy was alarmed and told Dad, "no way." He and Dad knew that Parnell and the vicinity probably were not ready for integration by a drunken pair like Del and me.

Del and I were told that we would leave about 9 a.m. on the day of departure. But at 5 a.m. that day, I awakened to find Dad standing over me in the room where Del and I were sleeping fully clothed, ready for the trip with our suitcases packed. Before I knew what was happening, I was in Dad's car, and he was driving us away.

"Wait, wait, Del's not here," I said.

"He's not coming," Dad replied as we sped away.

I was crushed. Later, Del awakened to find that Dad and I (and my suitcase) were gone. Leroy later told me that when he left for the Foot Long, Del was sitting on the couch looking rather dazed.

That was the end of the Del saga. When I returned a few days later, he had left Missouri to be with his father's family. A few years later, I encountered Del, and he informed me that I was a lying, rotten bitch (his words) and he never trusted anyone again.

My memory is fuzzy about most of the ride to Parnell. However, I do recall stopping at a restaurant in a very small Missouri town on the Iowa border. When we entered, all conversation stopped so everyone could look at the emaciated feminine figure (me) with an older man. How they stared in disapproving disbelief. Dad—seemingly oblivious to the patrons who so unnerved me—ordered pie and announced that the restaurant's homemade pies were the best between Parnell and St. Louis.

Upon arrival at Maplehurst Manor, Bernie viewed me with obvious disgust while Thomas M. was his always bubbly and cheerful self and told me about his girlfriend. Dad had not given me accusatory looks and had been absolutely kind.

The following morning, Dad asked me to accompany him on a walk around the perimeter of the farm to check fences for potential weak links, especially the electric fences that were being used extensively for confinement of cattle. I was so weak that I stumbled and nearly fell a few times.

I didn't realize that Leroy had alerted Dad of my declining health and constant drinking, and Dad had hastily arrived in St. Louis. Their plan was for me to dry out on the farm and regain some self-respect and common sense. Was this the first intervention?

Upon returning from my walk with Dad, I immediately began to plan for my hasty return to St. Louis. I thought at least my job in St. Louis was waiting for me. It was a Thursday, as I recall, and I knew I did not want to attend Mass on Sunday anywhere around there, especially Parnell.

When I told Dad I was leaving, it seemed his shoulders sagged in exasperation and he shrugged. He knew he couldn't hold me against my will.

I paid Bernie to take me to Iowa City Saturday morning to catch a bus to St. Louis. I called Leroy upon arriving at the St. Louis bus terminal. Disbelief and disappointment were in his voice, and he did not offer to pick me up. I took the city bus to 5006 Maple to absolutely no welcoming committee.

It seemed I suddenly had no friends. Louise and Nell had moved several streets away. Even my drinking partner—Del—was gone.

During the few days I was away, my job had to be filled. For a week, I contemplated, "What will I do?" One thing that always has been in my favor is that I could work circles around most coworkers—whether it be loading and mowing hay or filling carhop orders and working a counter. An inept nightshift worker was fired, and Leroy and the owner agreed that I was needed to fill that position.

My drinking then slowed to a trickle. I did my work well. Perhaps the intervention had been somewhat successful.

Patrick Leo returned from Vietnam in June 1967. He soon had a good job at the huge

General Motors assembly plant in St. Louis and started dating Geneva, the nurse he would marry in August 1968. Thomas M. was in the Army and stationed in Germany.

Dad had stopped the milking operation and a lot of the chores that Patrick Leo and Thomas M. had done. He lived alone.

Kenny and Marlene purchased and moved to the original Boland homestead, a mile south of Parnell. It was a mile north of their old residence, which they had rented from Aunt Marge Costello. Kenny and Marlene now had five children with the additions of Tim and Trisha.

Grandma Agnew was in declining health at the age of 80. She fell in 1967 and fractured her hip and had several setbacks. She also suffered from dementia.

On April 4, 1968, I was working the evening shift (5 p.m. to 1 a.m.) when word passed among the patrons at the Foot Long counter that Martin Luther King Jr. had been assassinated. Chills ran through me after it was announced that law enforcement was looking for a white man because I knew that would unleash an outburst of white hate. All was quiet that night, as it seemed reality had not yet set in.

The next day, Nell and Louise called and offered to take Leroy, Patrick Leo, and me into their home as a safe haven. They had heard from some hotheads—and word on the street—that any white folks who dared enter the area would be beaten and God knows what else.

Fortunately, we did not have to take them up on their offer since Leroy, Patrick Leo, and I were well known and regarded in the area. No threats were made toward us. St. Louis was one of the few major U.S. cities that did not experience fires and looting after King's assassination.

As 1968 moved on, a new employee was hired at the Foot Long. Opal, a beautiful Native American, was several years younger than her African-American husband, Jeremy. Jeremy was one of the nicest individuals I have ever met and one of the few devout African Catholics I've known. They had seven children. I found Opal to be a good girlfriend, as in someone to discuss clothes, men, etc. She also had wheels (a method of transportation) in the form of a van.

In August, Patrick Leo and Geneva Shepherd were married at the Cathedral Basilica of St. Louis on Lindell Boulevard. A lovely reception was held at The Cheshire Inn in Clayton, Missouri, on the edge of St. Louis. They rented an apartment in midtown St. Louis.

Patrick Leo, Geneva, and I visited Iowa in September 1968 when we all had days off simultaneously. We spent a couple of days at Dad's and also saw Bernie. When we visited Grandma Agnew, her conversation made no sense as her health had deteriorated badly. It was utterly devastating to observe Grandma in such circumstances. She had been such a very strong woman with a very sharp mind.

On the morning of November 8, 1968, Grandma passed away. Her funeral was three days later at St. Joseph's Catholic Church in North English, and she is buried in the Armah Cemetery. Leroy, Patrick Leo, Geneva, and I arrived the evening before the funeral and spent the night at Dad's. Leroy and I were two of the grandsons who served as pallbearers.

A gathering was held after the burial. The only upside to funerals is renewing old acquaintances with folks you would otherwise never encounter.

While I worked nights in the fall of 1968, Leroy began taking courses from H&R Block to learn tax preparation. He had sensed that he was never going to advance his career managing a drive-in restaurant. He could see the declining business.

On January 1, 1969, Leroy was hired by H&R Block. He also continued to come to the Foot Long to count receipts, balance the cash register, and put the money in the safe at night.

Leroy quickly moved up the tax-preparation career ladder. He was doing more taxes than the other preparers, and company officials could see he was management material.

In early 1969, both Nell's and Louise's families moved west to the suburb of University City. Louise and I remained friends until she died of cancer in the 1980s. I attended barbecues in her backyard, went to her children's school picnics, and sipped many quarts of vodka while relaxing on her front porch. She made delicious crispy fried chicken, wonderful spaghetti, macaroni and cheese, potato salad, sweet-potato pie, and hot-water corn bread, a family dish I'd never seen before or since. I wish I had the recipe. She was heavy on using red pepper, which she added to most everything.

Louise, David, and family actually moved into the apartment building where I rented a room when I first moved to St. Louis in 1953. When I visited Louise and her family, I slept in that very same room. It truly is a small world.

When Louise, David, and son Buck, who was a paraplegic, later moved to the suburb of Hanley Hills, Louise would call me every few weeks and invite me to spend the weekend with them. She would implore, "Gina, I'm so lonesome. I don't have anyone to visit with all day." Buck could not speak. I really admired Louise and David for the loving care they gave him.

Louise got a charge about my age—I was 37, but the wallet-sized photo IDs that I purchased through the mail and appeared legitimate didn't indicate that. When I would order one, all I had to do was send in a headshot photo and write out a birthdate, eye color, height, and weight. I visited her for years and never advanced in age—and sometimes got younger!

Louise sounded serious when she delivered one of her funniest lines ever to me. As I was leaving her house after a weekend visit, she called out, "Gina, don't stay away so long—next time you'll only be 15 years old!"

On a late spring evening in 1969, I was working the night shift with only one teenage male carhop and a very young male high-school student in the kitchen. Business had fallen off, and both the day and night staffs were downsized. Bessie and Thelma, longtime kitchen employees, had quit. They said they were afraid of walking home after work at 1 a.m., as they both lived within walking distance. Lil, the longtime night cook, was now the day cook as Minnie also had left due to the fear factor.

Around 10 p.m. on this particular evening, two neighborhood hoodlums, who I knew by sight, came to the counter. They were known drug users. When I went to hand their order to them, they tried to grab it and run without paying. I held on tight, and they failed in their attempt. But seeing that there were just two teenage kids and me on duty, they leaped the counter as I dashed to the phone to call for help. They bypassed the cash register—an antiquated machine that couldn't even be locked.

As they rushed for me, I retreated to the kitchen where I grabbed a butcher knife. They stopped in their tracks and demanded to know, "What are you going to do with that?"

Knowing I could not kill or stab another individual, I let the knife drop to the floor and we started to scuffle. One of them dropped the French-fry basket into the hot grease, raised it out, and swung at me. I moved, and he struck his accomplice. With that, everything stopped momentarily as they exchanged accusing words concerning the semi-hot fry basket.

As the scuffle continued, we moved next to the back door, and all three of us ended up outside. Next to the back door was a 10-gallon container with handles and a lid; it held disposed cooking oil. An approximate knee-high, chain-link barrier, which had been built to stop out-of-control vehicles, surrounded the Foot Long.

A large crowd had gathered in the drive-in lot, but no one offered to help me. One of the hoodlums pushed me, and I fell after backing into the chain-link fence. I found myself on my back. The accomplice picked up the half-full grease can and was bringing it down to smash my head.

With Herculean effort, I raised my arms and stopped the can from smashing my head. My farm tasks had made me very strong, and thank God, I used that strength at that time.

By then, I was very angry and said, "Now this has gone far enough." I struggled to my feet as they dashed into the dark alley.

New, less-friendly groups now lived in the neighborhood. After the incident, the faithful cook, carhop, and I continued our work. I do recall that it was a full-moon night, and I firmly believe and have observed several times that weird happenings occur on these nights. At the Foot Long, the oddest, strangest, and weirdest people would show up on those nights. When I was toiling after dark at H&R Block in later years, the very same thing occurred.

Leroy arrived shortly after the fracas. When the other two workers and I related the events of the night, he was so incensed that he jumped in his car and went out seeking the two would-be robbers. I later was able to recall the name of one of them, and Leroy also knew him by sight.

Leroy scoured a few neighborhood taverns but failed to locate them. I don't know what he planned to do other than confront them. He could be intimidating with his utter lack of fear and dagger-like remarks that he inflicted on folks who had done wrong.

My coworker Opal introduced me to Kolbe, a 19-year-old friend of hers. His smile was beautiful, and his personality was equally so. His light complexion was indicative of his mixed ancestry. He worked on and off as a roofer and in construction.

By November 1969, one of my jobs was to count receipts at the end of the night and close the Foot Long. It became nearly a nightly occasion that Kolbe would arrive at the Foot Long about 12:45 a.m., and he, Opal, and I would walk the 25 steps to my house so we could listen to records and have a few drinks. On about 50 percent of those evenings, Kolbe would spend the night with me.

One night in the fall of 1969, I was home alone at about 2 a.m. when I heard a very loud thud on the floor downstairs. Leroy hadn't arrived home for the night, as he liked to go on late-night spins (leisurely cruises along the city's highways and byways, as he relaxed and unwound). Therefore, I had failed to properly lock and secure the back door of the house.

Suddenly, a young man opened the bedroom door and burst into my darkened room. I saw his companion, Robber #1, as he passed the doorway in the lighted hallway and recognized him as someone who had engaged me in conversation in one of the neighborhood taverns. I didn't know his name.

Robber #2, who had burst into my room, held a razor-sharp knife to my throat, as I lay naked in bed. He told me not to move and to say nothing. He whispered, "I ought to f--- you right now." But he didn't.

Robber #2 kept shouting, "Where's the money?" Evidently, he thought we kept the Foot Long's day's receipts at home. Leroy had two steamer trunks in his room where he kept letters, cards, photos, etc., which were precious to him. Robber #1 forced the trunks open and was extremely surprised and dismayed to find no valuables. The valuables were in Leroy's safe-deposit box at a local bank.

I was unharmed, but they did leave with my portable record player. However, they left the speakers behind, one of which had fallen to the floor when they grabbed the player when they first entered. That was the noise I had heard.

On a late night that same fall, Leroy, a carhop, and I were preparing to close when three very young guys entered the carhop room. They frightened the young carhop, and one of them pointed a pistol at me and announced a holdup, "Give me everything in the register."

"Wait, I'll be right back," I replied, as I headed for the phone and the kitchen. Evidently they were nervous, and they fled into the darkened alley.

A couple of nights later, a customer said, "I heard you almost got yourself shot." He said he had heard from unnamed street-grapevine sources that if the would-be robbers could have zeroed in on me as I went to the phone, they would have at least taken a shot at me.

Oh, the thrills of working nights. The neighborhood was in rapid decline.

Early December 1969 arrived, and business at the Foot Long was bad. On the morning of December 6, the employees, including Leroy who had done so much to help the restaurant become successful, were told that it would be the last day of operation for the Foot Long.

The owner was leaving the property and told Leroy and me to be out of both the restaurant and our house as soon as possible—right away—because he was turning off the water, gas, and electricity that day. Leroy went out to find a place for us to live and to get a truck and movers. I began packing what few possessions we owned, leaving most things in the drawers where they were.

The owner definitely was true to his word as a flashlight and candles were all the light we had that night. It had turned unusually bitterly cold, and we were without heat and drinking water and couldn't use the bathroom or wash our hands. Leroy and I each put on our winter coats and two pairs of slacks and piled covers on the mattress. We huddled and I will say, for some reason, I had one of the most restful nights ever, not awakening until the morning gave us some dim light.

When the owner revealed to Leroy the previous morning that he was disconnecting all the utilities, Leroy pleaded with him to leave them on for just one more day. As the owner jumped into his car and sped away, he replied, "I'm sorry Leroy." Those were his last words to the Dawsons.

December 7 was Pearl Harbor Day and the end of our Foot Long era. The day was spent loading the moving van with two friends. Leroy had rented a four-room, second-floor, walk-up apartment at the corner of South Grand Boulevard and Arsenal Street, about six miles from our north St. Louis home, in lily-white south St. Louis. That alone was culture shock.

We had taken the small two-burner gas stove and the wall cabinets and counters from 5006, as well as the outdated living-room furniture and tables that the Foot Long owners had given us when I arrived in 1963. The television, my "Uncle Emmett" desk, three beds, and four mattresses were among the other things we loaded.

When Leroy and the movers left 5006 Maple for 3018 South Grand, I stayed behind to protect our items that were not yet moved. We had a fully assembled shotgun and, as I sat on a small chair still clothed in my sleeping winter garb, I cradled the shotgun across my lap. I was sitting back from the kitchen door with my gun-baby. The back door was open, as it was the same temperature outside as inside the heatless house. My intention was to discourage any looters who had seen the truck leave.

The owner pulled up about 10 minutes later; evidently he saw the truck leave and assumed we were gone for good. He got out of his car, squinted at the open back door, and cautiously approached. At that time, he detected me holding the shotgun. Wild-eyed, he ran for his car and sped away in haste.

Leroy and the movers came back and got our last little load and me. I then saw our cramped—especially compared with the eight-room house with a beautiful bathroom that we had left—new apartment. But I was very thankful that Leroy had found a home for us on such short notice.

After dark, when the movers had left, Leroy and I took a drive by 5006 Maple and the darkened Foot Long. How sad and forlorn they looked. Vandals already had broken the house windows, and a fire had been set in the basement. There were signs on the door that cautioned all to stay out, as it was a hazardous and unsafe building.

One of the many young fellows from the neighborhood came to Leroy's open window and extended his regrets that we would no longer reside in the area. He looked across at me on the passenger side. He had never seen me unshaven, without makeup, without my hair being styled and sprayed in place, or without a tight shirt-blouse.

"What happened to you? You sure don't look pretty now!" he exclaimed. With that remark, my depression descended on me like a mighty weight.

December 7, 1969, ended another eventful chapter of my life.

Leroy and I were invited to spend Christmas at Patrick Leo and Geneva's residence in St. Charles, Missouri, which is about 20 miles west of St. Louis. Patrick Leo and Geneva recently had bought a home and also had a baby daughter, Amista.

On Christmas morning, there was a covering of snow on the ground. I got ready and, of course, took a flask of vodka with me. Nips of vodka helped to temporarily blot out my depression and unpleasant reality for a time.

Dad had arrived from Parnell to celebrate at Patrick Leo and Geneva's house. After the turkey dinner, Dad, Leroy, Patrick Leo, and I played cards at the kitchen table. Our game was Pepper. When we got together, we used the North English pool hall Pepper rules that were in existence then (and probably still). Geneva took care of Amista in the dining room.

Leroy and I left for home around 8 p.m. after exchanging goodbyes. Shortly after leaving, I began to suffer chest pains, I could barely breathe, and my chest felt like a barrel was inside that kept expanding. Leroy said I got very pale. As I struggled with breathing, Leroy stopped the car and began massaging my chest while saying the *Act of Contrition*.

I soon broke out in a tremendously cold, very wet sweat and felt as if I had not one ounce of energy in my body. I slumped in the front seat as limp as a wet dishrag—totally devoid of strength.

After being alerted by Leroy, Patrick Leo and Dad came to 3018 South Grand the next morning. Since I no longer had any pain or chest stress, I convinced them that it was ridiculous to convey me to the hospital. A heart attack seemed so unlikely—I felt that heart attacks happened to older people. After all, I was only 38 years old!

But for approximately the next five months, I had absolutely no energy and struggled to get a few basics unpacked.

Taking a break at the Foot Long, 1967.

Leroy in our house, 1967.

At Dad's farm with Erma I in 1972. She followed me
around and always got first dibs from the bucket.

Dad and I in his front yard with his dog, Fala, in 1972.

In St. Louis with a friend's feline, 1973.

# Chapter 9

## 1970–1974

Leroy, who now went by "Lee," began full-time employment for H&R Block on January 2, 1970. He had been promoted to office manager and was responsible for overseeing four more city offices. As the first week of February 1970 rolled around, he became overwhelmed since companies had issued their W-2 forms and folks hoping for early refunds swamped the offices.

The tax returns had to be checked after they were prepared, and the checkers were falling behind. Therefore, about 10 p.m. on an early February 1970 evening, Lee arrived home with a large box of tax returns. He asked that I check them and handed me an "error pencil," which had purple lead so its marks didn't come through on copy machines.

My knowledge of a tax form was almost zero. I began to look through them and soon detected on what line each total was to be entered. Rental property was the most perplexing; I had no idea what was depreciable and didn't understand the depreciation tables.

By April 15, 1970, I had learned the intricacies of preparing a tax return, and thus I had a head start when I attended tax-preparation courses beginning in September 1970.

Between December 7, 1969, and April 15, 1970, I spent two weekends each with the Opal and Louise families. These were rather quiet times with nothing unusual happening. Lee had proclaimed that no visitors from our old haunts were welcome, as lily-white south St. Louis was still very segregated and prejudiced. Our friends from Opal's and Louise's families didn't want to venture to the south side either. Therefore, the Kolbe affair was over.

Dad came to visit around April 1970, and I went back to Iowa with him. I spent most of that summer in Parnell.

Thomas M. had returned from his Army stint with his recently wed wife, Denise. Denise, a teenager from California, was pregnant when they got married. Thomas M. and Dad were going to farm together, and Thomas M. and Denise resided with Dad at Maplehurst Manor for a short time. Denise was totally overwhelmed by the expectancy that she suddenly become a farm housewife.

Farm prices plummeted, and the price of hogs dipped. The downward spiral was the same with all farm products. Dad was unable to pay Thomas M. each week.

Thomas M. and Denise's daughter, Laura, was born in August 1970. Thomas M., Denise, and Laura moved to a house about three miles away, and Thomas M. commuted from there to Dad's. In December 1970, Denise and Laura left Iowa to visit family in California. Denise informed Thomas M. that he could join her if he wished, but she was not returning to Iowa. The farming venture had not been successful, and Thomas M. left for California the day before Christmas 1970 and hasn't been an Iowa resident since.

In September, I had left Dad's and returned to St. Louis to attend tax courses taught by H&R Block instructors. I passed the H&R Block course with perfect test scores, and I was hired to manage and prepare taxes at the West Florissant Avenue office in north St.

Louis, about 85 blocks north of our apartment on South Grand. A city bus went directly from South Grand to North Grand; it was an approximate 30-minute ride.

In early 1971, my coworkers included Bessie, who had been a cook at the Foot Long. Lee tried to find employment for his former employees and old friends from the Foot Long. Again, he was my boss.

I thoroughly enjoyed the tax-preparation job and met many very nice clients who I saw only once or twice a year. I also made a nice bonus of $1,400 that first year.

Thus began a period of 20-plus years of tax-season work. Then I would spend most of those summers in Iowa. I drew unemployment compensation for about 16 weeks in 1971 and in the following years when I worked for H&R Block.

So 1972, 1973, and 1974 continued in the same vein: my tax-prep job, summertime at Dad's, and updated tax studies in the fall.

When I was at Dad's farm, I hardly went anywhere, except Dad and I went to Mass either in Iowa City or Cedar Rapids (I refused to go to St. Joseph's in Parnell). My hair was dyed red, and I let it grow long. I looked completely different from my old Parnell days.

My social life consisted of a few evenings with Aunt Anna Agnew, who lived alone in the house she and Grandma had shared in North English. I also spent some afternoons at Kenny and Marlene's with their kids.

My drinking and social smoking were curtailed, although I did bring along cartons of Winston cigarettes to Iowa. Dad did not keep alcohol except for a fifth of whiskey that someone, usually a hunter who tramped his fields in search of game, had given to him. It often would last over a year.

Dad had a beautiful herd of cows—stock cows—whose primary purpose was to birth healthy calves each spring. Almost every year, he would use a different breed of bull. One year in early summer, I accompanied him to a farm in northeast Iowa; he had leased a bull for two or three months from its owners.

I recall getting a red Limousin one summer. Other years, there were Simmental, Charolais, Angus, Chianina, Brown Swiss, a Red Poll shorthorn, and my favorite, other than Bulba the Charolais that he had longer than the others, was a large-boned, dark red, gentle Gelbvieh that he purchased at the Sigourney sale barn. The combinations brought out the best quality of each breed. The offspring were of many beautiful colors. Dad had black cows that looked like Brown Swiss but didn't grow horns. His Charolais/Brown Swiss cow had the body of a Charolais, the milk production of a Brown Swiss, and an orange body color with Swiss ears.

Dad purchased Erma, a white Yorkshire-Duroc crossed sow, and five of her sisters from a local farmer. Erma was as tame as a dog and followed me about. She responded to her name, and she loved to be petted and have her ears scratched and tummy rubbed. When she gave birth to her piglets, she was never cross and trusted me completely when I handled them. I pampered her and let her drink fresh concoctions from the bucket before feeding the other swine. She also got the choicest ears of corn.

Unfortunately for Erma, like all meat-producing farm animals, she was sent to market when she grew older. Dad was practical and emphasized that farmers cannot "fall in love" with farm animals or they will go broke.

In a 10-year period, I also "claimed" Erma II, daughter of the first Erma, who had a Spotted Poland (breed) father and weighed 800 pounds when she was sent to market. Erma III, whose father was a Hampshire, was the last of the family as she died during the birth of her third litter. All the Ermas were very intelligent, would come when I called, and would rub their heads gently on my leg to ask for some "vittles" or some loving attention. I also had a special relationship with a sow named Pinky, who came before the Erma family.

In 1972, Lee was closing the H&R Block office at Union and Delmar Boulevards when he felt something rub against his leg. Startled, he looked down and saw a nearly full-grown tomcat, yellow in color. When he opened his car door, the cat hopped in. As he opened our door at 3018, ready to ascend the 20 steps that led to our living quarters, he shouted, "K, I found you a cat. I know you like animals."

"Delmar" was the name given to the very cuddly cat. He proved to me that cats are very intelligent. We had Delmar for 12 years. During that time, we were never concerned about mice or other rodents entering the apartment.

One day when I walked by the office of a physician, the doctor was out front.

"I love the way you walk," he told me. I got the message that it was more than my walking that intrigued him.

He would write prescriptions for anything I requested. My main request was for estrogen to make my hair thicker and lustrous (more feminine) and develop my breasts, which also became "lustrous." My skin became almost baby soft, and I had luxurious fingernails. When I visited Iowa, I wore big, loose-fitting shirts and a back brace around my chest to flatten my breasts. I quit taking estrogen when the changes became too much to disguise.

In St. Louis, I made a few friends as I made an occasional sally to the downtown all-white gay bars. One of those friends was a lawyer who had a crush on me. To me, he was just a drinking buddy.

Late in December 1974, I met Harlin, a 6 foot, 2 inch African-American young man who had just been discharged from military training due to insubordination. It seems I've always been attracted to bad boys. Usually, it seems, they were either on their way to or being released from jail or prison. I'm convinced that subconsciously I really wanted to help them—or did I wish to control them, as their chances of employment were greatly diminished? Since I don't do "whys" or "ifs," I'm not concerned.

Dad, still wearing overalls, 1976.

At Dad's farm in 1977.

With one of Dad's Brown Swiss steers, 1978.

Lee, 1978.

# Chapter 10

## 1975–1979

It no longer was unusual to see African Americans in the South Grand area where Lee and I lived. So we began to have black visitors. Beginning in January 1975, Harlin, the young man I had met a month earlier, spent many evenings and overnights with me.

In April 1975, Harlin was sentenced to 30 days in the city workhouse. He admitted to being present when his two accomplices stole a gun from a residence, and he took the rap for all of them. He wouldn't tell on his friends because being known as a "rat" in the underworld is as low as one can descend, and the "rat" is definitely ostracized. (Even criminals have a little code of honor in their systems.)

Harlin did not tell me about the charges until the day before he had to report to the workhouse. I was devastated. He brought his meager belongings to Lee's and my apartment because he would be unable to pay weekly rent in advance to hold his room in north St. Louis.

On April 11, 1975, the day Harlin was locked up, Ida Sampson made her appearance for me to prepare her taxes. Ida, an African-Native American nurse, was called "Mother Hen" because she seemed like everyone's mother. I became fast friends with Ida and her daughter Jan, aka "Mother Nature," and we still are friends to this day. They called me "sister" or "Gina," except when they thought I was really silly—then they called me "Phyllis," a take on comedian Phyllis Diller.

As I prepared Ida's tax form, she detected that I was bothered, and I revealed the reason was Harlin's imprisonment. She was very sympathetic. I completed her federal and state forms, and about 20 minutes after she left the office, she returned with a ham sandwich and a can of soda and insisted I eat before she left. From then on, she would arrive on April 11 each year to have her taxes prepared on our "anniversary" of friendship.

"Hen" would rush to the office and take care of me whenever I had an emergency. When I had an intolerable toothache, she took me to the dentist and then back home. She stayed with me until Lee arrived home from work.

Mother Hen and Mother Nature were very fond of Dad and called him "Daddy Dawson." Dad sold beef that he had raised to several of Lee's and my friends, including Mothers Hen and Nature. These friends knew they were getting the best meat that could be purchased.

On one occasion after Dad delivered meat to Mother Hen and Mother Nature, they cooked chicken for Lee and him. The ladies phoned me and said they would send some home for me via Lee and Dad.

As Lee and Dad ate, Ida's German shepherd, Dogella, hungrily sat near the back of Lee's chair. As Lee finished each piece, he gave the bones to Dogella. Lee let some audible gas escape a few times, and Dad finally said very seriously, "Dogella, you better move or you're gonna get shit on." Everyone roared with laughter. Dad could be such a comedian and storyteller. Ida occasionally told this story and was so tickled.

As for the chicken they sent home for me, Dad said Lee ate it as they drove back to our place. When I asked Lee for the chicken, his reply was "They must have forgot." It must have been really good!

I went back and forth between St. Louis and Dad's during these summers. Dad now employed a young farmer who helped with the livestock and farm tasks. But when I was at the farm, Dad started taking my help for granted and reverted to treating me like a kid. I was 44 years old.

I would go back to St. Louis for two to three weeks, and then Dad would call and ask me to return. In the summer of 1975 when I was in St. Louis for a few weeks, Harlin visited. He also wrote to me often when I was at Dad's.

September 1975 arrived, and I took tax courses again. The Halloween, Thanksgiving, and Christmas holidays were observed. Harlin and I had a happy candlelit repast on Christmas Eve.

On January 1, 1976, I began another year with H&R Block. By this time, I had many steady customers who would let no one else prepare their taxes. I was working from 9 a.m. to 5 p.m., Monday through Friday, no more and no less. I arranged to always have my last client done by 4:45 p.m. so I could catch the 5:10 bus heading south on Grand. When a client was waiting for me, I would tell him/her that someone on the nightshift could help. Nary a time did the client not say, "When will you be back?"

Harlin was coming by the apartment more often, usually arriving about 6:30 p.m. after work. I would greet him at the entrance, and he would say, "What's for supper?"

I was thrilled—I felt like a real housewife! I served lots of spaghetti (his favorite), macaroni and cheese, chili, and other dishes that provided leftovers for more meals. That was the reason I left work so promptly at 5 p.m. I wanted to be home in time to prepare supper for us.

When tax season was done on April 15, I received a sizable bonus of between $2,500 and $3,500. I had to live on that, along with unemployment payments, for the rest of the year.

I had a clerk-friend at the employment office who assisted me. Every six weeks, I had to appear in person at the office. On those days, I would be at the door at 8 a.m. with 50 or 60 other folks who had the same idea. When the doors opened, everyone rushed to get a number that was hanging from a peg—these folks could be very aggressive. However, my clerk-friend told me to nonchalantly walk to her desk and take a seat on the chair next to it.

I always took my clerk-friend a treat such as a pint of ice cream, cookies, a small cake, or candy. After perching in the chair next to her desk, I would put a large shopping bag, which held my papers and goodies, on her desk as if I were bringing her breakfast or delivering something. Therefore, I was the first person served. On the way to her desk, I looked neither left nor right at the assemblage with their numbers as I knew they were offended and pissed off. When I left, I followed the same routine.

In early spring, probably May 1976, Harlin arrived to spend the evening. It was a Saturday night, and I was dressed in an all-pink outfit. I was wearing a cheap, knockoff version of an expensive gold watch and, of course, I was made up as if I were going out on the town.

We were enjoying vodka and orange juice and watching television in my room. The drinks and ice were in the kitchen. As I sashayed down the hall on the way to the kitchen to refresh our drinks, I was surprised to see Lee sitting on the couch and a good-looking African-American fellow perched in one of the overstuffed chairs.

Lee suggested that I give his guest one of the cold home brews I had made the prior fall. The brews were very good if you like home brew (I don't). They were extremely powerful, probably 20 percent alcohol, as I used more than double the amount of sugar called for in the recipe.

I replenished our drinks, handed the guest a brew, and was returning to my room when he asked if I were a model and commented on my nice watch. When I got to the bedroom, I locked the door with the sliding-bolt lock, which I always did when I was inside.

About five minutes later, there was a light knock on my door, and Lee asked if he could get a cigarette.

"Do whatever he says," Lee said, as I opened the door.

I wasn't aware exactly what was happening until Lee's "guest" pushed Lee into the room. I recognized the large butcher knife from our kitchen that he was holding to Lee's back.

The guest was surprised when he saw Harlin, with whom I had just celebrated his 21st birthday, sitting on the bed with his back toward the wall. (I had my made-up single bed serving as a couch with several pillows next to the wall.) The guest began to berate Harlin for associating with such "low-life, no-good honkies" as Lee and me and ordered that he not move. The intruder definitely was not expecting to see another African-American individual in my room.

He demanded the watch I was wearing and announced that it was cheap and not real. The intruder had Lee remove his slacks, and then the intruder took Lee's money.

He had Lee get on the floor with his back to the proceedings and demanded that I unlock and open the closet door. The door was always padlocked, as I didn't want any of my overnight guests to have easy access to the closet.

In the closet were all my frilly, feminine clothes, shoes, and several belts. There also was some cash, perhaps $30 to $40, and a metal box that contained a stash of marijuana (which I didn't use) that I harvested the prior summer when visiting Dad on the farm.

The intruder entered the closet and started throwing my clothes on the floor while making fun of them. He threw the belts on my back, as he had me on the floor on my stomach.

"Wow, I bet you didn't know about this, bro," he said to Harlin when he discovered the marijuana. I was on my stomach and saw Harlin's surprised look, and Lee, unbelievably, made a quick turn of his head. He was immediately rebuked and told to look the other way.

With that, the intruder proceeded to hog-tie me with my belts as Harlin looked on helplessly. He knew he would be stabbed if he tried to stop the intruder. My wrists were bound behind my back, and I was told to lift my neck as a noose (belt) was placed around it. Then the other end of the belt was looped around my ankles that were up with my knees bent. The intruder knew that gravity slowly but assuredly would pull my head and feet down and I would strangle.

As the intruder finished that task, he announced that he should f--- me.

"This is what I think of you," he said as he urinated on me.

At that moment, I recall thinking, "I'll never wear this blouse again." Funny the things you think during a traumatic situation.

As the intruder stepped into the closet to reach up and take the metal box containing the weed, Lee, sensing the opportunity, scrambled to his feet and out the door. Sans pants, he fled down the steps and out to the sidewalk heading south. The intruder, wielding the knife, was in hot pursuit and almost caught Lee before he went out the door. But then, fortunately, the intruder headed the opposite direction of Lee and went north on Grand.

Meanwhile, Harlin had leapt from the bed and was close behind the intruder. When he saw that Lee had escaped, he bound back up the stairs, ran to the kitchen, and returned with a knife to cut the belts that bound me.

The police were called later, but since no one was dead and we only revealed that he had stolen my cheap watch and a few dollars, they didn't seem concerned. We didn't want to tell them that he had stolen a box of wild marijuana.

Lee had met the intruder in a downtown liquor store when Lee stopped to purchase a six-pack of beer. A conversation had taken place, and the fellow asked Lee for a ride home and added that he wouldn't mind having one of those cold beers. Lee then invited him to our home.

The intruder probably had noticed Lee's wallet, which always was stuffed with greenbacks of various denominations. Lee always trusted the young guys he encountered, much to his regret in later years.

When I checked the chair where the intruder had been sitting, I found the empty home-brew bottle stuffed in the back of the seat cushion. He had poured the brew under the cushion, and it was soaked. He never was interested in drinks—he was intent on robbery from the moment he saw Lee. This guy probably did get a good sum of cash from Lee's wallet, not just a few dollars that Lee told the police had been stolen.

A month later, I saw a story in the local crime newspaper, *The Whirl*, about this same individual tying two other victims, on separate occasions, the same way he had tied me. He didn't wait for either of them to die by strangulation—he plunged a knife into their backs. He had been apprehended and finally was off the street.

The summer of 1976 was spent on the farm with Dad. He still was very active and raised lots of hogs, some feedlot cattle, cows with calves at their sides in the pasture, 12 laying hens, and a few sheep. We were busy with chores beginning at 5 a.m.

Dad was taking pills for various, non-life-threatening ailments. I kept him on his pill schedule by parceling them out in daily pill containers. Some of his young helpers would teasingly call him a "drug addict" when he would show them the pills he was about to consume before dinner.

I found myself cooking, housekeeping, and choring, and I realized "never say never" again. Dad even asked if I would assist a young helper in stacking hay bales in the barn! I just couldn't refuse his request—he asked so nicely and even said "please." His saying "please" made my day, and I found I actually enjoyed the strenuous activity.

It also was nice to hear "thank yous" and compliments on my meals and cooking. Usually the comments from Dad's helpers were along the line that my cooking was just as good as a woman's.

One of the compliments that I appreciated the most came from Aunt Catherine Dawson. As we were eating dinner when she was visiting Dad in the 1970s, someone remarked that everything was in place and the entire dinner atmosphere was so pleasant and good. Aunt Catherine replied, "Gene is efficient in anything he does." She did not issue compliments often.

In the summer when I returned to St. Louis from Dad's, I was due for a personal appearance at the employment office. My clerk-friend was on vacation. When my turn arrived at the office, I could tell that the employee who called me to her desk just hated to see someone who wasn't actually physically laboring get a check. You would have thought it was her money instead of the government's. And of course, my employer, H&R Block, contributed to unemployment funds.

She scanned my search work list and quizzed me extensively. She remarked that I appeared to be depressed. She knew I was a veteran and had me sign a paper to take to the veterans' hospital. I assumed it was for a job interview.

With my flaming red hair, but sans heavy makeup, I presented the paper to a receptionist and was told to go to an upper floor. Upon arriving there, I unceremoniously was put in a room and a heavy door locked behind me. I gazed around to see vacant-eyed men, most of them in robes. A few were standing and gazing out the barred windows. I spoke to one of them as I took a magazine and sat down on a couch. He just looked back at me with a bewildered stare.

It then dawned on me that I must have signed a paper that put me in the psych unit for veterans with depression! I began pounding on the heavy door with the heavy-glass window until a doctor came. I informed him that I definitely was in the wrong place.

One lesson learned, for heaven's sake, is to always read everything, especially the fine print, before signing your name.

About mid-afternoon, I was escorted to a room where a white-coat-clad gentleman with some title of psych doctor was the only person present. He talked about depression and stated that the employment-office interviewer thought I was a candidate for treatment since I was a veteran and unemployed.

After he asked stupid questions—such as why I had to leave immediately—I informed him that I had to get home to cook supper for my husband. With that remark, he appeared taken aback and left the room. In a few minutes, he was back and said I could go. I suppose the hospital officials couldn't hold me against my will based on what an employment-office clerk recommended.

As I got on the elevator to descend to the lobby, about eight or nine doctors and nurses backed away and stared at me in dead silence. Evidently, they had heard about the crazy queen who demanded to be released to cook supper for her husband!

When I told the story to Lee and later to Patrick Leo, both of them found it highly amusing. They suggested that instead of just being queen for a day that I was queen of the psych unit for a day.

Terry Dawson, my oldest nephew, wed Marcia Brack on September 18, 1976, not far from Parnell. Lee and I arrived at Dad's too late for the wedding festivities, but we had a good visit with Aunt Catherine Dawson, who had come from Indianapolis. She had attended the wedding with Dad. Aunt Catherine announced that my brother Kenny, the bridegroom's father, was the most handsome man in attendance.

Harlin sent letters when I was in Iowa that summer, but "When the cat's away, the mouse will play." And that is what he did. By November 1976, I had become disillusioned with him and his incessant lies, and I demanded that he take his clothes and whatever else was his and leave my apartment. He called a friend and was gone within the hour.

After a good cry, I decided that *I'm Gonna Wash That Man Right Outa My Hair*—just like the song. That was the end of the Harlin affair.

Occasionally, Harlin would call to ask for another chance. He moved in with a woman for a time. He told her about me, but said I had a sex-change operation and was a real woman. She called me at work in early 1978. I was surprised to get her call and told her that I didn't have to meet her and my place of employment was off-limits.

I kept going out. After a night of barhopping, I sometimes awakened the next morning and couldn't recall how or when I got home or where I had been after my first destination. I would wonder if I had done anything stupid.

Jim & Kate's usually was my downtown bar of choice. It was not a gay bar, and the clientele ranged from executives of area businesses who dropped in after working hours to the pimps, prostitutes, male hustlers, pickpockets, gays, dykes, drag queens, and the just plain weirdos who all got along famously well.

But woe be the innocent wanderers who happened to enter. Occasionally they would be the victims of a strong-arm robbery in the restroom or be so overwhelmed by some of the clientele that they hastily departed—usually relieved of a watch, wallet, or cash.

When I had no memory of a night out, the next time I ventured to a bar, which usually was Jim & Kate's, I timidly would enter and slide up to a seat. I would start to relax if the bartender didn't give me any looks of disgust. Finally, I'd ask, "Did I do anything when I was here last time?" He would stop and say, "You just sat there like you are now." I suppose I had taken a cab home, as I usually did whether alone or accompanied. The guys I met usually were either going to or coming from jail, so they didn't have wheels.

When I went out one night in 1977, I was pleased with my outfit, my makeup was perfect, and my hair was styled and sprayed with every wisp in place. I had a black draw-string purse—in fact, I had two identical purses but, of course, carried only one. A little money (I usually kept most of it in my shoes), makeup, perfume, and cigarettes made up the contents of my purse.

I was having a pleasant time at Jim & Kate's that night when two underage fellows came to the bar. They said they were from East St. Louis and had walked across a Mississippi River bridge to the Missouri side. The nicer-looking young man asked if he could go home with me, but I told him he was too young.

The owner soon invited them to leave the bar. They ungraciously accepted his invitation. When the bar closed and I walked out with a couple of my gay sisters, the two young men were there and the nice-looking guy asked again if he could accompany me home.

I was a little suspicious since there were two of them. But I'm not really afraid of anything.

While "good looking" engaged me in conversation, the other conked me over the back of my head with a beer bottle and snatched my purse. I yelled unkind names after them as they hastily fled into a dark alleyway.

The beer bottle had broken—again proving I have a very hard head. I had a jagged cut across the back crown of my head, and blood gushed out of the wound as my friends took kerchiefs to stanch the flow and soak it up. Some blood trickled down my face.

I walked a half block to a cab, and before the driver could object, I was in the back seat. All he said was to not get any blood on the seat. At that moment, the door on the other side of the back seat opened. I thought it would be one of my "sisters," but it was a different good-looking guy who looked to be about 20. He started to wipe the blood from my face and said he was going to take care of me and make sure I was all right. I could tell he was sincere. We then sped away to 3018 South Grand.

The young guy was true to his word and cleaned the wound and got the blood flow stopped. The next morning, he told me that he had seen me several times at the bar.

I know the two who assaulted me had to be disappointed because my purse contained only about $2, a couple of cigarettes, and makeup. I hated the loss of the makeup for it was Lancôme!

That night, I decided that those thugs were not going to intimidate me. So after taking a couple of sips of straight vodka, I combed my hair over the wound, applied my makeup, gussied up in a different outfit (the other had blood on it), and got out the spare matching purse and filled it with everything the other contained—minus the money.

When I arrived at the bar, the patrons were amazed. They thought I may have gone to the hospital and could hardly believe I was back the next night. I was hoping those two would be back from East St. Louis and think they were seeing a ghost with the same hairdo, makeup, and purse. They weren't going to intimidate "Super Pussy"—my name for myself after Pussy Galore of the *James Bond* movies, who was quite gifted in combat.

I never saw them again, but there is no doubt in my mind that I would have recognized them. When something violent happens to me, it seems to print a perfect image in my mind.

In 1978, I really buckled down and was getting more steady clients. That year, I had my usual schedule of H&R Block and taxes until April, back and forth from St. Louis to Iowa in the summer, and the tax update in the fall.

Aunt Ann Dawson Conroy died in the spring of 1978. She was two years younger than Dad and a sibling with whom he had a close, loving relationship. She was 68 years old. I loved Aunt Ann; she was so pleasant and kind.

By the end of 1979, Patrick Leo and Geneva's family had grown to include John, Brian, Joe, Mike, and Mark. Thomas, born in 1981, would be their last child. They all joined Amista, the only girl of the siblings.

It was fortunate for me that all of their children were born after tax season, as I could spend time with them while Geneva was hospitalized and Patrick Leo was working days at General Motors. I think some of the kids may have thought I was a mean overseer, but I do have loving relationships with all of them. They now tell of the "abuse" I heaped upon them when they start telling their tales of growing up. I hardly recognize the stories—they have grown to preposterous proportions as they are told and retold and embellished significantly when I am the subject. I love their stories about others, too, but the stories concerning Maudie/Gene are no longer recognizable as they have grown both in length and outrageousness!

As 1979 came to an end, I had two good gay male friends. They were friends only, strictly for companionship and socialization. I never had been attracted to other gay men; my fascination and love were for masculine straight or bisexual men. Besides, my friends

Richard A. and Robert "Bobby Bare" were way too old for me. They were in their late 30s or early 40s.

I was 48.

I was stunned when I received my first mailing for senior citizens that same year. I thought, "For God's sake, I have not entered middle age yet!"

When I had turned 35, Louise asked me, "Gina, what are you going to do when you get to be 45?" She was speaking of my gay social life of glamour. At that, I said, "The same thing I'm doing now." I never thought that far down the line.

I had considered a sex-change operation many times through the years. The cost was a big deterrent. Another thing was that it would affect a great many lives other than mine. My Dad, brothers, Grandma, aunts, uncles, cousins, friends, and neighbors—what would they think? I wouldn't have felt like I could visit Iowa. What about a job? Lee probably would have stuck with me.

Well, it never happened, and I don't do "ifs." My Catholic faith, which was so thoroughly indoctrinated in my brain, was definitely against such surgery. By 1979, I was attending Mass again but shunned the confessional. I'm certainly glad my common sense rose to the top, and I didn't have the surgery.

I feel each individual should be free to make his or her own choice about gay marriage. For me, it wouldn't have been the right thing to do. Think of the divorces I would have had. As far as having a sex change, for some individuals it brings happiness and love of self, instead of sadness and loathing of who they are.

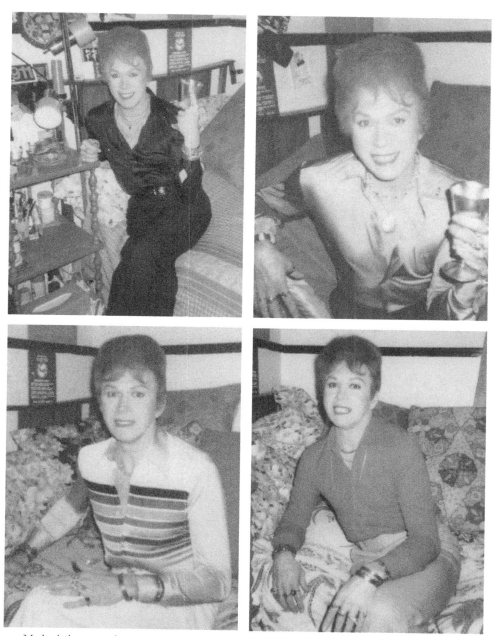

My bed also served as a couch in my room. These pictures were all taken in the late 1970s.

I am 53 in these photos taken at my apartment in 1984.
I enjoyed modeling my wigs, dresses, and jewelry.

# Chapter 11

## 1980–1984

On January 2, 1980, the H&R Block tax offices opened again, and I was extremely busy preparing tax returns for three generations of some families. I also started working the night shift.

I would take the Grand Boulevard bus early in the morning to arrive at 6:30 a.m. to file away returns and copies that had arrived via messenger Leroy Atkins in the overnight hours (we dubbed Leroy A. the "suitcase man"). Any supplies I had ordered, such as tax forms, toilet tissue, coffee, cups, sugar, and cream, had to be stashed in their proper places. This was the receptionist's job, but we always had clients waiting when she arrived at 9 so she didn't have the time. I also made the coffee.

My customers could observe that I was at work early and therefore would knock at the door. They would holler, "I know you're in there; I smell the coffee." Soon Lee deemed that my office open at 8 a.m. to accommodate the crowds.

I had customers who had moved from the St. Louis area and returned from Florida, Texas, Colorado, Kentucky, and California so I could do their taxes. They would proclaim, "Do you know how many H&R Block offices we passed on our way here?" I was impressed and thankful. However, I'm convinced they could have found someone to please them much closer to their homes.

When I did taxes, I always projected myself to be sitting right with the clients. I tried to jog their memories on every known deduction, tax break, and credit to which they were entitled under the federal and state tax codes. We prepared only Missouri and Illinois state forms in the area's branch offices. A very patient and knowledgeable lady prepared tax forms for the "foreign" states, which we called the states other than Missouri or Illinois, at another location.

All of my clients who could itemize, even if not by much, ended up using the long form, and most were refunded big bucks. After all, these clients had paid the withholding—the government was just using it interest-free until they reclaimed it by filing their tax returns.

The years 1980, 1981, and 1982 were very similar, except that back in Iowa, Dad began complaining about acute pain in his sides and back. He had cut down on his livestock population and no longer had sheep.

During one of my visits to Iowa, Dad and I somehow ended up talking about my childhood. Some readers may find it hard to believe, but I did not harbor any grudge against Dad for the physical punishment that he inflicted on me. I thought this was how all children were punished by their fathers.

But during this discussion, so many years later, I did say to Dad, "You know you hit me."

"Oh, I regret so many things I did," he replied sadly.

It was an apology for him. But I never felt that he owed me one.

Richard A. and Bobby Bare would arrive via city bus to 3018 on Tuesday and Friday evenings in the summers when I was home from Dad's Iowa farm. While I finished my final preparations before going out, Richard A. and Bobby would sit on my bed-couch with the large pillows and listen to the latest albums or eyeball television with their drinks in hand. Richard A. announced one night, "Miss Gina serves the coldest drinks, has the best television picture, the coolest room, and the softest, comfiest bed." I considered that a great compliment.

After a couple of drinks, we would call a cab and usually head for Jim & Kate's. I felt quite comfortable there and made friends with the various bartenders and owners. I always carried my lady purse, which held my cigarette case and lighter that was personalized with "Gina" emblazoned in rhinestones, a compact with a mirror, lipstick, lip gloss, three shades of eyebrow liner, and plenty of perfume. My favorite perfumes were You're the Fire by Yardley and Foxfire by Avon.

Of course, my restroom of choice was the women's and, when I went there, usually at least two women would ask to borrow my makeup. I really enjoyed Jim & Kate's and met various guys of interest there who became overnight guests. Many of them were transients or military men passing through St. Louis who had heard through the underground grapevine that Jim & Kate's was the place to hook up with whoever met your sexual preference test.

When we were at the bar, I noticed that Richard A. never sat on a barstool. His complaint was that his rear end was painful. Late in the summer of 1982, he finally went to a doctor as the rectal pain had intensified so much that it was almost unbearable. He immediately was admitted to the hospital and diagnosed with colon cancer in an advanced stage. For the next 2½ months, he was alternately at home, where his mother gave him the best care she could provide, or back in the hospital.

I hadn't seen Richard A. in about three weeks when I went to the hospital to visit him. I was shocked into tears as I viewed him—he had lost so much weight that he appeared skeleton-like. I spent time that evening with him, and he was sometimes delirious. I bathed his fevered face, and I let some water flow over his upper head and said: "I baptize thee in the name of the Father, the Son, and the Holy Spirit." Then I repeated it, adding, "Amen," as I didn't know for sure if an "Amen" was part of a baptism.

During one of our previous conversations, Richard A. had remarked that he wouldn't mind being Catholic. Baptism did not mean that he was Catholic, as baptisms are recognized by Almighty God and most Christian denominations. After all, I believe that all religions lead us to the same destination, back home with our Loving Creator. We just take different paths that lead to the same pearly gate.

Richard A. died in late 1982 and was buried at Jefferson Barracks National Cemetery in south St. Louis. May his soul rest in peace.

When 1983 arrived, it was the same routine. During tax season, I stopped all smoking and drinking and did not go out carousing any nights because I was becoming so busy. When the regional manager (Lee's boss) arrived from Kansas City for a St. Louis inspection, he asked to visit 3900 North Grand, my place of employment, to see the office that had a volume well over projections each year.

We were warned he was coming to visit. The "we" in the office were Albert and Brenda, the other preparers, and Erline, the receptionist. The four of us had been working together since 1974.

Lee advised me to wear a suit and tie instead of my usual jeans, shirt, and sweater. The H&R Block dress code was a shirt and tie for men, but I never abided by it. I felt my customers were more relaxed if I dressed in a way similar to their garb.

When the regional manager and Lee, the district manager, arrived one morning in early February, there were 15 people in the waiting area. I had a client at my desk, but Albert and Brenda did not have any clients at that moment. Managers hate to see clients wait because they don't want them to leave and go elsewhere. So the two managers suggested that Albert and Brenda help those in line. The clients in line squirmed uncomfortably and said they were waiting for me. Albert said, "They're not going to let anybody prepare their taxes but Gene."

I did not take appointments; I had learned that a third of the time the clients didn't show and didn't call to cancel. So my clients always waited patiently—they knew my procedure was first come, first served. They only would leave when there were seven or eight people ahead of them and they had time to dash across the street to Kentucky Fried Chicken. Many times, they would bring a box of chicken and fries back for me. They were a wonderful group of clients.

The regional manager decided that I should have my own office, receptionist, coffee maker, and all. Overnight, Leroy Atkins constructed an office for me in a room already in existence. The managers did not want potential walk-in clients to look in and be discouraged by a group of people ahead of them. It was a successful change, as I still had my usual clients and always some new folks who were recommended by them.

A nice bonus was forthcoming, as I brought in the most money of any H&R Block preparer in the St. Louis metropolitan area that tax season.

Patrick Leo had given his family's half German shepherd-half wolf dog, Duke, to Dad (Patrick Leo's family had two other smaller dogs). Duke was beautiful and very intelligent.

Dad drove a green (Irish) pickup, and Duke rode with Dad wherever he went. Duke would stand on his back legs in the back of the cab and look over the top. On hot days when Dad would transact business in a neighboring town, Duke would recline under the pickup in the shade. He waited patiently for Dad and never wandered away.

When Dad was at the farm, his two faithful companions were Duke and Daniel Boone, a great mouse-hunting cat whose tail and part of a back leg had been severed by a mower. When bad weather was forecast, Dan Boone would scratch on the door, and Dad permitted him to go to the basement where he slept on top of the warm hot-water tank.

My nephews John and Brian, Patrick Leo and Geneva's oldest sons, joined me on many of my 1983 summer visits to Dad's (only one visited at a time). Grandpa (Dad) would let them drive the tractor, and they rode with him in the pickup whenever he went somewhere.

One day, as I was cleaning the upstairs hall and chatting with John, then 12 years old, he declared that he thought I was gay. During the previous couple of years when he would tell me that I reminded him of someone, that someone would be either a woman or a man dressed in drag for comedy on television.

I agreed that his assumption was correct, and from that day—well, even before that— he and his siblings accepted me as I am. And I will declare that Kenny and Marlene's children never had any qualms about having a gay uncle—they've said they think it would be cool if everyone had one! I'm so grateful for this overwhelming approval by my nieces and nephews and their spouses and also my great-nieces and great-nephews.

Dad was one of the best storytellers. When I would visit him in the summers, he had the radio alarm by his bedside set for 6 a.m. It was so loud that it awakened me—I think the volume was set so high by design to not allow me to go back to sleep. I would bound down the steps, start the coffee, and get his plate, pills, cup, and saucer ready (he always used a saucer under his coffee cup).

Dad liked a few slices of bacon, always Morrell, thick cut. As the bacon sizzled and the coffee brewed, I would hear Dad, klumpety-klump, klumpety-klump, descend the back stairs. He would emerge, remarking about his rheumatism acting up. If his big toe hurt, it was going to rain. His toe ache was a very accurate predictor of precipitation.

After Dad had his first cup of coffee, he took his pills. Dad always had to have half and half with his coffee. If he remembered at night that he didn't have any for the next morning, he would get a frantic look, jump in the pickup, and speed to the Little Chicago Cafe in Williamsburg, six miles away. I think the owners must have ordered an extra carton of half and half almost every day, as he never returned empty-handed.

After the bacon was cooked nice and crispy, two eggs were fried semi-hard in the bacon grease. The toaster and coffee maker were on a small table just behind his chair so he could turn and reach both his toast and coffee.

After two pieces of toast popped up and were buttered—real butter, not margarine— the stories would begin. By that time, the pills, helped along by the hot coffee, had kicked in and the rheumatic legs had limbered. His stories could hold my interest, even though I had heard some of them as many as four or five times.

As Dad related the stories, I cleaned the stove, peeled potatoes, scraped carrots, and replenished his coffee. Then I would put a small roast, a two-pound roll of frozen hamburger, or something else that would slow cook into the oven for three hours.

At 9 a.m., he was ready to go outside to feed dogs Duke and Blueie and cats Daniel Boone, Tiger, and other unnamed felines. We would do the farm chores and physical tasks that needed attention, such as grinding feed for livestock.

At noontime, the oven meal was ready and, after dining, Dad would announce, "I'm through for today." After watching the noon news, he napped in his recliner for a short time.

He also liked to attend livestock sales at area sale barns. It seemed like Dad could find a sale almost every day of the week in a nearby town. Memories of those days and the stories make me smile.

Early in 1983, Dad's pains steadily grew more intense. He sold most of his machinery and his few cows and calves that he loved. (Cows are very calm animals, and if treated nicely, they become very tame.) When he would visit Lee and me in prior years, he would never stay more than two days, saying, "I have to get home and check on the cows."

After I went back to St. Louis in the fall of 1983, I had my usual tax classes. My employment office clerk-friend still collaborated with me to get my unemployment checks.

Another year had gone by, and on February 18, 1984, my 53rd birthday arrived. On February 17, after I left the office at 10 p.m., Lee, his assistant manager Arlene, and messenger Leroy Atkins decorated my office with streamers and "Happy Birthday Gene" signs. I was flabbergasted when I arrived early the next morning and was accompanied inside by three or four customers who had been waiting.

During the noon hour, I was surprised again as Lee, Arlene, and the managers from two other city offices entered with a decorated cake and ice cream and sang *Happy Birthday*. My dear brother always was so kind and thoughtful, and I was the recipient of more than my share of his love and kindness.

Nineteen-year-old Harry entered my office in mid-February 1984. When he arrived at my desk, I was impressed by his good looks. In addition to taxes, we discussed various topics including Michael Jackson, who was at the peak of his popularity. I had just purchased his album *Thriller*, and Harry suggested he would like to visit me and listen to it. I gave him my phone number but explained that I didn't have guests until after April 15, the end of tax season.

From that day on, Harry called constantly asking to come to 3018. I finally agreed that he could visit on the second Sunday of March. Sunday was my only day off during tax season, and I had to do laundry and try to catch up on the few drop-off tax returns I did for folks who weren't in any hurry (usually those who owed Uncle Sam).

He arrived about 1 p.m. as snow was falling. He told me of his family and childhood. My heart opened to Harry as he told of going hungry as a child, and that on some days, he had only a candy bar or a bag of chips for food. He related that sleeping in a chair in the home of his sister and her husband was very uncomfortable.

He stayed until about 5 p.m. From then on, until the end of tax season, I made an exception for him to visit each Sunday afternoon. That was the beginning of an almost five-year ordeal that ended only after Harry was arrested for armed robbery.

I put a photo of Harry and me on my desk. I met all of Harry's family. Harry's mother became very fond of me and called me her daughter-in-law. She would drop by my office and pull up a chair next to me as I prepared a client's tax return, which was annoying to both the client and me. When Harry and I visited the homes of his sisters, I always was in drag with wig and heels—the entire deal. They called me their sister and Harry's "Gina."

It was during this time period that I again became anorexic and bulimic, and poor Lee was worried about me. He said he heard me vomiting, not knowing it was self-induced.

I had purchased 35 beautiful wigs and at least 48 dresses for myself. A specialty dress shop on North Grand in the midst of the theater and entertainment district was my favorite. The lady owner let me try on the shop's dresses and then parade around and view myself in the full-length mirrors. The dresses were knockoffs of designer apparel and usually cost about $100 per garment. The shop owner had a framed photo of me hanging on the wall and several snapshots of me under glass in a display case. In all the photos, I was wearing dresses from her selection.

I also would go to Sears and buy three of the same dress in different sizes, keeping the one that fit and returning the two others. I did that about three times, and each time the clerks acted very unfriendly when refunding the money for the two returns. The dresses still had tags on them and had never been worn except when I tried them on. The fourth time I attempted the exchange-return transaction, the clerk said, "Wait one moment." She did not say "please."

In a jiffy, a very stern-appearing gentleman appeared. He said he would not take them back as they had been worn and he could see makeup on them. I declared that I personally knew the woman who tried them on and I knew for damn sure they had not been worn! He finally agreed to refund my money—providing I did not try to return goods again. I agreed, and I haven't shopped at a Sears since that encounter.

I followed the same procedure at the large Famous-Barr and Dillard's department stores. At Famous, I got my favorite gold lamé dress, and I bought my second-favorite dress, a very pale lavender brocade, at Dillard's.

I purchased shoes at a shoe store and had a pair to match each outfit. I went through many pairs of pantyhose; I would buy four or five pairs at a time when I shopped at Woolworths (where falsies and brassieres also were purchased). I usually purchased Lancôme makeup from Famous-Barr where the saleslady also gave me enough samples to keep me well supplied.

Harry would get jobs, such as doing maintenance or bussing tables, but they usually lasted only long enough for him to have enough money to buy a cheap used car. He also indulged in the pastime of smoking marijuana, which led to his indulging in more potent drugs.

When I tried to talk on the phone at home, Harry would snatch the phone from me. He would tell my friend, family member, or old flame—whoever was on the other end of the phone—to refrain from calling again. I lost touch with Bobby Bare, Mother Hen, Mother Nature, Opal, and the Louise family.

I had to face a new sadness in my life. When I visited Dad in 1984, he had been diagnosed with multiple myeloma, or cancer of plasma cells. I spent most of the summer of 1984 with Dad, occasionally returning to St. Louis for a week or two for employment-office appearances.

Dad was very depressed and lost interest in farm activities and most everything he had enjoyed. I would let a mother sow and her pigs into the yard and give them some feed near the front door so he could see them. He would barely glance their way.

I had to return to St. Louis for tax training in the fall, but Lee and I visited Dad at Thanksgiving, and Bernie also was there. Thomas M. and daughter Laura were visiting at the time. Dad hadn't seen Laura since she was four months old, so Laura and Grandpa really were just getting acquainted.

When Lee and I arrived after nightfall, Dad, Bernie, Thomas M., and Laura were playing Pepper at the kitchen table. I was amazed as I viewed Dad. The cancer had gone into remission, as that deadly malady often does. Dad had regained weight, his complexion was again a healthy, rosy glow, and his spirits were bright. I returned to St. Louis feeling much relieved and ready for a great tax season.

I'm not in drag, but I don't exactly look macho in this mid-1980s photo taken at Jim & Kate's in St. Louis.

A pose from my bed/couch, 1984.

The Dawson brothers in 1985. Front: Lee, Thomas M., and me. Back: Bernie, Patrick Leo, and Kenny.

Dad's personal items at Maplehurst Manor were auctioned off in May 1986.

# Chapter 12

## 1985–1989

When January 2, 1985, arrived, it seemed the bitterest cold weather of the winter came along simultaneously. Nephew Terry, who now was divorced, had come to visit and to consider working for H&R Block. His ex-wife, Marcia, had custody of their son, Jeff, who was born in 1979. But Terry decided he didn't want to be so far away from his son, so he returned to Iowa and soon had a new lady friend.

I was so overwhelmed with business and clients that I started staying at the office from Sunday nights until the following Saturday nights during tax season. On Sunday evenings, I would get a ride to 3900 North Grand. I took along five shirts, a pair of slacks, my make-up kit, an electric razor, and usually a large jar of peanut butter and a box of crackers for nourishment. Many times, my clients brought goodies for me.

When I stayed at the office, each morning a large piece of foam rubber the size of a single-bed mattress and enshrouded in a fitted sheet was rolled up and pushed behind a table in my personal office. An electric blanket and a small, electric space heater provided warmth for me at night.

Dad was revitalized in early 1985, so he purchased a tractor and some other machinery, had three or four sows with baby pigs, and had the mindset of a young farmer starting his first agricultural venture. He went into debt, as he borrowed money to do those things.

In April, he took a pickax to loosen some soil so he could plant a garden. The area near the old barn that was to be his garden site had very good soil, but it was firmly packed on the surface from years of livestock walking over it. A regular hoe and spade were not much help to prepare the soil for a garden bed.

The vigorous activity with the pickax was extremely taxing and strenuous, and he overdid himself. From that day on, he went into a steady decline that accelerated a little each day.

The cancer had returned with a vengeance.

In the summer of 1985, Bernie left for Minneapolis (where he was living) on the day I arrived. He had been with Dad over the winter months.

John, Brian, and Joe often were with Dad and me. Sometimes two nephews were with me at a time, and all three were with me on a couple of occasions. Grandpa loved his grandchildren, and he continued to permit them to drive the tractors and even the pickup if he were with them.

I thought Dad was too lenient with them. He let them drink coffee, use sugar on their cereal (not permitted at home), eat unlimited ice cream, and drink unlimited root beer (their favorite soda). It seemed he was enjoying being a kid again, as he would suggest to them, "We won't tell Gene." I feigned sternness and went along with the gag, knowing they wanted a rise out of Maudie K!

While I was back in St. Louis for a week in July, 11-year-old Brian stayed with Dad. Brian and Dad watched the news the night that Rock Hudson, the fine gay actor, announced that he had AIDS.

"I hope Gene doesn't get AIDS," Brian said.

Dad sat up in his recliner and asked why he would hope that.

"Well, Mom says Gene dates other men and has boyfriends," Brian answered mat-ter-of-factly.

Dad quizzed Brian extensively about what he knew from what I had said or insinuat-ed or what he had observed through the years. Brian gladly offered his observations of painted fingernails, rollers in my hair, etc., when I was at his house on babysitting missions.

Therefore, my 11-year-old nephew outed me to my dad!

Dad never mentioned that day to me, but on a couple of occasions, he did ask me just what "gay" means. He said there were some local women said to be gay. Dad also observed Iowa City having gay-pride events. I was evasive, played dumb, and changed the subject as if disinterested.

Lee visited Iowa that summer. Dad, Lee, and I went to Oskaloosa so Dad could get a new pair of shoes at a specialty store there. As Dad sat between his two gay sons in his pickup, he asked, "Just what is this 'gay'? I looked it up in the dictionary, and it said happy and jolly."

Lee hesitated, leaving me to answer.

"I suppose that's what it means then," I replied, quickly changing the subject as I point-ed to something I considered could be of interest. I thought to myself that it was too bad that I couldn't tell him he was riding between two of the gayest guys in St. Louis, Missouri, who also happened to be his sons.

But Dad must have suspected for years. He had intercepted letters Lee had written and sent to me at Maplehurst Manor shortly after Mother died. Lee told me the letters were very explicit. Dad never gave them to me.

I was afraid to tell him. He would think Lee and I would never escape the fires of hell, as that was the teaching of the Catholic faith and other denominations. It was much later that I finally realized that "God is love." He had created us in His image and likeness and would not create some of us as gay if only to toss us into the fiery pit. After all, what loving Father would push His own child into the inferno?

In August and September, I rode with Dad, usually with a nephew or two along, to the University of Iowa Hospital in Iowa City for his treatments to eradicate the cancer cells. The tragic thing is that the treatment also killed good cells.

Dad would drive to Iowa City, as he had loved to drive since he was nine years old. I drove on the return trip home as the radiation sapped all his strength. He then would sleep on his back with his mouth open, appearing dead to the world, for five or six hours without moving.

On October 1, I returned to St. Louis. I had missed tax school with Lee's blessing. The nephews were back in Missouri to attend school. Bernie returned to Dad's home. I had been back at 3018 South Grand for only a few days when I got word that Dad had been admitted to the hospital.

He had insisted on walking down the front-porch steps to enter the ambulance, nixing any assistance. He would not return to his beloved farm again.

On October 26, Dad entered the Americana Healthcare Center in Cedar Rapids. For a month, Bernie and I took turns with Kenny and Marlene to spend most of every other day with him at the care center. On November 25, the scheduled day for Bernie and me, an ice storm hit most of the state of Iowa. There was no way we could have made it out of the driveway, let alone get to Cedar Rapids.

Dad died at the care center without any family about 12:15 a.m. on November 26, 1985.

His funeral was held November 29 at St. Joseph's Catholic Church in Parnell. It was a loving, peaceful ceremony with standing room-only attendance. He was buried next to our beloved Mother in the rural Armah Cemetery.

For the next two nights, the wolf-shepherd dog Duke that Dad loved stood in Dad's driveway at sundown looking pinpoint in the direction of the Armah Cemetery. He howled like a wolf. I think he was calling Dad. Animals appear to be gifted with an extraordinary sense of perception.

Duke went back to Patrick Leo, Geneva, and family. Daniel Boone, the great mouse catcher, went to reside with Kenny and Marlene's family. Marlene loved kitties, and Daniel Boone joined her felines.

We not only lost our Dad and Grandfather but we also lost our safe haven and our extremely happy and peaceful visits to the beautiful farm and countryside. At the farm, it seemed that the sky always appeared blue, the air was smog-free, and the sun was bright and warm.

I had taken all of this for granted and now, sadly, it was gone from me forever.

A highlight event of 1986 was the sale of Dad's estate—the farm and everything he owned. At that time, there was a farm crisis in the country. Many farmers lost their land.

It was a trying time as we settled the estate after the sale. The good farmland and the beautiful house, which was a gem, were now owned by others. Dad's farm-machinery debt was repaid to the bank, and the final payments to the Federal Land Bank for the farm, which had been purchased in 1949 with extremely low interest rates, were made.

Back in St. Louis during 1986, Lee was robbed and nearly beaten to death while making a night deposit for H&R Block. He received many blood transfusions but was back to work within two weeks.

The year 1986 ended, and 1987 was calm. In 1988, Lee began to complain of severely chronic headaches and a complete lack of energy. He even took afternoons off—unheard of for him—to go home and rest.

By this time, Lee had endured all he could of Harry's and my late-night music and drinking at our apartment on South Grand. When I arrived home from shopping one day, Lee had cleared out his clothes and personal belongings. He rented an apartment on South Kingshighway to share with Bernie, who had returned to St. Louis (Bernie had been a carhop at the Foot Long for a few months after he graduated from Parnell High School). Lee left no address or note—he was just gone!

Harry was happy because he wouldn't have to lower the music volume and be concerned about Lee. I put Lee through so very much crap. He certainly had a strong brotherly love, hanging in there with support for me after all my shenanigans. I'm truly sorry for my actions.

On an evening in 1988, Harry and I sat at the kitchen table with drinks fixed. He also had rolled a joint. He turned to me glassy-eyed and suddenly began to assault me via fists and feet. He knocked me from my chair to the kitchen floor.

213

Harry jerked the wig from my head, took my lipstick and smeared it all over my face, and left me on the floor. He grabbed $15 that I had placed next to an ashtray and left.

One thing that was really upsetting to a drag queen—me—was having a beautifully styled hairpiece snatched from my head. It gave me a feeling of total nakedness and ugliness.

It was difficult to regain my balance while wearing three-inch heels and a tight gown. I then saw that I had a black eye, several minor facial abrasions, and a few bruises, but nothing major.

Harry didn't come around for a few days, but love is truly blind and I forgave him. What I didn't go through to feel accepted and loved. I always searched for acceptance and what I considered love—not realizing you have to love and accept yourself before you will find peace of mind and real love.

When Harry came visiting the next time, I didn't have a dress, high heels, or a wig on but had fixed my own long hair and wore makeup. As we sat at the table and I was sipping my vodka and 7UP, I detected his glassy-eyed look turned on me.

I decided to beat him to the punch. As he turned toward me, I clutched a cigarette lighter—knowing my punch would be more effective if I had a hard article in my fist. I proceeded to get the first blow unleashed and knocked him toward the wall. I was quick to my feet and got him in a headlock between my left arm and body. I then rained blow after blow on his head. I released him when he cried out in pain and begged me to stop.

He then regrouped and said, "Now, do you want a fair fight?"

"I've got more where that came from," I replied.

By now, we were in the dining/living room where a large couch and coffee table were located. On the coffee table was a beautiful figurine set that I had given to Grandma Agnew for her birthday one year, and Aunt Anna returned it to me after Grandma died.

Harry tried to land a blow on "Super Pussy" (me). I knocked him over the coffee table onto the couch, and as I leapt over the table between us, the figurine set was smashed. I got on the couch and again rained blows on his head as he tried to protect himself with his hands and arms. He started crying like a baby as he pleaded with me to stop, saying, "I'll never hit you again."

When I stopped, he continued to sob and tried to lie in my arms, gazing up into my eyes in disbelief and saying, "Gina, I never thought you had that in you. I'll never hurt you again."

I wanted to laugh out loud. I was so proud of myself. And I never again attired myself in a wig and dressy heels for him.

When he was about to leave the next morning, he stated, "You really beat me last night, but never try it again. If you do, you are dead meat."

Harry never hit me again, but I knew that he meant what he said.

Harry's friends included a former classmate, a small-time thief, homeless-teen Ben, and an ex-con who had just been released from the "big house," the main prison in Missouri.

I have to pinch myself when I stop and recall a couple of occasions around my kitchen table with his friends. I was completely in glamorous drag and didn't think anything about being in danger. Harry's friends all respected me, as I was their "dog's" (dog is a very good buddy) woman. In drag, they looked at me as 100 percent female.

It was early one morning in late 1988 when Harry and Ben stopped at a doughnut shop

These were taken in the kitchen of my apartment in 1985 and 1986. I had many wigs (obviously).

in south St. Louis. Upon entering, they announced a holdup with their hands in their pockets indicating they had guns, thereby making it an armed robbery. One of them accidentally broke the display case as he made his way to the cash register, which added destruction of public property to the crime. The other robber relieved the customers of their money.

They fled in Harry's car and sped north on Grand Boulevard. Not far from my apartment, they struck and knocked down a light pole, disabling the car. They fled across a nearby park, leaving their footprints in newly fallen snow and the car's ownership papers in its glove compartment.

Harry headed for his sister's abode; she was babysitting his young child. (In 1987, Harry impregnated a young girl; yes, he and I were together during this same time period.) At Harry's sister's home, the police found him hiding in a bed, huddled under the covers with his child. Harry immediately was arrested. The trial resulted in Harry receiving a 12-year sentence in the state prison system.

Approximately two or three weeks before the robbery, Harry and I were sitting at my kitchen table when he turned toward me and said, "You wish you had never met me, don't you? Well, you wanted me, you got me, and you're gonna keep me. And Gina, if you ever leave, I will track you down."

With that, a body-shaking chill raced through me as I thought, "He read my mind." I did wish I had never met him and wondered how I could ever rid myself of him. I lit candles at a local Catholic church, imploring Almighty God to take Harry out of my life.

Harry's sentencing ended that harrowing saga, at least for that time and the following years.

By 1989, Lee was in charge of 19 H&R Block offices, and Bernie worked nights for H&R Block as a messenger-suitcase man. With that many offices, Lee employed at least three nighttime suitcase men.

Lee's pains became more intense, and he sought out pain clinics to no avail. Finally, in the fall of 1989, Lee was told he was HIV positive brought on by tainted blood during his 1986 transfusions.

He was totally devastated. I, too, felt I was the recipient of a terrible blow. When he disclosed the dreadful news to me, I resolved that I would do all in my power to make his life as tolerable, peaceful, and comfortable as I possibly could.

At work at H&R Block, 1989.

With two of my pigeon friends, 1993.

Lee, Thomas M., and Bernie, 1992.

# Chapter 13

## 1990–1994

My drinking and social cigarette smoking stopped in 1990. The anorexia and bulimia were under control and no longer presented a temptation. No boyfriends or overnight or daytime guests were entertained. I had returned to the holy sacrifice of the Mass, confession, and reception of the Holy Eucharist.

In 1990, Lee and I purchased the property at 3123 Osage Street in St. Louis. It truly was our first home. We owned it outright, each paying $29,750 in cash, avoiding any interest payments. After we paid the moving expenses, I had approximately $800 in a checking account. I used almost all of my savings to purchase my share of the home.

The house actually was a duplex with individual units on the ground and top levels that were identically constructed and had separate entrances. We had both our closeness and our privacy. We had a full basement that had an additional bedroom and bathroom.

My possessions from 3018 were moved on September 1, and we emptied Lee's apartment two weeks later. I rented a U-Haul truck, and nephews John and Joe, Leroy Atkins, and a helper moved my belongings. Lee also rented a U-Haul for his moving day with basically the same crew with the addition of nephew Brian.

We had moved to the Dutchtown neighborhood, which was about 95 percent Caucasian then but is now a multicultural neighborhood, primarily African American.

The rest of 1990 was spent at tax classes, unpacking my 260 boxes, and getting my living space arranged. I also unpacked and arranged Lee's downstairs living quarters. We joined our new parish, St. Anthony of Padua, a quarter mile south of our home.

Our home was the new "House of Joy," the name I had given to 3018 South Grand. After the advent of caller ID—when I knew the caller would approve—my greeting would be "House of Joy, Maudie K speaking, in what way may I help you?" (These days, I use a more restrained "A pleasant good morning [afternoon, evening] to you," no longer indicating that joyful pleasures are on tap.)

Nephew John moved into Lee's and my basement room for a time. He went to work as a night messenger for Lee and H&R Block.

My heart went out to Lee at a manager meeting in December 1990. His address was about not discriminating against victims of HIV and AIDS. Some attendees murmured that they hoped they did not encounter anyone who had HIV or AIDS. There were so many misconceptions about the disease and how it is transmitted.

Lee had to speak on that subject against that background talk. He stood in front of the assemblage knowing that he was probably (he was) the only one in the room who was suffering with HIV, which eventually could turn into full-blown AIDS. However, since his address in 1990, many new drugs have been developed, and the disease sometimes can be controlled. Unfortunately, those drugs weren't available in time to help Lee.

My last tax year—1991—was highly successful money-wise, and I had not a single distraction.

In May 1991, Lee said he wouldn't be using our two-car garage (since I didn't drive,

I didn't have a car). He preferred parking on the street in front of the house because he thought it was safer than entering and leaving our alley-facing garage after dark.

Therefore, I converted the garage into a pigeon loft. I purchased my first six birds from Frandeka's Soulard Fish Meat Feed & Pet Shop, located in St. Louis's historic Soulard Market. I developed an enduring friendship with Jerry and Diane Frandeka. Through the ensuing years, I supplied pigeons for the pet shop when my flock was overpopulated. Diane and I had a barter deal; she would exchange bags of pigeon food for my birds.

I developed my own strain of pigeons that I called "HiGenes." They were crosses of many different breeds including Poulters, Homings, Fantails, Frillbacks, Scandaroons, Rollers, Archangels, and Egyptian Swifts. I sought to produce pigeons that had unusual and beautiful colorations with tame dispositions. Diane would remark on the beauty and health of my birds and said they were well behaved.

Later I integrated English Carriers. Pigeons have a homing instinct and will dodge gunfire and aerial predators, such as owls, hawks, and falcons. Pigeons were used extensively during World War I and World War II to send messages when other communications failed. Our enemies also had pigeon corps.

I had two other breeds later: Arabian Trumpeters and Thai Laughers. They don't "coo-coo" like other pigeons, but the Trumpeters "hoo-hoo-hoo" and the Laughers say "ha-ha-ha."

In 1991, just after dark one night, I had an encounter with a ladder in the pigeon house. Somehow, a half-grown cat had managed to get into my loft and devour several tiny, newly hatched baby birds. The cat wasn't old enough to tackle the adult pigeons, however, it did terrify them. For a couple of years, they would not fly to the upper north corner of the loft where the feline hid until I enticed it out the door.

I had climbed up an extension ladder to look for the cat, but I did not secure the extension hooks. The ladder began to slide down the wall putting me in peril. Just as it was sliding near the concrete floor, the extension began to come together, and I received a very deep and nasty cut on my right leg midway between the ankle and knee.

Nephew John, who was residing with Lee and me, heard the crashing ladder and came to my rescue to extract my leg. The wound eventually became infected because I failed to seek medical attention. Finally, registered nurse Geneva told me that my infection was similar to one that her mother had on her leg in a similar spot—which led to amputation.

Needless to say, I scooted off to visit my primary care physician, Dr. Timothy Mahood, and he fixed me up with antibiotics and salves. The only reminder I have of that incident is a small scar.

At my office, many clients thought Lee and I were the Bloch brothers, Henry and Richard, who are the namesakes of the company. When I overheard clients on the phone saying they were down at "Gene's" getting their taxes prepared, I thought the Bloch brothers might not approve of such individualism.

I overheard two assembly-line employees of General Motors discussing me as they waited their turns. One of them remarked, "He might be a funny bunny, but he can sure do taxes."

I had many, many favorite customers. Well, each was my favorite at the time I prepared his/her taxes. There were only two or three who made me think, "Ah, shit," when they appeared. If one of them were the first client of the day, it set the mood and the entire day seemed tense.

As it was, I grew accustomed to 10 to 12 pairs of eyes focused on me as they watched and hoped that I soon would have my current client's return finished. However, when their turns arrived, they would encourage me to "take your time, I'm in no hurry."

Saturdays were the busiest days, and the first Saturday of February, after W-2 forms had been received by company employees, was the busiest day of the year. Only the last day, April 15, and the other Saturdays of February were comparable to that day's crowd.

On Saturdays, I refused to open the door until 8 a.m. after all the preparers and the receptionist were on hand. On the first Saturday of February 1991, there were folks outside lined up 20 to 30 feet along the sidewalk. When the door was opened, it seemed an avalanche burst inside.

The clients did try to keep some order, but as people kept coming into my office and all 20 chairs were occupied and a few more people were standing, I had the sudden urge to scream and started to get dizzy. If there had been a back door, I would have fled. But there was no back exit, which was fortunate since I needed all the money I could earn. It was then that I determined that this was my last year working at this office.

I could do 20 to 22 tax returns working 11 hours each weekday. I had to work in a frenzy to do 16 to 18 to close at 5 p.m. on a Saturday. I would be fortunate to leave by 6 p.m.

At 8 a.m. one Saturday, I saw there were 28 people who had signed up to see me, and more would come in later. I told the last 10 on the list that I would not have time to prepare their taxes and someone else in the office was qualified to do them. Clients who came in later were advised the same. I don't think any of them went to another preparer.

For the rest of the tax season, I did every tax return I possibly could. Distractions were minimal, and I didn't have night guests.

I set records worldwide for seasonal H&R Block offices by writing more than $3,000 a day in tax returns three different times. There were special certificates for writing $2,000 in volume a day and I had many of those, but there were no certificates for $3,000 since it never had been achieved before.

When the year was over and the books were closed, I had prepared 754 tax returns. The bonus I received, in terms of working 40 hours a week, was equal to about nine months of work. I was so grateful since my savings had been depleted after buying the house. (The hidden costs that surface after purchasing a new home started for us when the first cold spell arrived in 1990. The furnace in Lee's downstairs apartment quit working.)

In late April 1991, nephew John and I went to the Block office where I had labored. We retrieved my foam mattress, electric blanket, and the rest of my personal belongings, officially ending my career in that office. I was 60 years old and burned out on doing taxes and working so many days nonstop for 3½ months.

I had wonderful friendships with my H&R Block coworkers and clients. Many invited me to barbecues, fish fries, baptisms, and weddings. They remembered my birthdays with cakes and cards. My coworkers Ada and Ella were especially kind. Ada occasionally brought chili or barbecue into the office. For five consecutive years after Ella became the receptionist, she baked a German chocolate cake for my birthday.

In 1992 and 1993, Lee was phasing in his replacement as manager. I prepared a few tax returns in the main office; the returns were for special clients that Lee had for more than 20 years. When he would explain that I was his brother, they reluctantly would agree that I could proceed. He proclaimed that I was better at tax preparation than he, but they didn't believe him. I was no better, if as good as Lee, at tax prep. They took a wait-and-see approach, but there were no complaints.

In 1994, Lee and I came to the end of our H&R Block careers. Early in March 1994, a banquet and awards ceremony was held and attended by the 200-plus employees who were under Lee's management. Lee was given several awards, and several of his peers and special friends thanked him and told humorous stories that included all the B.S. that goes with farewell dinners.

However, I noticed that he was not happy. The speeches of praise seemed rather like funeral eulogies. The humorous tales were not amusing to him. At one point, he turned to me and said, "What is he talking about?"

I received a beautiful watch signifying 25 years of service to the company. I had received a Block insignia ring for 20 years of service and an assortment of lapel pins for two, five, and 10 years of employment.

My retirement from H&R Block came at a perfect time for me since tax returns were beginning to be prepared on computers. In 1994, I had adapted enough to the Block computer tax program to prepare returns, but I could do them 10 times faster by hand. I had no hurry or pressure, as I did returns for Lee's special clients in a little private office. In 1994, I prepared only 80 tax returns, all on the computer.

After our retirements, I was delighted that I now could devote all my time to our home and to caring for Lee. I wanted to make his last years as comfortable as I possibly could.

Lee adjusted to retirement after a few months and started taking vacations, which he hadn't done for many years. He went to Atlantic City and Las Vegas, oftentimes with a nephew along. He also had time to visit our relatives in Iowa and attend the Armah reunion picnic in the summers.

Before his retirement, he would work on Thanksgiving, Christmas, and New Year's Day. He said he could get more work done and almost get caught up on bookwork since the phone was silent. I recall that we washed windows and curtains in one of his offices one Christmas Day.

In 1994, I was 63 years old and receiving Social Security checks. I had contributed to an individual retirement account (IRA) and had about $12,000 in it. I started to withdraw from it and put the money into a mutual fund. Soon after, the market took a hit, and my account dropped to around $8,600 in one day. Beware of the stock market unless you can survive the occasional sudden drop.

McToose had his own fenced-in area behind Lee's and my house. I am on the left and Lee is closest to McToose in this photo taken in 1995.

Lee and "McToose" in 1995.

Bernie (in plaid shirt) and me at my home in 1995.

Lee's and my home in 1995; I lived in the upstairs duplex and Lee lived downstairs.

# Chapter 14

## 1995–1999

After my retirement, I was occupied with caring for Lee and myself, cooking, cleaning, and tending a productive garden and the dozens of flowers that Lee would buy. We had so many tall cannas in various colors that they provided a privacy barrier around the backyard, and I embedded more than 600 tulip bulbs in the front yard. Soon there was no grass in the front or back, just flowers and vegetable plants. When they bloomed, people would stop their vehicles to snap photos.

Inside Lee's apartment were many African violets, which I learned to water from the bottom, and cactuses of many varieties. I found out that if I passed very near a cactus that it seemed to reach out to jab me! Mother-in-law's tongues practically filled his sunroom.

In 1995, I had a 10-by-15-foot concrete slab laid on the adjoining south side of the pigeon house. An 8-foot chain-link fence with a gate for an entrance, also covered overhead with chain link, was constructed for a pigeon fly pen/exercise yard. Up until that time, my birds were allowed to fly around the neighborhood and often sat on the neighboring house and its garage to the east. The owner got great pleasure from watching the pigeons, and some would perch right outside her upper apartment window.

I eventually decided that it was best for my pigeons to have their own fly space because when they were allowed to fly at will, they attracted feral pigeons that sought to integrate the group. The flock also attracted sparrows, starlings, and predators that loved to feast on pigeons.

Mr. Fantail was a brown Fantail (as the name implies) breed pigeon that died of a broken heart. His "wife," Speckie, fell victim to a virus. I tried to fix him up with another female, but he just stood around listlessly and finally stopped eating. He had been very active and lively until her sudden death. I found him dead on the nest that he and Speckie had "owned."

Prince was a male pigeon who rode on my shoulder whenever I was in the pigeon house. He used my shoulder as his perch and nuzzled my ear softly with his beak when I worked in the garden or backyard. I was sitting on the porch with Prince on my shoulder one day when a neighbor came over, blessed herself playfully, and addressed me as St. Francis of Assisi (the patron saint of animals).

I found a beautiful cream-colored Homing (breed) female for Prince to love, and they had many hatchings of twins. With the responsibilities of family, Prince abandoned my shoulder except for some very brief moments in the pigeon house. I no longer received friendly ear nuzzles, and he even would peck my hand if I tried to check his babies.

Lee rescued a baby goose that had been an Easter gift to a child. It had a broken wing, and Lee nursed it back to health. We found out that it was a gander, a male goose, when it matured. It followed Lee everywhere when he was in the backyard where the goose resided with his own house, self-feeder, and waterer.

His name was McToose, the Goose, or Goose-Goose McToose. He didn't like me very much and would threaten me by his voice and actions if he thought I was too close to Lee.

McToose even joined Lee on car rides. He would stand in the front seat of the car, which elicited stares of disbelief from other motorists.

Tame geese can be as intimidating as large dogs and will act as guard sentries if strangers approach their premises. In late 1995, McToose became too loud for the neighborhood, so he went to live on Patrick Leo and Geneva's property. They were living outside Moscow Mills, Missouri, on a property that had two ponds.

After McToose left our premises, Lee's interest turned to mute swans. Lee purchased an incubator and hatched three baby swans that he named King George, King Louie, and Queen Esther. We raised them in my pigeon enclosure. We covered the concrete floor with heavy cheap carpet as concrete is bad for swans to walk on. They had a "pool" (kiddie pool), and Lee purchased lettuce by the case for them. Swans defecate at the same rate as geese and ducks, which appeared to be every three to four minutes when they were young. What a green mess.

When they were feathered, the three swans also went to the ponds at Patrick Leo and Geneva's. Eventually, Queen Esther went to reside at a large pond in a St. Louis cemetery. Kings Louie and George were sold to other swan lovers.

Lee purchased the property to the east of our house (3119 Osage) in 1996 after the owner passed away. I installed a gate between the two properties and was in charge of acquiring a renter for the upstairs apartment, while Ella, an elderly lady, stayed in the lower apartment. I rented the upstairs apartment to a woman and her young son.

Lee never went inside the house at 3119 Osage; he bought the property for its two-car garage because he now had a second car. He had purchased a new Cadillac that he didn't want to park on the street. He drove the car, accompanied by nephews Brian and Joe, to Iowa to visit relatives and to show it off.

Lee had dreamed of owning a Cadillac for a long time, and now the dream was fulfilled. I rode in it once and was amazed as it had every amenity that I hadn't even imagined, and it felt as if I were riding on a cloud. He soon sold it and resumed driving his longtime favorite Oldsmobile.

On February 7, 1997, Bernie, who was employed by H&R Block as a night messenger, was hijacked as he unloaded his car at the H&R Block office on South Grand. The gunman wanted money and also demanded his keys. He told Bernie to get into the trunk of his car, which was open, as he had just removed the suitcase for the office.

When Bernie refused to enter the trunk, the assailant shot him point blank, breaking both arms, collapsing both lungs, and sending three bullets to Bernie's upper body—one nearly hitting his heart. Another lodged near his spine, which he carries to this day.

An alert customer at the restaurant directly across the street saw Bernie lying in the snow in the parking lot and called 911. He was rushed to Saint Louis University Hospital, and his life was saved.

Upon viewing him in the hospital bed, I let out an involuntary shout of shock. It seemed he had tubes protruding from all over his body and was swollen to what looked like double his normal size. My first thought was that he looked like roadkill.

After Bernie was released from the hospital, he spent six weeks at Life Care Center of Saint Louis. While he recuperated, Leroy Atkins and I moved his belongings to Lee's and my basement room that had been vacated by nephew John. Bernie lived there until July 1997 when he moved to the next-door downstairs apartment at 3119 Osage (Ella had moved to a retirement home).

By 1997, Lee had hired two young men to drive for him. He could only be comfortable in a car in a certain stretched-out position, and the driving position wasn't it. Keith or Jessie would drive him to stores to help him shop. They also helped him distribute feed to geese, ducks, and swans at several area ponds. Several restaurants and a doughnut shop saved their unused food for the birds. One restaurant would save dozens of leftover breakfast biscuits, and the doughnut shop had lots and lots of thick dough.

You should see waterfowl eating dough—well, maybe, it's just as well that you don't see it.

That fall, Keith became the owner of a "backyard" (not purchased from a dog breeder or a pet shop) male Rottweiler puppy named Bo. While Keith worked nights at a local restaurant, he left Bo with Lee for dog sitting. Lee fell in love with Bo and annexed Bo from Keith. Lee then bought another Rottweiler puppy for Keith.

Lee and Bo were inseparable, and Bo replaced McToose as Lee's riding companion. Lee had the back seat removed from one of his Oldsmobiles and replaced it with a large, wire dog cage.

The years 1998 and 1999 became more difficult as Lee's resistance to infections and diseases vanished. He now had full-blown AIDS. In December 1999, he was hospitalized twice but was able to return home for the Christmas and New Year's holidays.

The Immaculate Conception Church in Armah in the late 1990s. The church closed in the 1960s and was torn down in the mid-2000s. I often stopped to visit the graves of my parents and other relatives at the Armah Cemetery, which is on the church grounds, when I was in Iowa.

Since Lee didn't use our garage, I had converted it into a pigeon loft, complete with an outdoor area. This was taken in 1996.

These photos were taken after Lee's burial in the Armah Cemetery.

The five surviving Dawson brothers. Front: Kenny, me, and Patrick Leo. Back: Bernie and Thomas M.

The Dawsons with a few more relatives. Front: Uncle Kermie Herr, Aunt Theresa O'Rourke, me, Patrick Leo, and Aunt Mary Agnew. Back: Kenny, sister-in-law Marlene Dawson, Bernie, Thomas M., and sister-in-law Geneva Dawson.

# Chapter 15

## 2000–2004

Lee's 65th birthday was on January 4, 2000. He had told me he wished to see his 65th birthday, and his wish was granted. About 3 a.m. the next day, I called 911, and Lee left 3123 Osage for the last time.

Lee spent six weeks at Barnes-Jewish Hospital in St. Louis before his death on February 15, 2000. His cause of death was listed as coronary heart disease, pneumonia, and complications from HIV. He seldom, if ever, complained, and he accepted his terminal illness as "God's will be done."

In fact, two days before he died, I told him I wished I were a magician so I could take all his pain away. He looked at me very peacefully and said, "This is the way it's supposed to be."

On the day Lee died, I told him that I would care for Bo forever. He was like Lee's child, and I would treat him the same as Lee did.

My beloved brother left Parnell in 1953 with $38 in his pocket. Through his long hours of hard work, perseverance, and ability to learn, he became a very successful investor. When Lee died, his net worth was nearly $4 million. He set up trusts for his brothers and various charitable organizations. He remembered his nieces and nephews, and he was a benefactor to his parishes, St. Anthony of Padua in St. Louis and St. Joseph's in Parnell, and to the Armah Cemetery back in Iowa.

Loneliness arrived at his departure. Thank goodness, I had the pigeons and Bo. Bo and I eventually became the best of friends.

I got great support from Patrick Leo, Geneva, and their family, as well as Bernie, who still occupied the next-door downstairs apartment. Kenny, Marlene, and their family, especially Terry, were at my beck and call. Thomas M., his wife Martha, and daughters arrived before Christmas 2000 and stayed several days. Their very thoughtful daughter Esther, the youngest of my nieces and nephews, left a thank-you note under a pillow, which I found after they left.

Shortly after Lee's burial, I was sitting on the edge of my bed sobbing and in mourning, thinking of my dear departed brother. It was mid-morning, and the bedroom door was open. I could clearly see the hall just outside the door.

Suddenly, Lee was standing in the hall. He looked just like he did before he suffered from the horrible AIDS that claimed his life.

"K! Don't cry. I'm alright," Lee said in a very soothing tone. Then he added, "I've got to get back; I'm not supposed to be here."

I will swear on a stack of Bibles that this is a true story. No fiction here.

About a year before Lee died, he met Roy, a homeless man who lived in his car with his dog. Lee and Roy hit it off as they discussed their dogs. Roy was a jack-of-all-trades with his specialty being work on car engines. He installed new sidewalks for us at 3119 and did tuck-pointing and painting. Lee tried to find little jobs for him.

During my dear brother's final stay at Barnes-Jewish Hospital, Roy would drive me to visit Lee and return to get me when I was ready to go home. Until Roy's sudden death from a heart attack later in 2000, he would check on me daily to see if I needed to go anywhere or needed any work done. I purchased one of Lee's Oldsmobiles from the estate and gave it to Roy so he could get rid of the huge gas-guzzler he had been driving.

Leroy Atkins was my helper, too. He is a very good and kind man. He always responded immediately to each emergency I encountered, such as clogged drains, minor leaks, and malfunctioning toilets.

When Lee and I moved to Osage Street in 1990, the first person on the block to give us a smiling, cheerful wave of welcome was neighbor Jeanette Murray as she emerged from her little car. Naturally, her partner of many years, Joyce James, also was right there with a friendly greeting.

As the years passed, we became friends, but at first both Jeanette and I were still employed so we weren't at home so much. I would see her walk the couple's three dogs (the "old dude" and the "two gals," as I referred to them) in the park across the street. I also observed and loved the statue of the Virgin Mary that was in their backyard.

When Lee died, Joyce and Jeanette were very kind and sympathetic, and I was impressed as they entered him into perpetual prayers at the National Shrine of St. Jude.

On February 14, 2001, I was surprised to find a box of candy in my doorway with a card that read "Sweets for our Sweet!! Happy Valentine's Day 2001." On Christmas, they gave me a bag of wonderful Avon products fit for a queen. They always were kind and thoughtful and loved to present surprises.

Late in the morning of September 11, 2001, I picked a few tomatoes to carry down to Jeanette. I hadn't had the television or radio on all morning. She answered the door and said, "Isn't that awful?"

I wondered what she was talking about, but then I glanced at the TV and saw the footage of the terrible terrorist attacks. Jeanette was amazed that I didn't know about it. I always will remember that day, where I was when I first heard, and then watching the footage of the almost unbelievable events. It seemed like a horrible dream.

Occasionally, Jeanette and I attended Saturday afternoon Mass together at St. Anthony of Padua where we made the acquaintance of several parishioners. One time when I attended alone, an elderly gentleman came to my pew inquiring as to the health and whereabouts of my wife—Jeanette! As I explained that we weren't married, he and his wife nodded knowingly and said, "We understand."

They thought we lived together out-of-wedlock! Jeanette and I both got a big charge out of that.

Joyce and Jeanette's landlord would see me leaving their house and voice the opinion that Jeanette and I were seeing each other. Another neighbor asked Joyce if it were true that Jeanette and I were an item since she observed us leave for Mass together. I knew then that I really should be wearing my makeup or resurrect some of the heels, wigs, and gowns from my closet that I had worn in my heyday. We both were highly amused by the rumors.

In December 2001, Jeanette endured a terrifying mugging in her car right in front of her residence as she was preparing to drive away. The bold perpetrator carried out his dastardly deed in broad daylight. I think that was the straw that broke the camel's back, and Jeanette and Joyce decided to exit the neighborhood, no longer feeling safe and secure.

Jeanette started to carry a gun in her car. The way I found out was a little unusual. I had ridden to Mass with Jeanette, and when we were getting in the car to return home, she said, "Oh, I left the gun in the car during Mass."

"Where is it?" I asked.

"You're sitting on it," she replied. She had placed it on the front passenger seat with a small towel over it.

Evidently, it was a very comfortable gun for sitting or I have a tough, non-feeling butt from getting kicked so many times by my Dad for my youthful indiscretions.

In September 2002, I helped Jeanette and Joyce pack and move to Affton in south St. Louis County. I was very sad to see them move away, but I was happy that they would have their very own home. While I was helping Jeanette pack, she showed me a picture of her First Communion. I told her, "You look like a little angel." She liked that, and from then on I referred to her as "Little Angel." I also christened Joyce as "Joycestiffer," which had no particular meaning. I just liked the sound of it.

Jeanette sometimes called me "Rose Petal," but she usually addressed me as "Buttercup." When she would phone, I would answer, "Cup of Margarine, Queen of Everything speaking." She would reply, "You're real butter, not margarine."

They were happy in their new home and would drive into the city to transport me to their abode where Jeanette would serve steaks, baked potatoes, vegetables, and all the trimmings. Jeanette was a great cook, and I enjoyed several meals with Joyce and her. The evening would be perfect, but she always would think the food should have tasted a little better.

Father Bob Behnen came to my house in the 2000s, and we had coffee and doughnuts. He heard my general confession, as I tried to confess every transgression of my entire life that I could recall. He granted me absolution for all my sins and for what I thought were sins. He said, "They are wiped away; don't even think of them again."

With that, I felt a weight had lifted from my body. I actually felt lighter.

I "adopted" Father Behnen as my brother since he was slightly younger than I. When younger Franciscan priests or brothers were assigned to my parish, I would "adopt" them as nephews. I thought they needed a relative nearby since most of them were far away from their birth families. I realized priests and brothers are human just like me and need companionship. I no longer was in awe of them, although I still highly respected them.

When 2003 arrived, I went to my primary care provider, Dr. Mahood, for a six-month checkup. I had gained weight since my last visit as I had been eating too much red meat, chicken with skin, cheese, and ice cream. My legs and ankles were swollen. I couldn't even see my ankles and had been having sudden pains in my jaw. He made an appointment for me to have a stress test.

On February 19, 2003, I had a five bypass, open-heart surgery and a pacemaker implanted near my left shoulder. For four weeks, I was a patient at St. Anthony's Medical Center in south St. Louis County. Then I spent five weeks at Alexian Brothers Care Center several blocks from my home.

I had heard many horror stories about nursing homes. But the Alexian Brothers Care Center, overseen by Dr. Mahood's excellent care and dedication, is the reason (also prayers) that I got through this. I couldn't speak, swallow, stand, walk, or breathe on my own. I had pneumonia and uncontrollable diarrhea. I suffered from C. diff, which can be fatal.

Because of Dr. Mahood's care, the angel staff members who took care of me and cleaned my uncontrolled messes, the wonderful therapists who never gave up on me, and the prayers of my wonderful supporting family and friends, I did not become a permanent resident at Alexian. The therapists patiently made me stick to it and got me over the last hump. "No pain, no gain" is a very true saying.

Alexian Brother Richard, who was the supervisor of the facility, visited me when I first arrived via ambulance from St. Anthony's. He told me later that he thought I wouldn't last more than two days. God has blessed me so abundantly.

Patrick Leo and Geneva took me home on April 24, 2003. Bo nearly went berserk as I made my way to the house. Patrick Leo, along with Bernie, took great care of Bo and the pigeons during my convalescence. When I left for the hospital on February 19, I had 43 pigeons, and when I returned, there were 75—an increase of 32 in nine weeks!

Thomas M. had come from California to see me. He stayed at my house from early March until mid-April and then came back in late spring. Kenny, Terry, and Jeff came from Iowa and visited me in late March. Aunt Mary Agnew and her daughters/my first cousins Charlotte Pingel and Kay Agnew made an appearance in early April. Charlotte's and Kay's sister Rose Agnew, who recently had moved to St. Louis, visited often and brought food and fresh flowers.

Bernie sat with me from 6 to 8 each evening to be sure I was safely and securely ready for the night. Nephew John visited every Saturday. Patrick Leo and Geneva visited often, and some friends from the parish and my bank came by. Cousin Judy Harris Hilleman wrote inspirational letters.

While I was hospitalized and undergoing physical therapy, Jeanette and Joyce were faithful and cheerful visitors, even though Jeanette was suffering from lung cancer (she had been diagnosed in 2001, and the cancer was in remission). Jeanette always brought her St. Jude holy oil and would anoint me and say prayers imploring the Lord with the intercession of St. Jude (the patron saint of lost causes) to restore my health.

Thanks to their and all the others' prayers and words of comfort and encouragement, plus splendid health care, I'm still here. Without all the prayers said for my recovery, I'm thoroughly convinced that I would not have survived.

Joe Hoy, a dealer in exotic birds and animals, had a 30-acre spread of flat, prime farm-land near Nashville, Illinois, which is about 55 miles southeast of St. Louis. Lee and Joe had become friends because of their mutual interest in geese and swans. I had visited his country home where he resided with his sister, Frances. Joe became a good friend. We are just 11 months apart in age (I am older).

In addition to geese and swans, Joe had ducks, turkeys, miniature deer, llamas, alpacas, various breeds of sheep, cranes, peacocks, and at least 25 breeds of pigeons. I got started with some of my beautiful pigeons after getting birds from Joe.

In May 2003, Joe arrived at my home one evening so I could give him about 50 pigeons since my flock had increased dramatically in my absence. Joe had several pigeon lofts, a barn, and a brick building that had extensive pigeon facilities. Other small buildings housed his other birds and animals. A large pond on the property was habitat for his waterfowl.

My good friend Jeanette died in June 2004. Lung cancer claimed her life. Niece Tammy Dawson Bonnicksen, who recently had moved to St. Louis, transported me to the visitation, funeral, and burial.

It doesn't seem fair that Jeanette is gone since I am several years older than her, but that is God's will, which we must accept. I am fortunate to have become friends with Jeanette and Joyce.

Rottweiler Bo and I were the best of friends. When nephew Terry visited in 2004, Bo was OK with him the first day. For the next couple of days though, he stayed in the dog-house, looked sad, and didn't bother to come out as he always does when I'm alone. The day after Terry left for home, he was back to his usual lively self.

In the winter of 2003–2004, I slowly regained strength and had the confidence to write the first part of this book.

John and Mary Agnew Dawson's descendants and their spouses are pictured at a gathering after Lee's burial in 2000. I am in the middle of the front row with Brooke Gowin, one of my great-nieces, on my lap.

My dear friend Joyce James and me in 2009.

Bo and I grew very close after Lee's death. This was taken in 2008.

The logo on my jacket is mostly covered, but it shows a pigeon with the words "Gene's Loft." It was a gift from my friend Lana James.

Since I planted so many flowers in my front and back yards, there was no grass to mow. This was taken in front of my house in 2005.

# Chapter 16

## 2005–2009

In March 2005, Bernie moved to a 200-acre farm he had purchased in Iowa. I listed my next-door property at 3119 Osage with a Realtor since Bernie left one of its apartments and the other tenant purchased a residence. I spent about $1,800 to fix up the property, which included paying Leroy Atkins to paint all the rooms.

Many people arrived to view the house and property that included two blue spruce trees in the front and a thorn-less blackberry patch and beautiful vines growing on the fences in the back. In 2002, professional fence builders had installed 6-foot chain-link fences in both of my adjacent backyards. I wanted to make sure Bo would not be tempted to jump the fence.

On June 5, 2005, the house sale was complete and I no longer had the stress of being a landlord. Bernie and the other tenant had been fine renters, but I had others who had seldom paid their rent on time.

Needless to say, I was happy to lock the gate between the two properties.

In May 2005, I purchased some baby chickens—20 in all. They were pullets/female chickens, which became known as hens after they matured and laid eggs. I purchased a shed to hold feed and a very small henhouse. Jessie, the same young man who had driven for Lee, assembled the shed and henhouse. (He also helped me with errands and other tasks.)

I purchased some 6-by-6-foot chain-link panels and fenced off the west part of the backyard for the chickens. That began my laying flock of hens that I maintained for several years. The City of St. Louis allowed only four hens and no roosters—of course, I kept my favorites. The others I gave to Patrick Leo and Geneva as they had a flock of hens and a rooster.

In September 2005, I had extreme shortness of breath, and my cardiologist said the replacement veins-arteries had closed. This time, I entered St. Mary's Hospital in Richmond Heights where I had a successful procedure to insert a stent.

A month later, I returned for a second stent. During the procedure, one of my clogged arteries was punctured. Even though I was well sedated, it felt as if a kettle of hot water was racing through my body. The surgeon had to break the balloon that is used in such surgeries to stop the internal heart bleeding. That stent was not successful.

When the surgeon visited me the next day, he said he had seen the puncture of a main blood vessel only once before while watching an instructor. He said he called the instructor to tell him and related to him that "Your patient died and mine lived." I am truly blessed.

My nephew-in-law Bruce (husband of Tammy) visited me during my unsuccessful stent hospital stay. He saw all the monitors and special apparatus hooked to me and immediately fell to his knees at my bedside. He prayed audibly and said, "Gene, do you think you're going to make it?"

"Oh, yes," I affirmed. I never have seriously thought that I wouldn't survive any hospital confinement. I knew I always must remain positive.

In July 2006, St. Louis had damaging wind, lightning, and torrential rains—the storm had a lot of high volume. The top of one of my tall river birch trees was twisted off and hurled across the street.

The electricity was off for more than three days during one of the hottest times of the year. With help from nephew Joe, about $1,000 worth of meat and the entire contents of my chest-size deep freezer were discarded in the dumpster. It was depressing. I hadn't been able to resist bargains on meat, but I stopped hoarding it after that.

Those days without electricity were hard on people and beast, all of us suffering from an almost unbearable heat that was accompanied by extremely high humidity. When the electricity came on, there was a shout in the neighborhood like you hear when a football team scores a touchdown!

In 2006, a tenant of a neighbor came knocking on my door to ask if I would rent my downstairs apartment (where Lee had lived) to her. Why on earth she would ask was a puzzle to me. She knew that I used Lee's residence for overnight guests.

I explained to the tenant that I was leaving the apartment just like my deceased brother had it. I jestingly said, "I want it to be just like he left it when he comes back."

I never dreamed she would think I was speaking seriously until she suddenly turned, her heels clicking, and raced down the steps to her car parked in front of my house. As she click-clicked to the driver's side, she opened the door and shouted, "You leave him where he is!"

In 2007, I had eye-lift surgery. My eyelids had become so droopy that I couldn't see very well. Then I had laser surgery and cataract removal—suddenly it was as if I now saw a big-screen picture of my environment and the colors were so vivid! I didn't realize that leaves could be so green! After the eye-lift surgery, I thought I looked a few years younger.

My interest in genealogy always has been present. As a pre-teen, I would wonder about past grandparents and family history. Aunt Anna Agnew was my main source of information, but I did not record on paper what she told me. I think though that if a subject really is of interest to you, it is retained in your memory bank.

There are many who have been helpful in my genealogy compilation. I have been able to trace back to the 1600s to the Foxcrofts, who are ancestors of the Healy (Grandma Agnew) family.

Twila Gerard, who volunteers for the Iowa County (Iowa) Genealogical Society, was the first person I contacted to assist me, other than my niece Tammy and cousin Judy Harris Hilleman, who were far ahead of me in collecting information. Twila helped me immensely and introduced me to her younger sister, Lana Gerard James. Lana's sharp eyes and dedication to help resulted in a wealth of new information. She helped me locate branches of ancestors I thought never would be found.

Lana and her late husband, Walt, became part of my extended family, as have Twila and their sister Shelly. Nowhere else on this planet will anyone find three kinder, more thoughtful women with such becoming personalities. They volunteer for every project in their hometown of Millersburg and for the Iowa County Genealogical Society. To top it off, they are all super cooks and bakers. Aren't I lucky to have such great friends?

I remained in touch with Joyce James, who moved to southern Missouri in 2005 after she sold the house in Affton that she and Jeanette had purchased. Joyce purchased a double-wide trailer and had it placed on a lot that Jeanette's sister owned. Joyce loved the country and soon had seven dogs, two cats, and a miniature pony. Later on, I gave her some hens.

Joyce drove to St. Louis about four times a year and stayed with me as a houseguest. I enjoyed Joyce's visits, which always included stops at Jeanette's grave. We shopped and enjoyed Imo's pizza (her favorite), White Castle hamburgers, and fried chicken from Hodak's Restaurant.

At home, Bo began sleeping in my room in 2008 since he had grown old (11 years), skinny, and feeble. Eleven is old for Rottweilers.

I continued to provide pigeons to Diane Frandeka, raised lots of tomatoes, and shared eggs with my next-door neighbor Jill, who was a wonderful friend.

Nephew Thomas, who was home from his service in the U.S. Navy, married his bride Amy on May 9, 2008. I was the first in St. Louis to know, as he confided, "I haven't told Mom and Dad yet." This was Thomas's second marriage, the first one was just not meant to be, and his marriage to Amy later became unfulfilling in love for him. God does not expect His children to be unhappy in a marriage that wasn't meant to be.

Nephew Thomas took me to Iowa for the May 17, 2008, wedding of nephew Terry to Valerie in Cedar Rapids. We had a happy journey and stopped to visit Aunts Theresa Agnew O'Rourke and Mary O'Rourke Agnew before the weekend wedding. Bernie's hospitality was on display as we spent the night at his ranch-style home that overlooked his picturesque farm.

I felt that Thomas and I bonded on this trip. I had never been in his company as an adult, and he had matured into a very handsome, confident, intelligent man. His shining smile and great personality were similar to those of his older brothers.

The ceremony was beautiful and the reception was very enjoyable, as was the rehearsal dinner where I tasted prime rib for the first time. Yum, yum, yum.

On the day after the wedding, Thomas and I were invited to Lana and Walt's home for Sunday dinner. I hadn't met Walt or Shelly and had only met Twila for a moment and Lana for a second. When we arrived, Lana greeted us with hugs. Walt made us feel welcome, and Twila and Shelly were wonderfully charming.

When Lana and I had talked on the phone, during various conversations I mentioned my favorite foods and flavors. Lana has a memory like an elephant (very good), and when we sat down to eat, the table was laden with every dish I had said I liked. Tapioca, butterscotch pie, hickory-nut cake, and homemade ice cream were four of the favorites I had mentioned, among some others. We felt totally relaxed in the homey atmosphere. Several pictures were taken, and Lana sent food with us for later. What a wonderful time I had.

In the fall of 2008, Patrick Leo and I visited Iowa and stayed at Bernie's home. In the next two days, we visited second cousins George and Margaret House and first cousins Don and Patty Herr. We also saw Aunts Theresa O'Rourke and Mary Agnew, and Dad's first cousins (my first cousins, once removed, in other words) John and Vera Greene and

Frank and Theresa Greene. Dad had introduced Frank and Theresa to each other, and Dad detected sparks when they glanced at one another.

We visited Kenny and Marlene where Terry also was in attendance, along with visiting Walt and Lana James with Twila and Shelly Gerard. And we made trips to the Sigourney and Armah cemeteries.

It was a great trip, but I was totally exhausted when I got home. It took several days and nights to recuperate.

Bernie visited me the following spring. During his visit, I climbed a 4-foot aluminum ladder to check on a pigeon in a nest in the pigeon house. I had used the ladder in the loft for many years. On the concrete floor were a few bricks for pigeon perches.

The ladder buckled as I stood on the very top step, and I came crashing down. My head struck a brick straight on. My very hard head broke the brick into two pieces!

Bernie, who was in the backyard with Bo, heard the noise and rushed inside the loft. He helped me to my feet in my dazed condition and saw that I was bleeding from a large gash on the back of my head. Leroy Atkins had stopped by, and he and Bernie escorted me to the emergency room at St. Alexius Hospital. Fourteen stitches were required to close the wound, but thankfully an MRI showed no concussion.

I saved the two pieces of brick that fit back together like a puzzle. I truly have a very hard head. However, my short-term memory is not as sharp as it once was.

In 2009, I got tattoos on each upper arm. I was 78 and always secretly wanted a tattoo, but I had no idea what artwork I would want. Patrick Leo thought I had lost my mind. My nephews and nieces thought they were cool.

Aunts Theresa and Mary thought—and hoped—they would wash off. Aunt Mary tried to pull my shirt sleeve down to cover one arm, and her look was one that indicated I had fallen from a nut tree.

Old Bo and I often had spent time together on my front porch. But by 2009, he was getting weaker and did not come out. I had Leroy Atkins build a ramp to my upstairs living quarters so Bo could get up there. Before the ramp was added, he had missed a step twice and took a tumble backwards down the steps.

Back on the porch, I sat there by myself until three neighborhood teenagers occasionally started joining me. They were not invited. They appeared to like my cool, shaded front porch, but I thought they were getting too familiar with my habits and were asking lots of questions. I got the vibe that they really wanted to get in the house.

As they relaxed and sat on the porch one day, one of them stated that my abode looked spooky because of all the vines surrounding it. Right after that, something fell inside my living room and there was a noise. They sat up saying, "What was that?"

I nonchalantly—jokingly—said, "It must be that ghost throwing something."

With that, wild-eyed looks and all, they hopped off the porch and leaped down the steps. I never saw them again. When I made the ghost remark, I had no idea that it was going to eliminate my problem of the increasingly unwanted visitors.

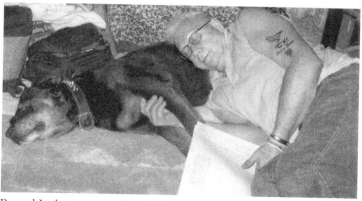

Bo and I take a nap together, 2009.

My oldest nephew, Terry Dawson, with Patrick Leo (middle) and me at my house in 2008.

I was 78 (in 2009) when I got tattoos on each arm—I always had wanted one!

I was so fortunate to become friends with Lana James, at the far right next to me. We are at her house with Bernie, Patrick Leo, and Lana's sister Twila Gerard, who also is a wonderful friend, in 2008.

Three Dawson brothers: Bernie, me, and Patrick Leo.

Bo-Peep joined my home in August 2010.
We bonded immediately, and she was a good
watchdog for me.

# Chapter 17

## 2010–2014

In early 2010, I signed a contract for a Life Alert bracelet. Thankfully, I never had to use it, and I actually wore it sparingly. I gave Jessie a key to the front-door lockbox, which held my door key, so he could let first responders in if I had to use the alert. Life Alert had his phone number.

One night in June 2010, Bo was on his comfortable bed on my bedroom floor while I sat on my bed, fully disrobed, observing television. But our solitude was interrupted when I thought I saw my bedroom doorknob slowly turning. I thought it was impossible, as I had secured all the outside entrances. As Jessie slowly opened the door and poked his head inside, I was in total disbelief as I clutched a blanket over my nakedness.

Behind Jessie were two police officers, one of them carrying a long pipe. Jessie had told them that there probably was a Rottweiler in the room with me. Fire-rescue personnel were in the hall. My next-door neighbor Jill had come over after hearing the siren (I didn't hear the siren since my house was so insulated that it was almost soundproof).

I somehow had accidentally pushed the alert button on the bracelet. It certainly worked as the responsible parties arrived very quickly! Afterwards, I was so shocked about the surprising commotion that I paid the contract off and returned the equipment because I was afraid I would unknowingly set off the alarm again.

On August 11, 2010, nephew Brian, who was alarmed at old Bo's declining health, arrived at my house with a 50-pound female Rottweiler that he had purchased on the Internet. The six-month-old puppy had arrived in St. Louis via plane the day before.

Old Bo accepted her. I think he was just too weak to object. I had to help him stand the last week of his life, and on the last day, he refused to eat or drink. I think he had taken himself off life support and was ready to die. He passed away on August 23, just eight days after he reached age 13.

The new puppy was named Bo-Peep. Bo-Peep could raise quite a commotion when people walked with their dogs in front of the house. She thinks she is the proprietor of all she can see and that she is protecting Maudie K from those "dangerous" animals. She is the same way with squirrels, loud garbage trucks, school buses, mail carriers, and anyone else attired in a uniform.

When Lana James and Roberta Voelkel, a friend of Lana's, visited me in 2010, Joyce James also arrived for a visit. I suggested that Joyce and Lana were relatives since they have the same last name.

Joyce, Lana, Roberta, and I visited St. Louis landmarks together. Since Joyce was familiar with St. Louis, she drove us to the Missouri History Museum. Joyce had Lana and Roberta holding on to their seats as she wove in and out of heavy city traffic. All the while, Joyce was vocalizing a steady stream of words directed at fellow motorists that disparaged their driving abilities, questioned their sanities, and blessed them with unsavory names.

At the museum, the Vatican Splendors display was on tour, and St. Louis was one of the stops. Seeing the exhibit was a once-in-a-lifetime experience.

Lana, who is a good Christian Methodist, and her sister Shelly toured my parish, St. Anthony of Padua, on an earlier visit. I had given rosary beads to Lana, Twila, and Shelly when I visited them in 2008. Lana says the rosary each day, asks St. Anthony for favors, attends Mass occasionally, which she did before we met, and is truly ecumenical, stating all prayers are prayers to Almighty God.

The evening after our visit to the history museum, Lana and Roberta enjoyed the banter between Joyce and me as we sat at my kitchen table. Both Lana and Roberta were so tickled by a remark made by Joyce that they both lost control and spit out a mouthful of beverage at the same instant.

Lana, Roberta, and I also toured the Museum at the Gateway Arch, and Roberta rode to the top of the arch. We visited the St. Louis Cardinals store and the gift shop at the Budweiser Brewery.

Not long after this, nephew Terry and I took a day trip to visit Joyce after she had been in a car accident. She had lost control of her vehicle as she rounded a sharp curve on a hilly gravel road near her home. Her vehicle landed upside down, and Joyce was pinned inside for 45 minutes until a passerby called for help. After her recovery, she had headaches for the rest of her life. Joyce also lost sight in one eye, and her sight was diminished in the other.

I sleep with my window open year around except when it is so hot that air conditioning is needed. I like fresh air, and I like to sleep in a cold room. My cousin Judy Harris Hilleman, a nurse, advised me to keep the air moving for better health.

So around 7 a.m. on March 8, 2011, as I was in bed with my bedroom window open as wide as possible, I heard shouting, "Open up, police!" Then shots rang out so close together that I couldn't count them. The shots were followed by a barrage of return gunfire. I could tell the two sets of shots were coming from different weapons or, at least, different locations.

The officers were two doors down where they had come to arrest my neighbor Carlos Boles. No wonder the shots sounded so close.

I hurriedly dressed. I was wide awake! More police cars arrived, and I went out on my front porch to get a better look. An agent ordered me back into my house just as I saw police in front of the entrance to Carlos's house.

I turned on the TV as the news media arrived and a helicopter buzzed overhead. I stepped back onto the front porch, and another agent advised me to go back inside but revealed that Carlos was dead. A U.S. marshal was killed during the attempted arrest.

A large crowd gathered in the park across the street and lines of police held them at bay. Most of the African Americans in the park assemblage were sympathetic to Carlos. One lady said that police picked on Carlos because he had a white girlfriend. Carlos's sister screamed and fell into a sitting position. Her photo appeared in newspapers worldwide.

Friends called to see if I was all right. My house was right up front in the news broadcasts on TV. Lana was speaking on the phone with the TV on when she glanced at it and saw my house—red front steps, vine-covered porch, and all. She immediately called me.

It shocked me how small the world had become. Lana was watching the very same thing more than 250 miles away that I was observing in person. Nephew Joe called as he heard about it on the radio as he drove a truck two states away.

Yellow police tape cordoned off the block for days, and I had to get permission to leave my premises. Evidence technicians swarmed Carlos's house.

Carlos always had been very respectful to me, addressing me as "Mr. Gene." Carlos, his mother, and his two sisters were friends of mine, and some afternoons I sat on their porch swing with them.

I felt safe with Carlos controlling the street thugs in the area. When Lana and Roberta arrived to visit me in 2010, Carlos observed their out-of-state vehicle parked in front of my house. Before they hardly had disembarked, Carlos and a few of his friends raced over to ask, "Are they friends of yours, Mr. Gene?" I assured them that they were, and Carlos directed his associates that the van was safe for as long as they were visiting.

I introduced him to Lana and Roberta. He shook their hands, welcomed them to the neighborhood, and told them they were safe as long as they were visiting Mr. Gene. If he had not given the order, Lana's van could have been entered and vandalized or even stripped of valuable parts; an out-of-state vehicle that was new in the neighborhood was like fresh game to street thieves and thugs.

After March 2011, Carlos's house eventually was boarded up, an eyesore to our peaceful street. Thieves removed anything of value. Occasionally, I saw cars with young, black, male occupants slowly pull up in front of it, almost as if the house were a shrine. Graffiti was scrawled on nearby walls, sidewalks, and windows, all against the police.

Afterwards, the neighborhood became almost too quiet. I had grown accustomed to hearing gunfire on most nights and even during daylight hours.

My poultry enterprise ended in 2012. I gave my last hens, Kim, Kourtney, and Khloe, to Patrick Leo and Geneva to join their flock. They were very beautiful Ameraucana hens that laid blue-green eggs. I had grown tired of fending off sparrows, starling pests, and predators.

In November 2012, I started going with Joe Hoy to auctions in the Missouri town of Old Mines, about 60 miles south of St. Louis. We would arrive about 10:30 a.m. for the noon auctions so we could see what was available, which included many animals and fowl. I usually would buy dog food that was sold for about half the regular price. Joe bought lots of odds and ends, as well as geese, ducks, and roosters.

I enjoyed our rides to and from Old Mines. Missouri has beautiful scenery, particularly in the fall. Joe told me his wild stories, and I supplied mine.

At the auctions, I became friendly with a lesbian couple who operated a large farm. I broke the ice with the women by speaking first and engaging in conversation. They soon were telling me about their first meeting and about their farm. They always helped Joe and me load for departure.

Joe and I also went to pigeon shows where I met many friendly, kind, and interesting people. When I attended the St. Louis pigeon show in 2013, I met James and Jan Willard, a wonderful couple who reside in Irondale, Missouri. Joe already knew James through their mutual interest in exotic fowl.

James gifted me with a very beautiful cock pigeon after Joe told him that I loved mixed-breed, unusual pigeons. Joe and James conspired to surprise me with Kormie, who is half Komorner and half Roller. Since then, James has given me my first pair of Arabian Trumpeters, who I named James and Jan. James also gave me my first pair of Thai Laughers and provided me with English Carriers and Fairy Swallows, which I borrowed until I had their offspring in my loft.

I have toured James's compound with nephew Terry and brother Thomas M. on separate occasions. The compound has many lofts, pens, and enclosures for his fowl. I have dined with James and Jan in their home, and they have broken bread at my house a few times. Jan and I exchange recipes, and James and I love pigeons with the same intensity. They are a super nice couple and accept me for who I am.

In 2013, Joe Hoy fell at his home. He was hospitalized in St. Louis after the fall and had some complications. Patrick Leo and I visited him at the hospital, and I was convinced that he wouldn't live very long.

Surprisingly, Joe returned to his residence, but he didn't emerge from the confines of his house for a few weeks. During this time, an invasion of a mother raccoon and her youngsters killed all but two pigeons in one of Joe's lofts, leaving their mutilated bodies strewn about.

On a Sunday in the summer of 2013, James arrived at my house, and we took hammers, nails, and other supplies and then traveled across the Mississippi River and journeyed to Joe's home. A sad sight met our eyes.

We caught all the remaining pigeons and attempted to repair the pens and lofts. I took four of Joe's rare Arabian Trumpeter pigeons to my loft with the intention of returning them when Joe could navigate himself. He was wearing leg braces and a medical boot.

In a remarkable about-face, Joe soon was back on his feet and again caring for a few pigeons and his rare animals and birds. He had recruited the help of two great-nephews.

I had my own issues in 2013. While changing a light bulb in my living room, I missed a step on my small stepladder and fell. The large bone above my right eye met a sharp edge of the coffee table. This time, I could see the wound and was able to stanch the blood flow. It healed nicely with many bandages that closed the opening.

At 3 a.m. on August 18, I awoke to the most miserable and uncomfortable feeling I had ever had. My chest, jaws, arms, and neck hurt worse and differently than ever before.

I knew I had to get to the hospital, so I put on clean underwear. I remembered that Mother had instructed my brothers and me to never go anywhere unless we were wearing clean underwear because we didn't know what might happen.

I dialed next-door neighbor/wonderful friend Jill and was hardly out the front door before we were speeding the seven blocks to the St. Alexius Hospital emergency room. Jill handled all the entry questions after I handed my insurance card to her. She called Patrick Leo and Geneva, and they arrived within the hour.

I had suffered a heart attack and was hanging by a thread. But I was back home in a few days after getting one more successful stent, although another stent was not successful. The clogged artery was almost like concrete, and the surgeon could not break through it. However, he said my heart was channeling a new artery next to the one that was impenetrable. I had no idea that was possible.

The body is a wonderful machine. I felt much better. In fact, in the year that followed, I had much more pep and stamina and no longer required rest and naps for the majority of each day.

After Joe Hoy was back on his feet, he couldn't wait to replenish his pigeon flock. I gave him several and returned his four Arabian Trumpeters. He attended auctions several times a week as far away as Decatur and Kankakee, Illinois.

I accompanied Joe to the Old Mines auction on the first Sunday of October. I had an overpopulation of pigeons and gave him 25 beautiful birds that day. The repairs James and I had provided had proven adequate, and Joe was acquiring many, many birds.

On October 27, Joe asked me to join his sister Genevieve and him at a restaurant in Caseyville, Illinois. After we ate and took Genevieve back to her home, Joe conveyed me back to my home where I had a few more pigeons for him.

That was the last time I saw my friend.

On Sunday, November 17, 2013, tornadoes roared across southern Illinois. Joe's home was directly in the path of a twister that struck with winds of up to 190 miles per hour. His home and all the buildings on the property were blown away.

Joe and his sister Frances lived in the house that was destroyed. They both died as a result of the tornado. Joe's body was in a field 100 yards from where his house had been.

I miss Joe and our outings together very much. We would talk about life in general and, of course, our mutual love of pigeons. He was a good friend.

On February 18, 2014, I turned 83. How blessed I was to be able to live in my own home and care for myself in most ways. Although I lacked my own transportation, my loving Patrick Leo made sure I got to medical appointments, Mass, and shopping. Many other people including Leroy Atkins also help. Leroy A. drops what he's doing if Maudie calls (he, too, refers to me as "Maudie").

Right around my birthday, Joyce fell at her trailer and went into a diabetic coma. She was taken to a nearby hospital, and she passed away.

I miss Joyce. We spoke via phone at least once a week. She called me her "Queenie."

In 2014, I disassembled my many pens in the backyard. I gave my 6-by-6-foot panels and gates to Patrick Leo to enlarge his chicken yard and fence his garden. My backyard then looked almost like it did when Lee and I moved to the house in 1990, except that it had the additional fences on the sides and the very small pen for growing tomatoes.

Roses of Sharon hedges and English ivy vines provided a privacy barrier. However, the privacy didn't extend to the second-floor porch-deck belonging to my neighbor Mary—she had an unimpeded view of my yard from there. If she saw me working in the backyard for an extended length of time, she wouldn't quiet down until I went in to rest. On hot days, she would order me to get in the house and out of the heat. Mary fixed Sunday dinner each week for her family and me. She passed away a few years ago and was a wonderful, caring neighbor.

In 2014, a 22-year-old pigeon-breeder friend took me on errands a few times. He gave me a friendship ring that he requested I wear always. But this friendship really was just a friendship; I'm 61 years older than him! That was the closest thing to courtship for me in my 84th year.

In August 2014, my North English High School Class of 1949, the "Forty-niners," gathered together to mark our 65-year class reunion. There were 14 present out of the original 34. I could not attend but spoke via phone with three of them and received photos from the event. As the years speed by, I have become very fond of my classmates.

Sixteen pills washed down with a cup of decaf coffee were my morning breakfast. Eight were vitamins and the others were prescriptions. Five more prescriptions were taken at bedtime. Nearly everyone I know older than 70—and many much younger—take prescribed drugs every day. (No wonder pharmaceutical companies do so well on the stock market.) I have taken my drug regimen religiously and credit the combination with keeping me functioning. How in the world did folks live to a ripe old age before the manufacture of wonderful pills, the answer to every ailment?

On fall Saturdays in 2014, I would spend almost the entire day watching football, except to leave for 4 p.m. Mass. What a plethora of games from which to choose! I would channel surf back and forth, to-and-fro, among the games in progress. Observing sports on TV is one of my main hobbies.

My other "favorites" are raising pigeons, Bo-Peep, genealogy, cooking, raising flowers, writing, and keeping in touch with folks via the telephone. I miss talking with Joyce James and Joe Hoy; I chatted with both of them quite often.

In 2014, I had visits from niece Tammy, Bruce, and Tad in March; niece Esther and great-nephew Alex in April; and nephew Terry shortly after that. Brother Thomas M. visited in June. Nephews Joe and Brian are occasional visitors.

Each Saturday that Patrick Leo transported me to Mass, Geneva sent along a home-cooked dinner for me. Patrick Leo also brought eggs, dried apples, and a variety of garden produce, as well as reading material.

In 2014, Lana James mailed surprises of money to me. I was instructed to use the money to buy milkshakes from White Castle, which she knew I loved.

I would have been lost without the phone. I would speak with Bernie and Lana every day; nephew Terry and niece Tammy twice weekly; Thomas M. and Esther approximately every 10 days; Aunts Theresa and Mary about every two weeks; and Kenny and Marlene pretty often. I also kept in touch with the rest of my nieces and nephews and my Agnew and Dawson cousins. And, of course, I would speak to Patrick Leo quite often by phone, too.

I occasionally speak to a few former "admirers"—when they have Maudie on their minds. But I haven't had an overnight gentleman visitor for a few years. Apparently, my wild days are over.

I like to keep up with my relatives and friends via the phone—no email for me!
This was taken in 2012.

Bo-Peep and me on the front steps of my house, 2017.

Bo-Peep and me in 2018, shortly after I was put on oxygen.

# Chapter 18

## 2015–

I finished writing every other part of this book in October 2014. There were many changes in my life after that.

In 2016, I was diagnosed with idiopathic pulmonary fibrosis (IPF). Not a good diagnosis to be sure. Two years later, I was feeling increasingly weak and realized that I was no longer enjoying my pigeons. So James and Jan Willard came to my house in June 2018 and took the pigeons back to their compound. It was then just Bo-Peep and me.

I felt worse and worse, and by August 2018, I was very weak and had trouble breathing. I ended up in the hospital and then a care center. I lost that round to IPF, but I am putting up a fight. When my doctor told me that I would not go home again, he said, "Your lungs are gone." I now live in an assisted-living facility, which is the next best thing to home.

Oxygen therapy is my 24-hour companion—it keeps me alive. In late 2019, I also was diagnosed with Myelodysplastic Syndromes (MDS).

Throughout the winter of 2018–2019, Patrick Leo and my nephews cleaned out my house. I brought as much as I could to my new home. On February 28, 2019, my residence on Osage was sold.

Bo-Peep joined the pigeons at James and Jan's country home. They take good care of her and the pigeons, and they are all happy campers there. Bo-Peep has a big doghouse and space, and it's a perfect setting for a dog.

In early 2019, my Realtor introduced me to Geoff Story, who is working on a documentary titled *Gay Home Movie*, which is about the history of the gay community in St. Louis. An article in *The New York Times* on June 23, 2019, included a photo of Geoff and me and discussed the progress of the LGBTQ community in the heartland. For the documentary, Geoff has interviewed me for 11 hours with lights, cameras, and a makeup artist. Hopefully, it will be shown at film festivals in the very near future.

My friendship with the James and Gerard family is great, and I speak with Lana nearly every day. I talk to Twila and Shelly quite often, too. Sadly, Walt passed away in 2016. Patrick Leo took me to Iowa for the funeral, and Bernie joined us there.

The telephone also keeps me in touch with Bernie, Patrick Leo, Thomas M., my nieces and nephews, and all my other relatives and friends.

Bernie had open-heart surgery in 2017 and recovered nicely. Patrick Leo and Geneva continue with volunteering. Patrick Leo suffers from Post-Traumatic Stress Disorder due to his frightful experience in Vietnam. Patrick Leo and Geneva visit frequently and do my shopping and running for me. Thomas M. lives in Torrance, California, and works on the docks. He shares his home with his daughter/my niece Esther, her husband, and son.

On February 10, 2020, I lost my second brother. Kenny passed away in North English with his loving family by his side. Due to my health, I could not attend the funeral, but my other brothers were all there.

At home in my apartment at the assisted-living facility, 2019. Behind me is an afghan created from a photo of the Dawson brothers taken at Kenny and Marlene's wedding. Only part of the afghan is showing in this photo, so it doesn't show all the brothers. But it does show Kenny on the left (my right), and Lee, Bernie, and a little of Patrick Leo on my other side. My drag photos on the wall flank a photo of my Great-Grandmother Catherine Dawson.

# Epilogue

What follows are observations of mine in random order. I wrote the chronological events of my life as accurately as I could from what my imperfect mind remembered for me.

"Love grows cold as queens grow old." True statement.

My belief is to live and let live, and for God's sake, not tell people how to live their lives in the name of religion.

I did not have a choice about feeling as if I should have been born female, and I did not have a choice about being gay. I never had the option of living a "normal" heterosexual life in rural Iowa. But thank God that my family always accepted me, and I was able to keep my Catholic faith.

In my experiences practicing a gay lifestyle, I found that my feelings are no less or no more romantic than any other person on this planet. I've been ugly-eyed jealous, hurt to the pit of my stomach, betrayed, and rejected. I've cried rivers of heartbreak and sadness. I've observed my straight friends experience those same feelings.

When I found someone for whom I really cared (not just a physical attraction, although that came first), I was as faithful as any betrothed. Then, when the relationship came to a disappointing end, I would want to kick my own ass for my blindness. Love is blind and can't see the forest for the trees.

Unfortunately, or perhaps fortunately, I was attracted to bisexual men who favored the feminine side of my gayness. The trouble was that most of them had girlfriends or wives and used me as the other "woman." Almost 100 percent of the time, when push came to shove, I was the one who spent more time alone. Some of them even promoted friendships between their girlfriend or wife and me. They wanted to have their cake and eat it too.

I would have pangs of guilt and suggest that these men and I really shouldn't have secret trysts. They invariably would reply, "What she doesn't know doesn't hurt her." After some affairs ended, I sometimes remained friends with relatives of my former beaus, and some were great friends for many years. I occasionally would see the former objects of my affection. But the flames had burned out.

All the gay people I have ever known were caring individuals. As a gay person, I changed diapers and cared for younger siblings, nephews, and nieces ever since I could lift a child. Gay individuals oftentimes are caregivers for elderly parents.

We come in all shades of color in all cultures and are in all the jobs of the world. We are everywhere and blend right into all segments of society. We are not dumber, smarter, prettier, or uglier than anyone else.

I used to hear people say "normal" instead of "heterosexual." What is normal to a straight individual is not normal to me. Normal is defined in the eye of the beholder.

We gay humans are God's children made in His own image and likeness. I don't think God would create gay, lesbian, bisexual, or trans children if He didn't have a plan for us. I don't think He wants to pitch His children into the fiery abyss.

Pope Francis is reaching out to gay individuals and wants the church to be more inclusive. The one line I especially remember from Pope Francis: "Who am I to judge?"

In 2014, I read that Catholic bishops, following Pope Francis's example, have become less judgmental. It's about time, as more and more young folk have abandoned the Roman Catholic Church, which kept followers in line for years through the fear of going to hell because of mortal sin. I have questions concerning those man-made definitions of sin, such as missing Mass if you aren't physically able or other elements prevent attendance. Jesus didn't preach in a beautiful building.

I don't feel I have any religion if I don't have questions regarding it. No one wants to be a sheep unquestioningly following the crowd.

Isn't God wonderful? How He loves us. We learn soon after birth that we don't live forever. We begin like a car—new, shiny, and running on all cylinders. God provides us "cars" with energy to make us run efficiently. As we get miles on us, He lets us get new "paint" jobs and replace our "pistons" so our "batteries" keep going for a time. But it is inevitable that we old "cars" will wear out.

But does the all-loving God Almighty junk us for scrap metal? No! He created us, and His son Jesus Christ died on the cross for all of us. So He takes us into His "old car museum" where we are instantly restored. We don't even need "fuel" anymore. We are there with the Father, Son, and Holy Spirit from then on.

God is everywhere and knows all, sees all, and loves all equally and always. There is only one God, but He has several aliases. He is known as the Great Spirit, Allah, Buddha, and many more titles. They are all the Creator. We all are made in His image and likeness. We must love our brothers and sisters in Christ, wherever they reside in this world.

If you believe in your prayers, they will be answered. Really, what is the use of praying and asking God for help if you don't believe He will answer you? My main intercessors are Saints Jude, Anthony of Padua, and Francis of Assisi.

I realize that you don't have to be on your knees to pray. Prayers can be said anywhere, at any time. My rosaries often were said while lying in bed or while sitting on the front porch with Bo-Peep. I don't forget to thank Almighty God for His graces and blessings, for being my Creator and salvation, and for becoming man and dying on the cross for my sins and all the sins for all time.

Does your mind wander when you are saying prayers? I certainly have that lack of concentration. For example, if I'm praying the rosary, I'll suddenly come to the realization that I'm on the fourth decade and have been on cruise control since the first. I didn't miss a beat evidently. I hope those lip-service prayers are heard also! I think my best prayers are when I ask or thank God spontaneously for favors, if His will be done, or for petitions already answered.

Some of my favorite things are the smell of brewing coffee, the taste and smell of vanilla, bacon frying, train whistles and the hum of train tracks in the quiet nighttime hours, the musical sound created by pigeons flapping their wings, the beautiful voices and organ of St. Anthony of Padua's choir, and any rendition of *Ave Maria* or *Danny Boy*. Even the sound of locusts, which bothered me as a child, I like to hear every few years.

On the opposite side, one of my pet peeves in prior years was the total disregard of the importance of being on time by some of my work associates. At least it was a good lesson in learning patience and temper control!

I hate being late. I would rather not attend at all than be late. That especially goes for attending Mass or any function that has a crowd. I like to arrive at appointments a half hour early if at all possible. I want to be the first in the door before Mass. Patrick Leo used to take me to most of my medical appointments and to Mass, and he, too, likes to be plenty early.

I do pride myself on being well organized. Every item has its place, and I try to put things back as soon as I am done with them. As I would sit at the kitchen table (my favorite spot for reading, writing, and watching TV, as well as dining), I could reach most anything I needed from my rolling chair. I had cheap reading glasses scattered throughout the house.

I've been on both sides of the coin of caretaking. I've had to make decisions for Dad and brother Lee, and I felt I had 100 percent support from my brothers. Their input helped immensely in the decision-making and eased my conscious. Caregiving certainly has its rewards with the looks of thanks in the eyes of the patient and knowing you did something to make your loved one feel better.

I have found it really, really heartbreaking to see a strong individual, who seemed indestructible in all ways, melt away right before my eyes. Or to see the person who could jump higher, run faster, and always assisted others, using a walker. But I think the saddest of all is watching the sage from whom you sought advice lose his/her common sense due to dementia.

Our Father, Almighty God, through the words of His son, exhorts us to visit the sick and bury the dead. I feel I can pray for the souls of my loved ones just as well at home as I can standing at a gravesite. After all, they are not there. They are more likely to be sitting with me at the kitchen table than in a lonely, snow-covered, windswept, or sweltering cemetery.

Bad dreams plague me and have since I was a child. When I had a fever, I sometimes had a terrifying dream that I was inside something like an egg and couldn't get out. I would feel like I was practically suffocating. I also would dream that I was inside a tombstone but could tell it was light outside and could hear murmuring voices. It was very hot in there to the point of almost burning. It was truly terrifying.

Falling from a tall building is a more recent recurring dream. Just as impact is imminent, I coast to a soft landing but awaken with my heart pounding. Another unpleasant dream involves becoming entangled in electrical wires—each way I try to move, another electric wire is ready to shock the hell out of me. I have practically kicked a hole in my bedroom wall and almost broke my toe when "surrounded" by attacking dogs or sows in my dreams.

Since I had open-heart surgery, bad dreams have become almost nightly occurrences. In my dreams, I'm pushing a stuck car or am washing load after load of laundry in an old-fashioned washing machine. I am tired the next day as if I had actually physically exhausted my entire body.

The worst dream of all, and it is recurring, is that Dad and I are arguing bitterly. I know we had a contentious relationship in my early years, but I couldn't have loved him any more than I did in the last 20 years of his life. I sought his love and approval for 54 years, and it was not forthcoming. Those dreams seem so real that I'm sometimes in tears when I awake. Sometimes I've made him cry in the dream—that is the dream that is most dreaded.

Isn't it fun to give? What a delight it is to see the joy that an unexpected gift brings to a recipient, and it gives me even more joy as the giver. I appreciate each and every gift I get, but I especially appreciate the thoughts behind them. When I was younger, I would tear open an envelope and read the first page of a card. I didn't take time to "smell the roses" and read the verse inside. Now that's the first thing I read.

Be sure to show appreciation to deserving individuals by giving praise and compliments often and lavishly. Have you noticed the encouragement a compliment or deserving praise does for folks? I still remember compliments that my Uncle Harry Agnew sent my way directly or when he was sure that I heard as he was speaking with someone else.

I feel very blessed to be the firstborn in John P. and Mary Agnew Dawson's family and the firstborn grandchild on both the paternal and maternal sides of my family. I got all the grandparents, aunts, uncles, and obviously my parents all to myself for at least 1 year and 10 months. I've been able to enjoy my brothers all the days of their lives. I've been on earth to greet every first cousin.

Since I'm firstborn, I was around after each new brother arrived. Then I would observe each brother become the cutest baby I had ever seen and then continue to be blessed with good looks. I would wonder why I was unattractive with immense, floppy ears, a small, pin head, and sissified ways that were very natural to me.

I was very bashful and embarrassed just about any time that attention was focused on me or even if I was just acknowledged by an adult or someone I admired from afar. I think my self-consciousness and lack of self-respect started about the time I entered third grade. Kids can be cruel, perhaps not intentionally, when they are teasing or when little remarks that are detracting are magnified and dwelled upon. It especially hurts when a person is very sensitive and wants everyone to love him or her.

Thank the Lord that common sense and acceptance come with advanced age. I used to be too concerned about what people thought of me and tried to please everyone but myself. Patrick Leo reminded me, "Maudie, most everyone thinks about themselves nearly 85 percent of the time. They're not concerned about your looks or actions." At least long term, they are not.

Now—especially since there have been a couple of times when I've been "hanging by a thread," as my cardiologist said—I've stopped to smell the roses, drink in the beauty of God's creation, accept my fellow men and women as they are, and accept myself as I am. I don't give a crap what others think of me. Well, I actually do, for I don't wish to offend anyone.

There is a little good in the worst of me and a little bad in the best of me. Now I love myself. I've found that now that I'm confident, I've made many friends. I've found that what I thought were looks of disapproval from others were views of hesitation about whether to speak or not to an insecure individual, such as I. Now I make sure to wear a smile and greet people as soon as I see them.

I think part of my longevity is a result of my exposure to germs from as soon as I could play outside. Kids nowadays don't get exposed to germs like my brothers and I did, so they don't build any immunity or resistance. Just think of the fun a child misses by not playing in the dirt and/or a sandpile with its buried treasures.

As a child, I thought cancer, heart attacks, and other health problems happened to other families. I thought the Dawson and Agnew families were immune to all but pneumonia after Aunt Winnie Dawson died from it at age 17 when I was four.

When Uncle Leo Agnew was killed in World War II, the families seemed more vulnerable. Then our medical hardships and tragedies began. Kenny was thrown from Beauty, a frisky horse, and later required surgery. As a young child, Thomas M. was badly burned when a pan of boiling water tipped on him. Mother died after being burned in a household accident.

When Thomas M. was about 12, he also was thrown from a horse, and he suffers back stress and pain today. Patrick Leo lived the horrors of the Vietnam War and has a Purple Heart for his wounds. Multiple myeloma claimed Dad's life. Bernie was carjacked and survived up-close bullet wounds. Lee died after battling HIV and AIDS. Kenny just passed away in February 2020 after suffering from congestive heart failure. I've chronicled my health problems in this book.

All of my uncles are gone. My only living aunt is Elisa Baldonado Dawson, who was born in 1922. Aunt Theresa Agnew O'Rourke died in 2015 at the age of 94, and Aunt Mary O'Rourke Agnew died in 2017 at 97. As of 2019, I have lost many first cousins: Terry Costello, Michael Costello, Eddie Harris, MaryAnn Harris Petermeier, John Harris, Rita Harris Brenner, Margaret Herr, David Herr, Charlotte Agnew Pingel, John Agnew, Bob Agnew, Jim O'Rourke, Marsha Hartzell Stillwell, Joe Conroy, Billy Dawson, Steve Dawson, Tom Dawson, and Martha Dawson Swanson. May their souls rest in peace.

My conclusion is that we are just like any other family. We are average and definitely not immune to tragedy! God does not burden us with more than we can bear. We are all working our way to heaven and how we handle obstacles in our paths is part of the trail to paradise.

It was a blessing to have brother Lee as my boss. I usually worked by my own rules, and anyone else would have fired my ass for the shenanigans I pulled during the Foot Long days. Perhaps Lee felt sorry for me since he knew I had been fired from two other jobs. Dad asked him to look out for me, he revealed some years later. It seems as if Dad also asked Patrick Leo to do the same. They are both carrying out Dad's wishes.

I wouldn't have been able to live in and maintain my Osage home if Lee hadn't purchased it with me. After Lee died, I wouldn't have been able to pay the taxes, insurance, and upkeep if he hadn't set up a trust for me. I think Lee probably got the large guard dog, Bo, with me in mind.

Before I moved away from my house in 2018, Patrick Leo and Geneva saw to it that I had transportation anywhere I needed to go—even though it is a 110-mile round trip to Osage Street and back to their home.

Kenny, Bernie, and Thomas M. were thoughtful with their many telephone calls and visits. But I don't think Dad charged them with looking out for me.

Phrases from my brothers and me:
"Yep" —Kenny
"Whatta ya got?" —Lee
"They seem to be" —Bernie
"Strange, indeed" —Patrick Leo
"Jesus loves you" —Thomas M.
and
"Lord have mercy" —K (me)

I don't do "ifs." It is a word that shouldn't be in the English language as far as I'm concerned. "If" has caused guilt feelings, feelings of inadequacy, and shame for me until I finally realized to disregard the word.

What is done is done. Move right along.

I've learned—nearly too late—that stress can be as dangerous as physical ailments to the health of your heart and, therefore, to your entire body. You have to employ steel-strong willpower to defeat stress. Nothing is going to stress me out again.

By that, I mean that fear is not going to run my life. I refuse to live in imagined fear.

When I was young, even into my 30s, I worried about dropping through that trap door to hell. I was concerned that God was a punishing God. Remember when you mildly misbehaved as a child, and you would be reminded that God was watching you?

Some priests gave sermons that emphasized punishment, fire, and brimstone. So I went to Mass because I was living in fear that I most definitely would be on the "Down for Eternity escalator" if I didn't.

I think if you treat your neighbor and everyone else with love and friendship, there is nothing to fear. Refuse to fear the future, either long term or immediate. Stay positive always. Negativity enables unpleasant things to occur.

Fear not, and you'll be happy. Be the very best you can be.

# The Last Words

Life unfolds as it is supposed to, and there is nothing we can do about the events that have transpired.

However, I am sorry for my many transgressions. It is impossible to amend to everyone who deserves my apology, but I hope they have forgiven me.

I'm sorry to Almighty God for everything that I did that caused Him pain and pray for His forgiveness. He died for our sins so that we, with sorrow and asking for forgiveness, will be saved. Those are comforting thoughts and give me peace of mind and tranquility.

This is it! I've "blah, blah, blahed" and "yada, yada, yadaed" enough. Thanks for hanging in there with me.

So long for now.

Thanks for taking time to read this book. I truly did my best to "tell all" as honestly as possible.

If you are so inclined and have time to give this old queen some honest feedback, please leave a customer review on the book's web page at www.amazon.com. I would be most appreciative!

Made in the USA
Coppell, TX
06 December 2020